The Girl in the Window
and Other True Tales

THE GIRL IN THE WINDOW
AND OTHER TRUE TALES

An Anthology with Tips for
Finding, Reporting, and Writing
Nonfiction Narratives

Lane DeGregory

With a Foreword by Beth Macy

THE UNIVERSITY OF CHICAGO PRESS
CHICAGO AND LONDON

The University of Chicago Press, Chicago 60637
The University of Chicago Press, Ltd., London
© 2023 by Lane DeGregory
Foreword © 2023 by The University of Chicago
Published 2023
Printed in the United States of America

32 31 30 29 28 27 26 25 24 23   1 2 3 4 5

ISBN-13: 978-0-226-82537-3 (cloth)
ISBN-13: 978-0-226-77127-4 (paper)
ISBN-13: 978-0-226-82538-0 (e-book)
DOI: https://doi.org/10.7208/chicago/9780226825380.001.0001

Library of Congress Cataloging-in-Publication Data

Names: DeGregory, Lane, author. | Macy, Beth, writer of foreword.
Title: The girl in the window and other true tales : an anthology with tips for
    finding, reporting, and writing nonfiction narratives / Lane DeGregory ; with a
    foreword by Beth Macy.
Description: Chicago : The University of Chicago Press, 2023. | Includes
    bibliographical references and index.
Identifiers: LCCN 2022037312 | ISBN 9780226825373 (cloth) |
    ISBN 9780226771274 (paperback) | ISBN 9780226825380 (ebook)
Subjects: LCSH: Creative nonfiction—Authorship. | LCGFT: Creative nonfiction.
Classification: LCC PN3377.5.R45 D44 2023 | DDC 070.4/44—dc23/eng/20220830
LC record available at https://lccn.loc.gov/2022037312

♾ This paper meets the requirements of ANSI/NISO Z39.48-1992
(Permanence of Paper).

CONTENTS

FOREWORD

Beth Macy

When I began my career as a newspaper feature writer in 1986 fresh out of journalism school, few people were writing the kind of stories I aspired to tell—socially relevant pieces that not only illuminated the issues of our time but were also so deeply entertaining and moving that you felt fortified and more enlightened by having read them.

They changed you, in other words. As James Baldwin put it, "You write in order to change the world, knowing perfectly well that you probably can't, but also knowing that literature is indispensable to the world. . . . If you alter, even by a millimeter, the way people look at reality, then you can change it."

The stories in *"The Girl in the Window" and Other True Tales* have this kind of power. They are the life's work of Lane DeGregory, whom I consider to be the Jimmy Breslin of our time.

For more than two decades, Lane has written at the pinnacle of narrative journalism but not from expected literary establishments like the *New York Times* or the *Atlantic* or the *New Yorker*. She's worked in a midsize market at the *Tampa Bay Times* (formerly the *St. Petersburg Times*), a newspaper with a long-standing reputation for cranking out great writing as well as winning several Pulitzers, including one for Lane's 2008 story about a feral child whose odyssey inspired the title piece of this collection.

As her former longtime editor Mike Wilson describes Lane's place in the pantheon of narrative writers: "She's a local journalist with national importance." But her stories aren't local or national, he adds. "They're universal."

This book comes at a critical moment in storytelling, a time when newspapers are shrinking and folding at record rates and a slow-simmering brew of political rage, growing inequality, and disinformation threatens our very democracy. The collection also demonstrates Lane's unparalleled range, from investigatory enterprise stories to pure features that both spin off the news and stand alone for their depth and timelessness. What they all have in common is that they help you better understand your neighbors—all your neighbors—and, more important, they make you *feel*. Their strength originates from the way Lane squarely locates herself *among* rather than *above* the people she meets, armed with her legal pad, an insatiable and genuine curiosity, and a quest to understand rather than judge.

She is empathetic without being naive, never shying away from the mistakes people make. Like the best writers I know, she participates willingly, even joyfully, in the editing process—even if it means accompanying busy editors as they're walking out to their cars.

I wasn't surprised to learn that Lane grew up in a family where the newspaper was read aloud every morning, where Woodward and Bernstein were deemed heroes, or that her stated goal at the age of five was to become a reporter. Rather than market-hop from one media outlet to the next as many ambitious young journalists do, chasing bigger salaries and larger audiences, Lane staked out a single postage stamp of soil, as Faulkner called it, planting her roots deep in the sandy western Florida earth.

This is not always easy, especially when you're working full-time while raising kids. Early in our newspaper careers, Lane and I both watched from medium-size newspaper markets as our mostly male colleagues got the primo assignments, often earned more money, and did not have to deal with being confined to stories that were deemed "soft" for a part of the paper that had only recently stopped being referred to as the women's section. Some of our male counterparts had stay-at-home wives who packed them lunches complete with little cheer-up notes.

We did not have to dance backward in high heels, but we did have to squeeze our interviews in between daycare drop-offs and sick-kid days and convince our bosses that we weren't napping or watching daytime TV when we wrote from home because it was quieter and easier to actually think. *And* we had to do the barrier-busting work of redefining whose stories were deemed newsworthy beyond the white-guys-in-ties officialdom that still, in my opinion, pervades too much of history's first draft.

And yet the first time I met Lane in the early 2000s, we were at a small narrative storytelling conference on the Outer Banks of North Carolina, marveling that our bosses were actually paying us to talk shop in a beach house with a near-limitless supply of beer and fried seafood. She had just published "Diving Headlong into Sunny Eden," the first story in this collection.

I remember being floored not only by how she found the story — while riding the bus for another story, then quickly pivoting to the better story in front of her — but also how she managed to nab the deliciously intimate dialogue near the end of the piece. As the couple took the first beach swim of their young lives, I wanted to know how Lane managed to record what they were saying to each other several hundred yards from shore.

Well, duh, she just walked right into the ocean with them — in her jeans. Talk about immersion journalism!

While many of us at that writing workshop have gone on to publish books, Lane keeps mining the earth beneath her sandals for the lucky readers of the *Tampa Bay Times*. At subsequent conferences where we've crossed paths, I've asked Lane if she ever wants to ditch the newspaper gig, as I did in 2014, and join us. But she has always deflected because she really, *really* loves her job.

What she loves most is people. "For all her acclaim and awards, she's driven mostly by 'I've gotta do justice for this person. I've got to make sure that when they read this, it feels genuine,'" said Maria Carrillo, who edited Lane at the Tampa paper and, earlier in both their careers, at the *Virginian-Pilot*. "She still gets twisted in knots about this, which is great." Though now retired from editing, Carrillo continues to cohost the popular writing podcast *WriteLane*, wherein Lane dissects literary journalism through the lens of her own stories.

This collection comes at a time when, ironically, more young people than ever are interested in joining our storytelling diaspora, writing not just for print but also for newer forms like podcasting or screenwriting for streaming services. Every time a politician calls journalists the "enemy of the people," I'm buoyed to learn that more people want to become part of our narrative writing tribe.

This book will help them learn the craft from a journalist working at the height of her powers—making the extra phone call, turning every page, being patient both with her subjects and herself (for as the great Robert Caro has advised, "Time equals truth"). Lane's Tips & Takeaways that accompany each story are generously offered and so goodie-laden that I found myself thinking as I read them: I wish I had known this starting out.

I wish I'd learned earlier to lean on photographer colleagues as my second pair of eyes, as Lane routinely does, or about her unique way of structuring her notes, or about the best ways to collaborate with editors—Lane has clearly benefited from her close working relationships with Carrillo and Wilson.

During the reporting for "The Girl in the Window," Wilson told Lane that she was not to return to the newsroom until she'd interviewed the biological mother of the feral child, which Lane resisted doing. "He was not going to let me off the hook on that," Lane told me. "He insisted that we couldn't really know [the girl] until we found out what was happening with the mother. I hated her for what she'd done, but that was a huge revelation to me—'get all sides'—and I'll be forever grateful to Mike for that."

For people who just crave reading great nonfiction yarns, this book will not disappoint. It shows how important feature writing is to the health of a democracy, especially as so many economically hammered newspapers in smaller markets try to make do with dwindling staff that now rarely cover more than crime, breaking news, and high school sports. Newspapers were once the civic glue of a community, and I truly believe that the *Tampa Bay Times* and other, newer nonprofit startups can be a critical part of the solution to problems stoked by social media echo chambers.

As this collection proves, shared narratives like the ones Lane tells nurture empathy and understanding, qualities that are in short supply today. A 99-year-old who's still going to work every day, the non-autistic 12-year-old twin whose heart is pure, a sister driven to the brink of violence, even a fan at a Stormy Daniels strip show.

As Wilson, now at the *New York Times*, describes it, "Lane's storytelling is fueled by her love of people. She is simply fascinated by everyone. I've never seen anything like it. She gets stories by chatting with waitresses and convenience store clerks and perfume saleswomen. As a journalist I had often heard the saying 'everyone has a story,' but I thought it was hyperbole until I worked with Lane."

Annie Dillard wrote, "You were made and set here to give voice to this, your own astonishment." *"The Girl in the Window" and Other True Tales* deserves a special place among the best books about writing, next to Stephen King's *On Writing*, Anne Lamott's *Bird by Bird*, and Tracy Kidder and Richard Todd's *Good Prose*.

Lane DeGregory has given readers and writers alike a bird's-eye view into her own astonishment. And that, gentle reader, is a complicated, wonderful, and life-changing place to be.

Beth Macy
Roanoke, Virginia
April 2022

INTRODUCTION

A feral child finds a family. An old bottle washes up with a note inside. A boy's stuffed elephant flies out the car window.

I wrote these stories for a daily newspaper in Florida. Years later, I still receive emails about them from readers across the world. And from writers wanting to know: How did you do that?

This anthology is my answer. It is for people who enjoy reading true tales, for writers of all types trying to improve their own work, and for teachers and editors eager to help. These are the stories that hundreds of readers have reacted to, that countless journalism students have studied. They are also my favorites.

The *Tampa Bay Times*, formerly the *St. Petersburg Times*, has long been known for pioneering literary nonfiction and consistently producing some of the best feature stories in the country. The newspaper is more than a century old and is owned by the nonprofit Poynter Institute, which trains American and international journalists.

Since 2000 I have written for the *Times*, led classes and webinars at Poynter, and traveled to colleges and conferences across the country and around the world to teach other journalists, editors, professors, students and writers. In recent years I have also hosted a podcast, *WriteLane*, where my longtime editor and I share stories and talk about ways to find, report and write nonfiction narratives.

For years, people have been asking me if I had a book with my stories and the stories behind the stories. Now I do.

Some of the pieces in this collection are short, reported and written in a single day. Others are projects I worked on for months. A few are off the news. Most are about the struggles of ordinary people, recounting loss and love, pain and perseverance, tragedy and triumph. All of the stories are set in Florida. But many could have taken place in your backyard, wherever you live.

I hope they feel universal and timeless.

I also wanted the book to include not just my stories, but the kinds of advice other writers often ask for. As I was planning it, I thought about questions from classes and conferences where I've taught:

Where did you find that young couple who just arrived in Florida?
How did you get the murderer to talk to you?
Did you really hear those girls talking in the woods?

I decided to use the stories themselves to answer these questions. Since I wrote them all, I can offer background no one else can about how I found the couple on a bus, wrote the murderer a letter, went camping with those girls. I share these insights through the book's structure and several special features.

The book is divided into three parts: "Short Stories," "On Assignment" and "Narratives." These reflect different story forms familiar not just to journalists but to other writers. Many of the short stories were reported and written in a couple of days; others took more time but are told in tight frames. Most of the ones on assignment came from editors asking me to find a unique angle on a news event—something any writer can do in any medium. The narratives are more immersive, taking readers into new worlds, introducing them to people who are suffering, struggling, celebrating. All sorts of writers can learn ways to find similar compelling characters to use in their own work.

At the center of each chapter is one of my stories, reprinted as originally published. The stories are all framed by some bigger theme related to how I found, reported or wrote the piece, in chapters such as "Talk to Strangers," "Listen to the Quiet" or "Use Their Voices." I offer general advice on this theme along with background on how the story came about in the sections "Before the Story." For several key pieces, I also include "After the Story" segments recounting what happened later, either to the people featured or because of the story or both.

Then there are the annotations in the margins. Each story contains ten to twenty Tips & Takeaways tied to specific details, sentences or passages. In these annotations I take readers behind the scenes of my reporting, organizing and editing processes. And I share thoughts that might help people navigate their own journeys to tell stories, such as "Go along for the ride," "Compare memories" and "Have the last word."

Finally, three "Spotlight" features—one in each part—gather my most essential advice on finding ideas, reporting, writing and editing. Some of these suggestions appear in more detail in the Tips & Takeaways throughout the book, but the "Spotlight" features bring it all together, along with visual aids.

The annotations and other special features offer instruction for all sorts of storytellers—for journalists who write for newspapers, magazines and book publishers; for people who make podcasts, TV shows and documentaries; for anyone interested in immersing themselves in real-life stories and deconstructing the process of creating them.

These stories can be used as teaching tools in newsrooms, high school and college classes, and workshops. And by any writer who wants to learn how to develop ideas, set scenes, organize notes, write memoirs and find their voice. For each story, there is also an episode of my *WriteLane* podcast posted to the Poynter website, offering additional insight into some aspect of the story.

The book also can be read by people who just want to dive into good stories, who crave narratives that make them think, laugh, cry—and connect.

No matter which of these you are, I hope this collection will entertain and inspire you.

PART

01

SHORT STORIES

Narratives don't need to take a lot of time or space. I often have to work within strict word limits. But even when I have more flexibility, it's sometimes easier to write stories that are tightly framed around a single scene or moment, zooming in on who a person is or what's at stake.

And readers love quick hits, stories that strike them and stay with them—especially when the writer makes readers feel like they're there and makes them care.

I have spent weeks with people, reporting on their lives, then decided to focus on a few hours—before, during and after something happened—as in the story of a teenage boy begging for a family. Everything else became background or got left in my notebook.

Most of the stories in this part, like the one about the young couple fleeing winter, were reported in one day, written the next. Some I reported and wrote the same day. They're all under 1,600 words. Two of the ones that gained the most attention are under 800 words.

Sometimes, a little says a lot.

With wages from their Wendy's jobs,
Dan Marinko, 20, and his girlfriend
Jenna Solterman, 18, fled Wisconsin's
winter for Florida's sunshine and palm
trees. Photographer: John Pendygraft

TALK TO STRANGERS

Be nosy, sit by
the old woman on
the bus; everyone
has a story

Diving Headlong into Sunny Eden:
A Young Couple Flees Winter

Reported in one afternoon; written the next day. Published May 30, 2011

BEFORE THE STORY

We were riding the city bus, reporting another story, when the photographer and I noticed this young couple kissing and pointing out the window at things they had never seen, like pelicans and palm trees.

We eavesdropped for a while, then asked them their story: they had taken a Greyhound across the country, fleeing the frost of winter, seeking sunshine and salt water.

They had never seen a beach.

So we ditched the other assignment, which we could come back to the next day, and followed them on their quest to see the seashore.

This illustrates an adage I firmly believe in: Journalists are like paramedics—we're always on call. Even if we're chasing another story, we have to be alert to narratives unfolding around us.

Public transportation is a great place to witness strangers on a journey and find stories. You meet people on the bus or subway that you might never encounter otherwise. And you can hold them captive, asking questions, at least until their stop.

This couple was on a mission and clearly amazed by the new world they had awoken into. I wanted to capture their wonder.

I also wanted to remind readers in Florida what a wild, wonderful place we live in. It can be easy to forget how special your surroundings are.

THE STORY

MAKE A MOVIE. Try to envision story openings as if you were directing a film: What's the first thing you want your readers to see? Where should you focus the camera? Starting with sunrise—squinting into the dawn, transitioning between dark and light —seemed like the perfect place to dive in. A new day. A new beginning. Sunshine streaming across Jenna's pale forehead.

CONSIDER CULTURAL REFERENCES. Allusions to popular songs, movies or TV shows can be problematic if not everyone recognizes them. But when the references are mainstream—and the details are telling—they can provide insight and context. This couple was so young that the girl carried a *Hannah Montana* purse. And their frame of reference was so small, their only connection to anywhere tropical was through cartoons like *SpongeBob* and *Finding Nemo*.

PAINT A PICTURE. To understand why Dan and Jenna ran away to Florida, you have to know what they wanted to escape. In one paragraph, I give readers a glimpse of their Wisconsin town, where it is, how small it is, how awful the weather is. I just Googled those facts and got excited when I found the town slogan: "Where the North Begins."

They woke to the sun streaming through the bus windows. He glanced out the glass and grinned.

She buried her face in his sweatshirt. "Too bright."

He remembers every detail. They were curled together on the front seat of the Greyhound, between his battered duffel bag and her Hannah Montana purse. For three days, they had been traveling south. It had been dark since they left Atlanta.

Now, squinting in the blinding dawn, he saw that they were cruising over a long bridge. On both sides, small white waves capped the bluest water he had ever seen. Ahead, there was land—a wide causeway lined with tall palm trees.

Palm trees! Just like on SpongeBob.

He draped his arm around his girlfriend's thin shoulders. He kissed her pale forehead, then both of her eyelids. "Look," he said softly. "We're here."

Welcome to Florida.

A week earlier, they had been in Wisconsin, working at Wendy's. Outside, hail was pelting the parking lot, blanketing everything in ice.

Dan Marinko, 20, was angry. He remembered saying, "Why does it have to be like this again?"

"I know, right?" Jenna Solterman, 18, had answered.

They had grown up in Portage, halfway between Madison and Green Bay. Nine square miles of prairie, with 9,728 people and a prison. The town slogan: "Where the North Begins."

Winter, there, lasts almost all year.

Dan had said, "It doesn't have to be like this."

Neither had ever been out of Wisconsin. They had never seen a beach, never felt sand shift beneath their bare feet.

But Dan's Aunt Helen had sent postcards from St. Petersburg: A pelican on a piling, tan girls on golden sand, warm sun sparkling on the gulf.

"I don't know much about Florida," Dan had told Jenna. "Except everyone says it's paradise."

There comes a time when a guy just has to dust the dirty snow off his Air Jordans, grab his girl and go.

That weekend, while snow piled up outside the drive-through, the young couple worked overtime. On Monday, they put their paychecks together: $530. On Tuesday, they each packed a pair of jeans, two T-shirts and shorts. His tent. Her hair-straightener.

They left everything else in her room they shared at her mom's house. They didn't tell her mom that they were going, or that they weren't coming back. Jenna slipped a photo of her mom into a sock.

Wednesday morning, when a friend dropped them at the Greyhound station in Madison, the air was 39 degrees. Jenna shivered in her hoodie. Dan held her hand. They bought two tickets to St. Petersburg, wherever that was. Total cost: $388. That left them with $141, a bottle of water and a half-pack of Marlboro reds.

"It's going to be great," Dan kept telling Jenna. "You'll never be cold again."

THINGS THEY CARRY. When you run away with only a backpack, what do you bring? I asked Dan and Jenna to show me everything they brought with them, so I could see what was important enough to carry along. Money, of course, was crucial—how long could they make that last? But I especially loved that Dan brought his tent—he knew they might be homeless. And Jenna brought her hair straightener and slipped her mom's picture into her sock.

Millions of people have done this, decided all their troubles would disappear, all their dreams would come true, if they moved to the land of eternal sunlight.

Dan and Jenna set out for the same reasons folks have flocked to Florida for more than a century: To stop shoveling snow. To escape. To start over.

They weren't worried about unemployment rates or hurricanes or oil spills. They were young and in love and they had each other. All they needed were a few waves. And a tan.

"In Florida," Dan told Jenna, "they say you can eat oranges right off the trees."

SOAR ABOVE. Between providing background in the second section and returning to the narrative in the fourth, I wanted to rise above the specifics of this story and make it universal. Everyone who visits Florida has that moment when they realize they've landed in paradise. This couple's motivation was the same one that draws millions of visitors every winter.

She sobbed as the bus pulled out of the icy parking lot. Over her shoulder, she watched Wisconsin fade behind them.

"What about sharks?" she kept asking. "What about alligators?"

He is broad-shouldered and outgoing, with homemade tattoos inked across both forearms. His sideways grin is endearing: Leonardo DiCaprio with a *Dumb and Dumber* haircut.

She is slender and shy, her blond ponytail streaked with hot pink. On one hand, her fingernails are blue; the others are black. She wears a tiny diamond ring he bought her at Walmart.

BURY THE BACKSTORY. There's this formula to TV true-crime stories: start with the murder, then go back to when the victim was born and work forward, chronologically, to the crime. I find it better to get the readers invested in the character, action and setting before making them flash back an entire generation. In this story, I don't tell you how the couple met or anything about their relationship until the fourth section. And I fast-forward through that, to get back to the story quickly.

ASK: ARE YOU SURE? When Jenna told me Dan was on probation and wasn't supposed to leave the state, I asked them both: Are you sure you want to share your story in the newspaper? I wasn't going to call the cops or turn him in. But I wanted him to know that he could get caught if someone read that he'd skipped town. He insisted that no one in Wisconsin would see the Florida paper.

He still can't believe she said yes.

They met through Jenna's brother, and have been together for more than a year. Jenna knows all about Dan's past. He told her how, when he was 9, his dad shot and killed his mom, and how he and his brother went to live with Mom's sister, Aunt Helen. Everything was okay until Aunt Helen got divorced and moved to Florida.

Dan was 11 when she sent him to foster care.

Jenna knows Dan has done stupid stuff: got kicked out of high school for carrying a pocket knife, stole a convertible whose owner left keys in the ignition, got in a fight in jail. She knows he is still on probation and wasn't supposed to leave the state.

But she loved the way he called her beautiful and kissed her eyes and promised to take care of her, to take her away.

For the first time, she imagined a world without winter.

———

The air was thick the last Friday in April when they stepped out at the St. Petersburg bus station.

Dan and Jenna felt like they had landed on another planet, where everything was sticky and green and the sun was so close you could feel it frying your face.

Dan shoved up his sweatshirt sleeves. Jenna pulled sunglasses from her purse. They checked a map, found a stop near Aunt Helen's trailer park, and bought transfer tickets to the city bus.

While they waited, Dan steered Jenna toward a sandy median. "Look," he said, pointing at a palm tree. "They're real!"

———

THROUGH THEIR EYES. Watching this couple drink in their new landscape, basking in that wonder and joy, was delightful. Through their eyes, I saw things that have become so familiar to me that I don't appreciate them anymore. I zoomed in on details as they discovered them: a blue heron, a hibiscus bush, a pelican.

After we have been here for a while, it's easy to forget what a weird, wonderful place we live in, where blue herons wander through gas stations and bushes bloom all year.

We crank up the AC, close our blinds and watch TV. Instead of venturing into the Eden outside.

This young couple had journeyed more than 1,350 miles to find Florida. Now that they were here, things seemed so surreal.

"Look! What's that crazy bird? It's got a scoop bill," Jenna said, pointing, as the bus ambled west along Bay Pines Boulevard.

"I think it's a pelican," said Dan.

"What's a pelican?"

"You know," he said. "Like on *Finding Nemo*."

———

They reached the stop by Aunt Helen's house about 1:30 p.m., found a sign for her over-55 trailer park. But before knocking on her door, Dan wanted to go swimming.

They were close now. He could smell it. The breeze blew in salt and seafood. So they set out walking west, to find the beach.

He paused by a hibiscus bush, plucked a scarlet flower and tucked it behind Jenna's ear. "There," he said. "Now you're a Florida girl."

After a while, they ducked into a pizza place. "How far to the beach?" asked Dan. The waitress told them 3 miles.

That was too far to hike, especially carrying all their bags. So they went back to the bus stop and got on the first bus they saw.

It carried them across another bridge, then turned left toward Madeira Beach. Strip malls and souvenir shops flew by. They passed an ice cream stand, high-rise condos.

Suddenly, Dan jumped up. "There it is!" he shouted. Between two low buildings of the Surfs Inn, a sliver of sand stretched all the way to the water. "Look at that!"

He pulled the overhead cord. The bus driver eased the door open. And, carrying everything they owned, the young couple from Wisconsin walked into the afternoon sunshine.

They followed a short walkway, climbed four concrete steps and stopped. Sunbathers were scattered along the shore; skimboarders splashed in the shallow swath; farther out, a sailboat drifted beyond the breakers. "Oh wow," Dan said. "It's so much more than I thought." Jenna nodded. She didn't know what to say.

All their lives they had been surrounded by land, the whole country hemming them in. Now, they were at the edge of everything, about to dive in.

"Come on!" Dan said, kicking off his Air Jordans and sprinting toward the water.

Beneath their bare feet, the sand was soft and hot. They didn't have bathing suits, so they ran into the water in their shorts, laughing and leaping the little waves.

"It's so warm," she said. "I thought it would be cold."

"I told you," he said. "We finally made it. Look at us! We're in paradise."

Behind them, the tide crept up the beach, erasing their footprints. In front of them, the gray-green gulf stretched forever.

She jumped up and threw her arms and legs around him. He kissed her, tasting the saltwater on her lips. He had never tasted saltwater.

DON'T INTERFERE. It was incredibly hot that day in Florida. Dan and Jenna had no idea how to get from the bus to the beach. The photographer and I so wanted to help them, to shorten this long walk to nowhere in the sweltering heat, but we couldn't tell them they got off at the wrong stop or were going the wrong way. We had to follow them trying to figure it out themselves because we didn't want to change or even influence the story.

SLOW DOWN. A wise editor once told me: "Just before the climax, brake. Slow down. Make readers wait for that rising action to crest." Anticipation builds excitement and makes the payoff so much more powerful. I could have skipped right from the bus to the beach. But by following the couple as they zigzagged across town, boarded another bus, passed strip malls, souvenir shops and condos, readers take the journey with them. That way, when Dan and Jenna finally saw the sand, it was even more incredible. Like finding Oz after following the yellow brick road!

AFTER THE STORY

Dan hadn't told his aunt he was coming to Florida, bringing his girl-friend and planning on crashing on her couch for a while. When they showed up, Aunt Helen didn't welcome them with open arms.

She put up with the couple for a few days, and they got to spend more time at the beach.

Dan's probation officer didn't see the story. So I didn't have to feel guilty about outing him.

But when Aunt Helen caught them smoking pot on her patio, that was the last straw. She called Dan's probation officer—who hauled him back to Wisconsin. Of course, Jenna followed.

GET A LIFE

Go to festivals, join
bowling leagues,
mine your friends

Zeke the Labrador: An Intuitive Dog Saves His Owner

Reported over two days; written the next day. Published December 15, 2015

BEFORE THE STORY

Having a wide, diverse social circle is incredibly helpful for finding story ideas. If you mostly hang out with other writers, you won't meet people to write about or who can introduce you to those people. Whatever your interest or hobby, get with a group of others who enjoy the same things, listen to their conversations, tell them you're always on alert for good stories.

One of my friends who lives halfway across the country, who knows I love dogs, told me about a friend of hers who has a cousin in Florida, and the cousin's husband had this incredible old dog that had saved his life—more than once.

Zeke only lived a few miles from me, but I learned his story through a web that spanned five states. Tell your friends to tell you stories. Everyone knows someone who knows someone else worth writing about.

And make sure you check the stories out, vet them with the subject's spouse, friends and coworkers.

Zeke's story seemed too good to be true, so I knocked on a lot of neighbors' doors to gather and confirm key details.

Gerald Rittinger wanted a dog for
companionship. He had no idea Zeke
would save him, again and again.
Photographer: Scott Keeler

THE STORY

The first time it happened, Gerald Rittinger was driving to buy his gravestone. His diabetes was getting worse. Doctors had just diagnosed him with prostate cancer. They gave him six months.

Gerald's wife, Jeanne, was in the passenger seat of their Lincoln that day. Their puppy, Zeke, was supposed to stay in the back seat. But the yellow Labrador kept putting his big paws on the console between them, inching forward.

They headed north on Interstate 75 to his family cemetery in Kentucky. After about three hours, Zeke stood up and began barking. "Down! Zeke, get down!" Jeanne scolded, tugging at his collar. Zeke leapt up, nuzzling his wet nose against Gerald's neck. Licking his face.

Laughing, Gerald tried to push away the puppy. But Zeke wouldn't back off. His barking got louder. The dog became so agitated that Gerald had to pull off the highway.

Seconds later, Gerald had a seizure. "If he had still been driving," Jeanne said, "all of us would have been killed."

That was 12 years ago. Gerald had his headstone engraved, planted it in the graveyard, then came home to die. But Zeke wouldn't let him.

When Gerald met Jeanne more than 30 years ago, he was running the National Museum of the U.S. Air Force in Dayton, Ohio. She was a real estate consultant who trained other Realtors.

She told him she was afraid of dogs. Never had one, never wanted to get to know one. Then they met a neighbor, who had a chocolate Lab she learned to like.

After they moved to Florida in 1995, after Gerald's Type 2 diabetes got so bad that he had to take insulin four times a day, and Jeanne had to travel more for work, she decided to get a dog so Gerald wouldn't be so alone.

"Zeke chose us," said Jeanne, 60, a warm, wiry woman who seldom sits still. "He was only a month old, in this pile of puppies in a playpen. But as soon as he saw us he broke free and ran to us, wagging his tail."

The second time they went to visit, when the Labs were ready to be weaned, Zeke seemed to remember them. He raced to Gerald and rubbed his soft head against Gerald's leg. "You could see

LET THEM START. If you want to put the people you're interviewing at ease, let them tell the story their own way. Where they start their tale often helps me figure out where to begin. Instead of telling me about how she met her husband or how they picked out their puppy, Jeanne jumped right into "The first time it happened..." And she gave such great detail, it transported me into the back seat of their Lincoln.

PROMISE SOMETHING. Try to end your first section with a question or quest: What's going to happen? What's at stake? What comes next? That way you won't lose readers while you weave in background, before you return to the narrative. Knowing that Zeke wouldn't let Gerald die signals that there will be more rescues.

INCLUDE JUST ENOUGH. It's great to know too much. Sometimes the hardest part of writing is figuring out what to leave out. I spent hours talking to this couple about their childhoods, courtship and careers. But when I started writing, I realized readers only needed three biographical details: how they met, what they did for work, when they moved to Florida.

USE HURDLES. It would be easy to assume that someone who has a big old dog loves dogs. But when I asked Jeanne if she'd always had dogs, she shook her head—and told me she'd always been afraid of them. That tension let me set up the idea that Zeke helped win her over.

it in his eyes," said Gerald, 74. "He has this way of looking at you, like he knows something."

ANTICIPATE SKEPTICS. When you know someone might question the veracity of your story, offer evidence to dispel their doubts. I knew not everyone would believe that a dog could sense when its owner was about to have a seizure. So I researched articles about Diabetic Alert Assistance dogs and included the *National Geographic* quote to explain what dogs can be trained to do.

Dogs can be trained to find bed bugs and bombs, to sniff out survivors after earthquakes. Others can detect cancer cells in urine samples.

"Some dogs can smell odors given off by humans with diabetes," a *National Geographic* article reported in 2009.

Diabetic Alert Assistance dogs are specially bred, trained from birth through their first year, says the website dogs4 diabetics.com. Getting one certified costs about $10,000. "The process requires a properly trained dog, as well as a trained handler."

Zeke never had any training, except for the basics at puppy kindergarten, where a police officer at St. Petersburg College taught him to sit and lie down.

"He never really even got 'fetch,'" Gerald said. "He just ate the Frisbee."

His best trick, everyone thought, was dancing on his hind legs for a Pup-Peroni treat.

Until he saved Gerald. Again. And again.

LIMIT DESCRIPTION. I used to spend an inordinate amount of time trying to describe people and places. But a little goes a long way, especially if there's something distinctive to include. If all you know is that someone has emerald eyes, or a pencil-thin mustache, that might be enough. Zeke's anvil head, butterscotch fur and angel wings brought him to life.

Zeke grew to be a big boy, packing on 115 pounds. His head got wide and flat, like an anvil. Across his shoulders, the butterscotch fur faded into two white arcs. Jeanne calls the markings his angel wings.

When he was young, he used to wander around the Broadwater neighborhood of St. Petersburg. He learned which houses had kids, which people had dog biscuits. But he would always head home to check on Gerald.

Sometimes, the dog sensed plummeting blood sugar and seizures before they happened, in time for Gerald to take a glucose tablet, or call 911. Other times, Zeke didn't get any warning. He would find Gerald slumped in a chair, or sprawled on the living room floor. If Jeanne wasn't home, he would sprint through the garage to knock on a neighbor's door.

ASK ABOUT BEFORE. Report about what things used to be like, so you can contrast them to now. Gerald told me that Zeke's hips hurt, so I asked what had changed because of that—poor old dog could no longer get up on the bed and sleep with his people. And when I asked Jeanne about how their walks were different, she shook her head and said, "Zeke used to lead."

"He's a wild character. I don't know how he knows. He just has this way of sensing when I'm in trouble," Gerald said. "Maybe he smells something in my sweat, or a change in my breath. Maybe he just feels me panic."

One night, Jeanne was sleeping beside her husband when

Zeke jumped onto the bed and yanked her arm. Jeanne turned on the light. Gerald's mouth was drooping, his face slack. He had just had a stroke. If she hadn't called an ambulance then, he wouldn't have survived.

"I know of 30 times, at least, that dog has saved his life," Jeanne said. "All the paramedics know Zeke."

———

The old yellow Lab is almost 13 now. In the last few months, he has lost 20 pounds. His muzzle has faded to white, like his angel wings. His hips hurt so much, he can't jump on the bed.

But every morning after breakfast, he hauls himself up to nose Gerald's knee and let him know it's time for a walk. It's often the only time the two leave the house.

They move slowly, side by side. Jeanne watches them cross the yard. Zeke used to lead the way. Now he trails behind Gerald, limping, crisscrossing the street to find slices of shade.

After they pass four houses, Zeke starts wheezing. "It's okay," Gerald says softly. "You just tell me when you're done."

As they make their way down the street, neighbors come out to pet their favorite dog. "He's a hero. Absolutely," said Ray Ockuly, who lives a few doors down. "All these years, he's what has kept Gerald alive."

"Zeke looks out for everyone," said Kirk Price, who lives nearby. A few months ago, when his 11-year-old daughter fell off her bike in front of Zeke's house, the dog got up from the yard, licked the girl's leg, then lumbered to her home and pawed at the door until her mom came. Thinking Zeke wanted a treat, she turned to go into the kitchen.

Instead, the dog clamped his mouth around her hand and took her to her daughter, who was still sobbing on the sidewalk. "I've never known a dog like that," Price said.

Barbara Klinowski also lives on the block. One day this summer, she was coming home when she saw Zeke standing in the middle of the street, barking. "What are you doing? Let's go home," she told the dog.

"He led me back to his house, where I found Gerald barely holding on," she said. "I called Jeanne, but if I hadn't found him . . ."

After 10 minutes, Zeke plops beneath a palm tree, panting, and looks up at Gerald as if to apologize.

"It's okay. We can turn back," Gerald says. He waits a mo-

BE PATIENT. Some people have a hard time just watching and waiting. But it's important to be still and let things unfold. Seeing how long it took for Zeke and Gerald just to cross the street was devastating. But their pace was perfectly matched. I witnessed Gerald's encouragement and affection when he rubbed his best friend's heaving sides. And I saw, through it all, Zeke's tail never stopped wagging.

KNOCK ON DOORS. Corroborate what people tell you, add other voices and examples when you can. The more sources you have, the closer to the truth you get. And readers appreciate knowing that you didn't just accept one couple's story without checking it out. We saw several neighbors on our short walk. I talked to them on the sidewalk. Then I knocked on six more doors. Everyone hailed Zeke as a hero. Several had their own rescue stories.

HAVE THE LAST WORD. It's easy to wrap up stories with a quote, especially a good one. But a colleague once chastised me for being lazy. "You're the writer!" she said. "Don't you think you can come up with something better than whatever someone tells you?" Not always. But now, at least, I try. And I spend a lot more time on my endings. Jeanne's quote would have worked. But I went back to the gravestone, and the idea that Zeke's and Gerald's names would be etched together.

ment, rubs Zeke's heaving sides, then heads toward home. The old dog stumbles back onto his feet and follows, tongue lolling, tail wagging.

Some people have suggested putting Zeke out of his misery. But Jeanne knows that once she loses her dog, her husband won't be far behind.

"Whoever goes first," she said, "they're going to be buried together."

And she's going to add Zeke's name to Gerald's tombstone.

03

EXPLORE RITUALS

Find faith, follow rites of passage, focus on holidays, be with those who can't celebrate

Finding the Right Words: A Boy Buys His First Valentine

Reported in one afternoon; written the next day. Published February 13, 2014

BEFORE THE STORY

Celebrations and somber gatherings offer opportunities to cross cultures and connect readers through similar experiences and universal themes. Write about weddings and funerals: love and loss; baptisms and Quinceañeras: birth and coming of age.

Each family has its own rituals, and intergenerational get-togethers, around holidays especially, give context and chronicle change. How did Grandmom celebrate graduation? What will Christmas look like for the new immigrant?

It's also interesting to explore outliers: those who have to work while others are worshipping, those who don't believe — or care.

One year, just before Valentine's Day, a friend told me about her 12-year-old son, who was agonizing about buying a card for his first crush. There was a new angle on the holiday and a scene I could witness.

I made plans to go with my friend and her son when they went shopping over the weekend. But on Friday, in the middle school

Austin Erickson wanted the Valentine for his first girlfriend to be special. But most cards aren't written for 11-year-olds in love. Photo: Melissa Lyttle

cafeteria, the girl dumped him. There went my story. But then I did what I often do when I'm desperate: I posted a plea on Facebook:

"I'm looking for an adolescent boy or girl who is going to buy their first real Valentine . . . Someone who would be willing to share his or her love story with me."

Within two hours, I had 30 leads: friends of friends suggesting neighbors and kids from the soccer team, all kinds of moms I didn't know offering their own children as subjects.

I met Austin at his home, interviewed him in the living room, then asked to see a picture of his girlfriend—and his bedroom. You can learn a lot about someone just by looking at where they live. On the walls, I saw posters of *Star Wars* and *Batman*. On his dresser, there was a swimming trophy. Austin laughed at some of my questions. He told me, "Women are complicated."

THE STORY

In the passenger seat of his mom's SUV, Austin Erickson sits silently, clutching his wallet, watching as his subdivision slides by.

"So Publix?" asks his mom, turning onto the highway. "Target?"

Austin, who is 11, doesn't look at her.

"The Hallmark store," he says. "This has to be special."

Normally, Austin hates going to the Hallmark store, waiting for his mom and older sisters to sift through Vera Bradley bags while surrounded by all the candles that are supposed to smell like rain.

Normally, Valentine's Day isn't a big deal to the sixth-grader who loves *Star Wars* and *Batman* and Minecraft.

"But now that I'm in a relationship it seems more important," he says Tuesday afternoon.

"I want to impress Sarah."

Sarah. He says her name like a sigh. Her last name starts with a K. He just can't pronounce it.

She lives six doors down, in a beige house a lot like his. They met the first day of Seven Springs Middle School, at the bus stop.

Their courtship started like so many young couples': "I remember the date, it was Sept. 4th," Austin says. "Her friend came up to me and said, 'If Sarah asked you out, would you go?'"

Austin hesitated. He could tell she's smart. "That's impor-

GO ALONG FOR THE RIDE. My favorite way to report a story is in two parts: First, interview someone in their home. Look for photos and plaques, books and mementos, note the neatness. Then observe them doing something, going on a quest or journey. I asked to jump into the back seat as Austin's mom drove to the strip mall. I listened as they talked about what he was after and his feelings. I used that conversation to hint to readers why this was a big deal.

PRESENT TENSE. I initially wrote this story in the past tense since it happened a couple of days before Valentine's Day but was going to run that day. My editor suggested we try it in the present tense, which can make readers feel like they're along for the ride. It's a much more intimate, immediate voice—and hints more toward the universal experience. This could be happening right now.

FIVE SENSES. We sometimes forget to use all our senses when we're reporting. But smell, touch and taste can transport readers in powerful ways. When I asked Austin if he liked going to the Hallmark store, he said no. So, of course, I asked him why. And the first thing he said was because all the candles are so stinky, they give him a headache. "What's the worst?" I asked. "Rain."

CHANNEL YOUR SUBJECT'S VOICE. Austin had this endearing mixture of adult vocabulary and adolescent insight. And he took himself very seriously. So early on, I knew I wanted to tell his story with words he would use. "Her last name starts with a K. He just can't pronounce it." His quotes also were wonderful. So I used more of those than I normally would.

tant," he says. And she has a good sense of humor. "When she laughs, everyone around her can't help laughing."

It took a few seconds to decide, he says. "I'm a very busy person: I swim breaststroke, I'm a green belt in karate, I have church and Boy Scouts and I get straight A's and I'm going to go to the University of Florida and be a lawyer." Then he looked at her again. "Yeah, I can probably do this."

So Sarah's friend told Sarah and Sarah started giggling her great laugh and they've been together ever since: six months, which in middle school time equals forever. "I'm her longest relationship," he says. "Max and her only lasted a month. We've been going out all year."

They've never actually gone anywhere, not even to each other's homes. "I'm worried about meeting her dad," Austin says.

GET THE BRAND NAME. When Austin told me he and his girlfriend played games while waiting for the bus, I could have left it at that. But as the mom of two then-teenage sons, I knew how different games say different things about the kids who play them—and that the device they play on matters. So I asked, "What games?"

Their relationship revolves around the bus: waiting for it, sharing a seat, playing Flappy Bird on her iPod. Sometimes they hold hands. They can't eat lunch together because they have different schedules. "She's an older woman, in seventh grade," he says. "But we're the same height, so it's okay."

After school, they hang out at picnic tables, waiting together for a glorious half-hour, from 2:50 until 3:20 p.m. "Good thing we have the last bus!" They talk about their teachers, other kids, his swim team, her little sister. "Everything, really." She brings him peanut butter crackers.

They never fight. "Why should we?" They have hugged but never kissed. She was the first to say, "I love you."

"We were waiting for the bus and the school resource officer was giving us a ride in his golf cart but there weren't enough seats and I didn't want Sarah to have to stand," he says. "So I held on to the back and she said, 'Austin, I love you, but you're going to die.' She was kidding about me dying. But I'm pretty sure she meant the 'I love you' part."

———

DON'T INTERRUPT. You never really know what you're going to need until you start writing. So take in everything, from the lights to the carpet to the song that the stuffed pig sings. I didn't want to intrude on Austin's expedition, so I just followed him around the store, picking up the cards he put down, so I could write down the sentiments he had discarded.

He follows his mom through the parking lot at Mitchell Ranch Plaza, into Deb's Hallmark, where stuffed animals grin on tall tables and racks of cards stretch in a red sea of sentiment.

"I want to get something personal," Austin tells his mom. "I mean, I should know her enough to get something she likes."

His mom smiles. "Well, what does Sarah like?"

"She likes me!" says Austin.

He has been saving for months, his Christmas money, wages from walking the neighbor's dog. In his black wallet, he has

$100. "You're not going to spend it all on Sarah?" says his mom, half-asking, half-scolding.

"No," says Austin. "But I don't want something that looks like it's been bought on a budget."

Austin and his mom walk past a croaking frog, a barking dog, both holding stuffed hearts. "Oh, look at the pig!" says his mom.

Austin squeezes the pig's hoof and it starts dancing to The Cupid Shuffle. "Now if they have a cow, I might get that," he says. "Sarah has a cow lunchbox. So she must like cows."

He wanders through the card section, past cartoons of old ladies telling fart jokes and photos of wiener dogs making puppy eyes. He shows his mom a card shaped like Darth Vader with the tagline: *The force is strong between us.* He puts it back. "I know this is about her."

In a section called, "Romantic Love," he finally finds a cow: just its face on the front, black and white, with wide eyes, a pink nose. Inside, it says, "I want to sMOOOch!"

"Oh," he says, closing the card. "It's about kissing."

They don't make Valentines about holding hands.

———

He vetoes a sparkly headband, passes on a personalized pen, never even considers a candle. For a while he holds the stuffed "Qupig," but after listening to four verses of The Cupid Shuffle, he sets it back on the shelf, declaring, "I don't want her dad to kill me."

Instead, Austin chooses a box of Whitman's chocolates. "What girl doesn't like chocolate?"

And a card with a winged pig, whose nostrils are shaped like hearts. *I hope you have a happy Valentine's Day*, says the front. Inside, the pig flaps its hooves, saying, *I squeally do!*

"That will make her laugh," he says.

Hearing her laugh is worth way more than the two hours of dog-walking wages this will cost him.

"Do you think it's enough?" Austin asks his mom in the car. "Just chocolates and a card? I mean, I know I have to write my own message to her too. That'll be the hard part."

That's always the hard part. Especially when you're 11 and you really like this girl and you don't want anything from her except for her to like you back—not even a kiss, not really, not yet—and you have no idea what to say or how to say it.

And the only B you have ever gotten in your whole life was in writing . . .

EAVESDROP. Of course, Austin and his mom knew I was there. Of course, they saw me shadowing them. I got such great, immersive detail just writing down their conversation. And whenever I had a follow-up question, like what they were thinking or feeling or laughing about, I jotted that down in my notebook with an arrow to come back to later. You often get better insight listening than interviewing.

ASK EVERYTHING. When a boy tells you he walks the neighbor's dog, don't just get the dog's name—ask how much he charges per hour, so you can know the extent of his wealth when he buys an expensive card. When he tells you he gets straight A's, don't just ask what his favorite subject is—ask which is the hardest, and if he's ever gotten a B. And since it's a Valentine story and this is his first love, you have to ask if he's ever been kissed. Or wants to be.

BOOKEND. You need to know why someone is attracted to the other person if you're going to write a love story. For Austin, it was his girlfriend's laugh. That was one of the first things he mentioned about her, and something he returned to again and again. So when I heard him tell his mom that he finally chose that card because it would make her laugh, I decided to begin and end his descriptions of his girlfriend with that laugh.

EMBRACE THE UNKNOWN. For Austin, the hardest thing about buying a Valentine turned out not to be choosing the card but finding the right words to write inside. I desperately wanted to know what he wrote, but he wasn't going to write it with me hanging over him. So I was going to call him the next day, but my editor thought it was better not knowing, leaving the question lingering with readers to let them fill in their own blanks.

Beyond the specific Tips
& Takeaways embedded in
the individual stories, here
is more in-depth advice
about finding ideas.

FINDING IDEAS

Stories are everywhere, you just have to be open to them.

Get out into the world, walk through a new neighborhood, talk to an Uber driver, look around and wonder. Then ask.

Some of my best ideas come from my life outside of work and have nothing to do with news. I find stories while I'm watching ball games with my kids, walking my dog, listening to my husband's band.

Festivals and fairs are brimming with characters and crowds. See who's celebrating Arbor Day or selling bathtubs in an expo booth. Who would do that? And why?

Reading what's posted on walls also helps. Check bulletin boards at libraries, recreation centers, coffee shops. Pick up free papers and flyers. Subscribe to newsletters from different towns, nursing homes, nonprofits—ideas will come flowing into your email. Social media groups also are full of stories, especially neighborhood ones. Join as many as you can keep up with. They're good places to fish for subjects, to get directed to possible sources. And it's an easy way to scroll through other people's thoughts, complaints and kudos.

Being part of in-person groups also inspires ideas. Whether you go to church, play in a pool league or meet with a book club, let everyone know you're a writer and are looking for stories. Ask: What should I write about? Who do you know?

A good narrative needs four ingredients: Character, Action, Setting, and Theme—or CAST.

CHARACTER

Write about people, not issues
Explore a town, building, corporation
What hasn't been done?
Look for stakeholders—everyman vs. outlier
You need access, insight, introspection

ACTION

Something has to happen
Can I watch it unfold? Recreate it?
Find a quest, question or complication
Show tension, motive, fear
What's at stake?

SETTING

Give a sense of place—movie openings, transport readers
Use a drone-level overview or just a single window
Can you go there?
Recreate the place—Google Earth, old maps, photos, weather reports, census data

THEME

One word
Universal connection
Why of the why

Whether you're covering an event, writing about an issue or profiling someone, it helps to consider stakeholders, to see as many perspectives on the story as possible.

I often make a diagram that looks like a childish sun. In the center of the circle, I put the idea or assignment. On each ray coming out of the circle, I list people who might be involved in or care about the subject. All of those people can provide ways to see the story.

Stakeholders

Once I was assigned to write about the Miss Florida beauty pageant. The runner-up from the last two years was from St. Petersburg, where I live. Other reporters had written profiles about her over those years, so I was trying to find another way in.

With her in the center of the circle, I brainstormed about who else might have something at stake: Her mom, who had started entering her in beauty pageants when she was a toddler. The caterer, trying to feed skinny girls who weren't eating during the three-day pageant. Her personal trainer, who had become her boyfriend.

I settled on the "Svengali" who chose her outfits and followed him as he took her shopping for the evening gown.

04

WONDER, WHO WOULD EVER?

Find someone doing
a strange or dirty job
and ask: Who does
that? Why?

Meet the "THE" Guy: Flag-Bearer of the Rodeo

Reported in one long day; written the next. Published June 13, 2007

BEFORE THE STORY

In old Bud Light radio ads, the announcer raised an invisible beer to workers doing the strangest jobs. I'd be listening in my car, cracking up thinking: Who picks up the golf balls on a driving range? Who designs wrestlers' capes? Who cleans out porta-potties? And why would anyone do that for a living?

Every awful job has a story. Find someone doing it, spend a day watching that person work, dig in deep about what they get out of it—and you'll have a "day in the life" narrative that takes readers into worlds they have never thought about.

The stories can be in the shadow of someone important: Who digs a president's grave? They can illuminate a larger news story: Who takes photos to document a murder scene? Or they can draw you to something peculiar: Why would anyone want to run a business picking up dog poop?

For this story, I was writing a travel piece about a Disney-fied dude ranch and took my two school-age sons to the little rodeo.

You can't always believe the guy in the white hat. Meet Grant Mason, *left*, and Ike Stein, who's really the good guy. Photographer: John Pendygraft

While watching four horsemen ride across the ring, carrying flags, my boys got the giggles.

One guy was "God," one was "Bless," one carried the final flag, "USA." The other rider's banner said simply "The."

"Wouldn't you hate to be the THE guy?" my older son said.

Later, when I told my editor about that conversation, he said, "Well, who is the THE guy?"—and sent me on a mission to find out.

THE STORY

At the end of the rodeo, Lee Greenwood's anthem blares through the speakers at Westgate River Ranch: "I'm proud to be an American . . ."

The crowd stands. The music builds. As the singer asks God to bless his country, four horsemen gallop into the dusty arena, unfurling 7-foot-long flags.

The flags are red, with white letters rimmed in blue sequins. Each man gets a word: GOD. BLESS. THE. USA.

You wonder: Who's the THE guy?

Think about it. The dude two horses ahead gets to be GOD. The next rider is BLESS. The cowboy at the end is Mr. USA. The third horseman isn't even a noun or a verb. He's just an article. Superfluous—except for grammatical purposes.

Who is the THE guy?

You ask Leroy Mason, who runs the rodeo, if he knows him.

"Sure," Mason says. "He's my son, Grant."

So on a Saturday in June, you meet Grant and his parents for lunch at the ranch. They take off their cowboy hats. Grant blesses the chicken fingers.

He's 15, been riding horses since he was 2. He was home-schooled until last year, when he enrolled at Lake Wales High so he could join the ROTC. Finished the year with a 3.9 GPA. Wants to go to West Point.

He's not what you had in mind. You were expecting some lackey who wrangles calves and lives in a mobile home with his girlfriend, her kid and a bunch of dogs.

"Grant doesn't want to be a cowboy, and I'm thankful for that," says his dad, who used to be one. "Been on the road most of my life. We moved here so Grant wouldn't have to grow up like that. Now he has a permanent home, land, horses." Mason smiles at his son.

"He doesn't know how blessed he is."

SECOND PERSON. This wasn't a story about me or my experience. Anyone who went to that homespun rodeo might have wondered the same thing. So I didn't want to use the first-person point of view. But the third-person perspective felt too official. I just wanted to take readers along with me on the journey of discovering who this guy was, so I wrote to "you."

SET EXPECTATIONS. Before I even started reporting, I had a picture in my mind of what the THE guy would look like, who he would be. By sharing that early in the story, I made sure readers knew the stereotype I was assuming, so that they would be as surprised as I was when that was broken—then proven true. Of course, I made it "You were expecting . . ." instead of "I was expecting," which seems more inclusive and hopefully less judgy.

LISTEN FOR CONNECTIONS. Four words launched the idea for this story. So throughout my reporting, I keyed in on references to those words—and their ideals. We didn't get into God, but during lunch, Grant "blessed" the chicken fingers and his dad said, "He doesn't know how blessed he is." When you make those connections, they reward the readers. And they help foreshadow the plot twist to come.

You watch Grant get the animals ready for the rodeo. He works with a guy named Ike.

Grant's cowboy hat is white. Ike's is black. Grant doesn't shave yet. Ike has a droopy mustache. Grant's shirt has dry-cleaner creases; Ike's wilts with sweat.

The teenager and the ranch hand cover more than 300 acres on horseback, flushing bulls from pastures, driving cattle.

Mostly, the THE guy leads.

Ike brings up the rear.

A half-hour before the rodeo, you're waiting at the deli for a piece of pizza. Ike comes up and asks what sort of story you're doing. You tell him you're here to write about the guy who carries the THE flag.

Ike looks confused. "Well, that would be me."

What? you ask. How can Ike be the THE guy?

"It wasn't by choice," he tells you. "They just handed me that flag four years ago, and I've been carrying it ever since.

"But for some reason, tonight they asked me to carry BLESS. Usually, Grant's BLESS."

You find Grant's mom outside the ticket booth. Tell her about your conversation with Ike.

Judy Mason hesitates. "Oh, that Ike," she says softly. "He'll say anything to get in the paper."

As the rodeo riders get ready, you thread through them, asking: Who carries the THE flag?

Ike, says a bull rider. That would be Ike, says a trick rider. Ike, says a steer roper, then the rodeo clown.

Barrel rider Caity Wall tells you she choreographed that closing number years ago. Her mom sewed the flags. Her husband is GOD.

"The THE guy?" she says, laughing. "Oh, that's always Ike."

At the end of the rodeo, as Greenwood's anthem blares through the speakers, GOD gallops into the arena.

Next comes Ike, bearing BLESS.

Grant follows, gripping THE.

"I'm proud to be an American . . ."

Afterward, you track down Ike.

His last name is Stein. His horse is Topper. You had it about right: He's 25, lives with the girlfriend, her kid, three dogs.

During the week, Ike takes care of 2,500 cattle. Weekends, he works at the rodeo. He's the guy who opens the bull chutes and prods the steers.

"I'm just the grunt," Ike says. "You don't want to write about me. Write about Grant."

But Grant is BLESS (except when reporters come).

You're the bridge between God and country, Ike.

The genuine article.

OTHER VOICES. Sometimes people in the background know more than those in the spotlight—or at least are willing to share more. Chat up the secretary for the city council, the janitor at the statehouse, the clerk of the court. I had asked Grant's parents about him and talked to other people organizing the rodeo. But it wasn't until I finally talked to Ike that I realized I needed to ask everyone I could who the real THE guy was. Those queries strengthened the story and gave me more good details— including who choreographed the horsemen's galloping entrance and who made the flags.

LISTEN TO THE MUSIC. The patriotic anthem that blared through the rodeo's closing number was familiar enough that I figured most readers would know the reference. And the message of being proud to be an American seemed to summarize what that whole pageant was supposed to be about. Including snippets of songs adds sound and texture to a scene, and helps immerse readers in the moment.

Anthony Moran holds on to his
brother, Ryan, in church. The
12-year-old twins are inseparable,
despite their vastly differing abili-
ties. Photographer: Keri Wiginton

05

ESTABLISH INTIMACY

Make a connection, build trust, have a conversation: dogs, kids, cars

A Brothers' Bond: Autism Ties Twins Together

Reported in two days; written in two. Published January 25, 2009

BEFORE THE STORY

I was at a church, covering a baptism, when the boy behind me started kicking the pew. I turned around. He was wriggling, thrashing, then started squealing. The boy next to him wrapped his arm around him and began rocking, whispering that everything was okay.

They looked about the same age as my sons, then around 12. When they walked out of the sanctuary, I followed them. On the playground, I watched them swing—then found their mom to ask if I could talk to them.

Of all the people I talk to for my stories, adolescent boys are the hardest. Most don't want—or don't know how—to have a conversation. They make me feel like I'm bothering them. To find a way to connect with people, talk about things that interest them first before you ask your questions. Ask about what they like to do, where they hang out, whether they have pets. Young people often open up when you ask about video games or movies. Older people love to talk about their kids and granddads.

I sat on the floor while one of the boys played Minecraft, just watching. I told him my son loved that game and also has a brother close to his age. Eventually—without turning from the screen—he told me about his twin.

THE STORY

He waits for his brother and mom to sit down, then slides into the wooden pew beside them. Anthony Moran always has to be on the aisle.

When your 12-year-old twin brother peels off his shirt during the offering, you want to be on the aisle so you can get him out of there. Fast.

"Did you bring his candy?" Anthony asks his mom. She reaches into her purse and pulls out a Ziploc filled with cough drops. "And his drink?" She retrieves an Iron Man sippy cup.

Anthony looks at Ryan, who is unbuttoning his pants. "No," Anthony says gently, shaking his head. "Not appropriate. No one wants to see our bellies here."

Anthony Moran is blond and earnest and super serious for a seventh-grader. He gets straight As at Peniel Baptist Academy.

He speaks softly, always in plurals: We, us, our. Like many twins, he thinks of himself as half of a pair.

The other half has brown hair and wide blue eyes and a boisterous giggle.

Ryan Moran is in speech therapy and special ed at Ochwilla Elementary. He seldom says whole sentences.

All his life, Anthony has been his voice.

FIND MEANING IN DETAILS. Always gather as many specific details as you can, but when you start writing, choose only those that say something important. I didn't describe what the boys were wearing or their house, but when I saw their bunk beds, the contrast between the Game Boy and the diapers hit me. These twins were at such different places in their development.

The boys live with their mom and dad and two dogs in a little house with a big yard in Interlachen. They share a room with bunk beds. On the bottom mattress, Anthony's Game Boy case sits next to Ryan's box of diapers.

The house has a third bedroom, but Anthony has never asked for his own space. "Why should I?" he said. This way he's there in case Ryan needs him.

Their mom, Jayne, 50, is studying to be a teacher. Their dad, Paul, 63, is a stained-glass artist. He is not at church with them on this December Sunday because of his part-time job stacking produce at Publix.

"Aaarrriiiaaah!" Ryan shrieks as the minister greets the congregation at Trinity United Methodist Church.

Anthony reaches across his mom and clasps his brother's shoulder. "Soon," he says. "We'll get to sing soon."

ESTABLISH INTIMACY

The twins are fraternal, born 15 minutes apart. As toddlers they climbed slides, played catch, chattered away.

Then Ryan began to regress, his parents said. He stopped talking, seemed to withdraw.

After endless tests, doctors determined that he had "a pervasive development disorder." When Jayne went to enroll her boys in prekindergarten, she first heard someone say the word "autistic."

"I just sat there crying and crying: He can't be," Jayne says. "But he is."

She worried: What kind of life will Ryan have? Will he know he's loved? What will happen to him once we can't look after him?

She agonized over Anthony: How would having a disabled twin affect him? Would he be teased? Would he resent Ryan?

Anthony sees his childhood in scenes: That time at Burger King, when he got so scared. The day in first-grade P.E. when he got so mad. The night the mayor gave him an award.

In every memory, Ryan is the main character.

"We were 5 years old, and we were playing in that bin of plastic balls at the Burger King," Anthony said. "Then Ryan was gone."

While his parents scoured the restaurant, Anthony ran out the door. He knew where his brother would be: in the middle of the highway, "just turning circles." Anthony looked both ways, crossed the stream of cars and grabbed Ryan's hand.

"He used to always run away," Anthony said. "But I'm faster. So I can always bring him back."

Anthony's parents never ask him to look after Ryan. He does it because Ryan is his brother and he needs him.

Okay, there is another reason. But he really doesn't like to talk about it.

Today's sermon is about Christmas and Walmart, how they don't have to go together. The best gifts, the minister says, are those you can't buy.

"Aaarrrooo!" Ryan gets louder. He picks up his sippy cup, throws it onto the pew. Anthony leans toward his mom, "We're out of here."

He packs Ryan's drink in the plastic bag. Then he takes his hand and leads him out of the church, onto the playground.

FIRST TIME. When you're writing about someone trying to overcome an obstacle, it's important to know when they first realized they'd have to face it, what they thought then, how their perception and worries and resolve have changed over time. It doesn't have to be much, just a scene or insight they encountered early on in their struggle.

CREATE QUESTIONS. To keep people reading, give them something to wonder about. Ask a question near the top of your story, or before you share a bunch of background. If they need an answer, they'll plow through information to get it. I wanted readers to think about why Anthony was so devoted to his brother, but that was the payoff. Here, I just hint that he doesn't want to talk about it. Why?

"Yeeeaaayaaa!" Ryan squeals, flopping into a swing.

Anthony takes off his glasses and folds them into the Ziploc. "Want me to push you?" he asks Ryan. He unwraps a cough drop and holds it out. "I brought you some candy."

———

Most of the time it's good having a twin, Anthony insists. You always have someone to talk to, even if the other person can't really talk back.

Ryan understands everything. "Only sometimes he doesn't care what you're saying, so he walks away." And he can speak "when he wants to," Anthony said. "One time when we were in the bathtub he said the whole pledge to the flag."

Ryan will catch a ball, but he won't throw it back. He'll rebound your basketball but won't shoot it. In Little League Challenger baseball, he'll run the bases—but only if Anthony runs with him. "He's always thinking about other things, so he can't concentrate," Anthony said. "It must be weird to be in his world."

The best thing about Ryan is that "he does stuff that makes you laugh." Like one time at the pool, he walked over to this man and just started sniffing his feet.

It's annoying when you're trying to do algebra homework and Ryan sneaks up behind you and shouts "Baaa!" just to scare you. "But Ryan just thinks he's being funny, so you can't get mad."

Jayne worries that Anthony tries to do too much. She wanted him to go to a support group for kids with autistic siblings, but Anthony refused. "I don't want to be around kids that complain." Even when Ryan is hitting him, Anthony just takes it.

The only time Anthony gets upset is when he feels he has to defend his brother. Like that day in first-grade gym class.

"For the longest time, Ryan wouldn't hug anyone," Anthony said. "But one day he came running up to me at P.E. and started hugging me. All the kids, even the teacher, started laughing." Anthony got so mad he screamed. "You don't know him!" The next day, he brought in a book about autism and read it to his class.

In September, Anthony won Student of the Month and the mayor invited him to the City Council meeting. The room was crowded when the family arrived.

"Ryan just started freaking," Anthony said. "Dad had to take him out of there.

"As I get older, things like that don't bother me as much," Anthony said. He stopped. "Well, they do. I just don't show it."

GO LOW. When you're interviewing someone, never be above them. If the person is seated, don't stand. I often sit on the floor to be less obtrusive while watching a scene unfold. When I'm talking to kids, I always go to their level. Many don't want to make eye contact. So I'll even be behind them while they're playing video games if that makes them more comfortable to talk.

PUT IN PAUSES. Speeding up and slowing down sections is one of the most important parts of writing. I never had trouble fast-forwarding, including a bunch of information or ideas at once. But I always had trouble slowing down. A wise colleague advised me that I wasn't noticing "the nothing." Write down when people stop, or stare at the floor, or don't answer. Those can be telling moments, too.

ESTABLISH INTIMACY

The only thing that kind of stinks about having a brother like Ryan, Anthony said, is that your parents won't let you stay home alone.

Some of Anthony's friends can stay without a sitter for hours. After all, they're almost 13.

But Anthony's folks haven't even gone on a dinner date in three years. They feel it's asking too much to give him sole responsibility for his brother.

A few Saturdays ago, Anthony got up early with Ryan and let his parents sleep in. He changed his brother's diaper, gave him a bath and made him toast. Then he put on a Barney video in their bedroom and went into the den to play PlayStation.

Soon after, Ryan padded into the kitchen and put a bag of popcorn in the microwave. He turned it on high and set the timer for . . . who knows how long.

"The whole house filled with smoke, and I got in big trouble," Anthony said. "I deserved it, though. I should've been watching him."

By the time church lets out, the boys have climbed up on a blue platform overlooking the parking lot. They watch their mom coming toward them.

"You ready?" Jayne asks.

Anthony climbs down the ladder, then reaches up for Ryan. "You're okay," he says.

He grabs the Ziploc bag and fishes out his glasses. As her boys rush down the sidewalk, Jayne thanks God. At times like this she wonders: What will happen when Anthony starts dating? When he goes to college?

What will he become? And what will become of Ryan?

Ask Anthony those questions, and he looks angry. Nothing will change, he says. He can't imagine life without his other half.

But what if you fall in love with a girl who doesn't want Ryan around? "I would never like a girl like that."

What will happen when your parents aren't around to take care of Ryan? "He will always, always be with me."

And what do you want to do, Anthony, once you're grown? "I'm going to Harvard," he says. "I'm going to medical school to become a doctor. I'm going to find a way to cure autism, so people like Ryan can talk."

USE THEIR VOICE. The easiest way to find your voice for a story is to adopt the voice of the person you're writing about. I normally wouldn't say "kind of stinks." And I don't remember if those were actually Anthony's words. But I wanted to capture the essence of the way he talked—a smart adolescent. And I needed to convey what mattered most to him. I asked about the negative aspects of having an autistic twin, and for him, it was more that he couldn't stay home without a babysitter.

GUILT IS GOOD. Ask people what they did wrong, what they got in trouble for, what they feel guilty about. That insight is helpful to understand your subject's mindset but also can make great scenes. Many turning points, or learning points, revolve around a new understanding that develops after something negative happens. Anthony was forthcoming about his mistake and felt awful.

GO WITH GOD. Even people who aren't religious pray: to pass this math test, land this job, save Grandma. I was with this family at church, so I knew they talked to God. But I didn't ask what they were praying for. That came from another question. When I asked the twins' mom what she was thinking while she watched her boys that day, she surprised me. She wasn't praying for them. She was thanking God.

FIRE QUESTIONS. Shooting a string of questions off all at once helps engage readers' curiosity and picks up the pace of your writing. I condensed some of Anthony's answers and used his clipped quotes for others. I like the rapid rhythm of a Q&A—especially when the answers are so succinct and poignant.

And if your brother could answer, what would you ask him? "I'd ask him, 'Do you want to be like me?'"

When you're Anthony, you worry about things. Math tests, for one. And whether the dogs are digging up the yard and eating the pool toys. And when you go to the park, you never know when somebody might call your twin brother a retard.

"I mean, I know everyone in the world isn't nice. But Ryan thinks everybody loves him," Anthony says.

"Maybe he wouldn't want to be like me."

Anthony buckles his brother into the van and turns on a Sesame Street video. Ask him again why he's so devoted to Ryan and at first he doesn't want to talk about it. A moment passes while he looks out the window.

Finally he says, "I think about it all the time." He hands his brother the sippy cup.

"I mean, we're twins. I could have been him."

ASK AGAIN. I asked Anthony why he was so good to his brother at least 10 times, and he kept evading me. I don't think he wanted to really think about it. But that was the question that had driven me to the story, so I knew I needed a good answer. Finally, I think, I wore him down in the van. It helped that he was distracted and didn't have to look at me. When he said that last quote, and I realized the why, I cried.

06

DON'T JUDGE

Ask for advice, stand
in their shoes, how
not why

The Truth Is Flexible: Learning
How to Panhandle from the Pros

Reported in two days; written the next day. Published July 8, 2009

BEFORE THE STORY

At every busy intersection around Tampa Bay, you'd see them: hot,
hungry, desperate-looking people of all ages and races standing on
the corners, holding handwritten signs, asking for handouts. It was
the height of the Great Recession, and a perennial situation had become a crisis.

Motorists yelled at them. Cops tried to keep them out of the
street. City officials considered banning them, making panhandling
an arrestable offense.

Everyone was taking sides: Should you help? Or shake your fist?

I kept driving by, wondering: How much money can they make
in a day? How long do they hang out? Do they compete with each
other? Are the stories on their signs true?

Most of their backstories were similar: addiction, mental illness,
jail. So when I pitched this story to my editor, looking for a different angle on the issue, I told him I wanted to focus on how they did
their jobs.

A photographer and I interviewed about 30 people, some work-

If you want to stand on a corner, flying a sign, professional panhandler
Roderick Couch has plenty of pointers. Photographer: John Pendygraft

ing alone, some in couples, others as teams. We sweated with them beside streetlights and stoplights, asked about what worked and what didn't, the highs and lows of the job.

Instead of looking down at them for begging or calling them out for their lies, we asked for tips about how they worked.

THE STORY

You have to go to work early. That's what they call it, going to work.

Get there by 7 a.m. or some guy who says he's disabled, or some woman who claims she has kids, will steal your slice of sidewalk.

You want an interstate off ramp: lots of traffic, an overpass for shade. Or a busy intersection with a long stoplight.

And you need a sign: your life story summed up on a soggy square.

Better yet, make two signs, so you can be whatever you need to be.

"After a while, you learn what works," said Roderick Couch, 28. He was in a wheelchair outside a St. Petersburg Walmart last week, clutching a sign that said, "Disabled." The word was in quotation marks, as if the writer were crossing his fingers. Couch limps but can walk 100 blocks of U.S. 19 in a day. He hasn't worked since he got out of jail.

His girlfriend, Jazmine Saldana, 24, held her own banner: Homeless. No quotation marks, but maybe there should have been. Since the couple started panhandling in November, they have had enough money to sleep in a motel all but one night.

"You have to know how to fly," Saldana said. That's what they call it, flying a sign.

Every day, from dawn to dusk, they're out there. From Seminole to St. Petersburg, Clearwater to Carrollwood, hundreds of panhandlers brandish their makeshift billboards across Tampa Bay. Their weathered faces and sad signs have become part of Florida's landscape.

There's the elderly African-American man who swears he fought in 'Nam. His hat reads "U.S. Air Force." His sign includes the Marine motto, "Semper fi."

There's the bearded white guy whose cardboard claims he was "layed off." And the young guy with the red goatee and

LEARN THE LINGO. When you're trying to transport readers to another world, or convey another culture, it's important to tap into the vernacular and listen for colloquialisms. Whether you're going to a baseball game or a cooking competition, each has specific language. Make sure you understand what the person is saying. And help your readers understand the meaning.

SEED DOUBT. Some of the best characters are flawed and unreliable. I needed the panhandlers to trust me enough to let me in and explain their process. But I wanted readers to know that I didn't believe everything they were saying, especially their backstories. You don't have to aggressively challenge their claims. But alluding to conflicting military allegiances, you can hint that the truth is elusive.

"Anything helps" sign who hangs out by Tampa's Bayshore Boulevard Publix.

Every day, you see more.

Around Tampa's Hyde Park alone, panhandlers say they can count at least 200 of their kind. In St. Petersburg, off I-275, nine people compete for shifts at one intersection. Turf wars erupt. A 60-year-old man who uses a walker recently shoved a 49-year-old into the bushes. "He knew I owned that spot under the tree."

Maybe you feel sorry for them: Times are tough. It could be me.

Maybe they make you angry because they want handouts.

Homeless or not, desperate or not, they all have their strategies, each one forged in the blast oven of the streets.

"Panhandling isn't just a job. It's an art," said Cliff Stewart, 49, who has worked the I-275 22nd Avenue N exit in St. Petersburg since he got out of prison two years ago.

You have to know what moves people most: beer and God.

You have to learn the rules. What to do, what to avoid doing. You have to set quotas. And know the right words.

Police say: Stay on the sidewalk. Wait for people in the cars to call you over.

Panhandlers say: If someone else is waiting to fly a sign, you have to rotate out every half-hour. If you leave to get a drink, you forfeit your shift.

Try to make eye contact. People in BMWs and Lexuses won't look at you, the panhandlers say. People in beaters give the most. When someone gives you money, that's a hit. Or a lick. Try to look friendly but not too happy. Remember, you're hurting.

Don't smoke or drink beer or scratch yourself. Don't wipe your nose or pick your scabs. Who would want to slide money into that hand? Stand on one foot sometimes so drivers will think you're not drunk; your eyes are bloodshot because you've been crying. And just because some hippie gives you a baggie of mushrooms, it doesn't mean you're going to trip.

"People hand you all sorts of things," said Damion Ogdee, 29, who works the Hyde Park area. He has gotten Budweisers and Pop-Tarts, cigarettes and T-shirts. His buddy once scored four tickets to a Poison concert.

Women give more money than men. Female panhandlers fare better but have to put up with obscene propositions. "If I was doing that," said a thin young woman named Sarah, "you think I'd be out here holding this sign?"

ACKNOWLEDGE ANGER. This story, I knew, would evoke sympathy from some people, rage from others. I had to walk a fine line between those extremes. I tried not to make readers feel sorry for these folks. And I needed to give a nod to those who hated them. It helps to anticipate readers' reception and address it early in your story. Then you can just let them draw their own conclusions.

DO'S AND DON'TS. This section was so much fun to write, like a "how to" of panhandlers' best practices. The single question that sparked these sentences was "What do I need to know out here?" That query works whether you're following a surfer or a senator. And it makes whoever you're interviewing feel like an expert, gives them incentive to impart inside information.

CAST A WIDE NET. For other stories, I might have zoomed in on a single panhandler or corner. For this story, the photographer and I decided to fan out to as many places as we could, see how methods changed from place to place. We learned how similar people's processes and rules were. The more places you visit and people you talk to, the more authoritative your writing will be.

She was at the 22nd Avenue N off ramp in St. Petersburg. Her cardboard said, "Stranded! Trying to get home." With all the competition, it's no longer enough to be generically needy.

"The more specific your request, the more people can relate," said Sarah. "That way they think they're really helping."

Two debates divide the panhandling community: Stay on one corner or float? Wheelchair or walker?

If you always work the same sidewalk, regulars get to know you. If you float from spot to spot, your face—and your story—stay fresh.

Some say wheelchairs increase people's pity. But if you're in a chair, you can't get to the cars. Wheelchair Dave, they say, did better with his cane.

"A lot of people out here aren't sincere," said Roderick Couch, the "disabled" ex-con. "That messes it up for the rest of us."

According to Couch, there are low-class panhandlers "who sleep outside and won't even clean themselves." And high-class panhandlers "who might even work a little on the side, so they don't really need your money."

"Me and Jazmine," he said, "we're middle-class. We believe in washing our clothes and our butts. We got morals."

Like everyone else interviewed, they have criminal records. He served time for stealing from the Spring Hill IHOP where he worked. His girlfriend was arrested for prostitution.

Your sign is your voice. You have only a few words to get sympathy at a stoplight.

Scrawl your messages in magic marker on the back of a Listerine box or a pilfered "Home for Sale" placard. Highlight your words with crayons. End your pleas with three exclamation points.

Are you homeless? A vet? A single dad? A widow? Do you have an ailing mother or pet? All the above?

One guy parades his limping dog. Another says he sends half his money to his 2-year-old son. One admits he stays out just long enough to collect enough for smokes and a six-pack.

"I don't need much. So I don't have to stay out here long," said Jeffrey Buzzard, 49, who lives behind a St. Petersburg church. In the back of his dirty camouflage shorts, he carries three signs. His morning pitch says "Layed off." His evening placard: "No work today." Like he tried. On Sunday, he flies: "Got God? Need daily bread."

Other professional panhandlers swear by the two-sign minimum. You have to watch the cars, switch it up. When Cliff Stew-

SEEK CONTROVERSY. Tension heightens stories and gets readers more invested. Ask what people argue about, what upsets them, what issues divide them. The conflicts don't have to be big, political or religious. Panhandlers squabble over turf, cleanliness and sincerity. They even have their own class system.

ASK, THEN CHECK. Ask people you interview if there's anything in their background you should know about and give them a chance to come clean. Then, of course, make sure you verify their criminal history to see if their story checks out. Most of these panhandlers admitted they had been arrested but were vague about what they had done.

QUICK QUESTIONS. So many of the panhandlers' signs had questions: Why lie? Got God? I embraced that language, wanting to echo their attempts to draw in drivers—and show how they tried to appeal to people's sympathies.

art sees an older driver at 22nd Avenue N, he holds: "Homeless Vet." For people who look like they party, he has: "Why lie? I need beer. God bless!"

God and beer. If you don't like one, he says, you're bound to like the other. And you'd be surprised how many people love both.

Though their signs say they're homeless, few panhandlers seem to sleep outside. Most make at least enough for a can of beer, a piece of chicken and a cheap motel room. The typical daily take falls between $60 and $100.

Couch and Saldana say they each collect about $80 a day, more than they would make flipping burgers or stocking shelves. They don't have to punch a clock, ask for a lunch break or pay taxes. "A while back, a woman gave us $400," Couch said. "Tell me where you can make that in a day."

Ogdee, outside the Bayshore Publix, sets his weekly quota at $800. His income has never fallen short in the four months he has held "Homeless. Anything helps. God bless!"

"I'm paid a week in advance on my rent," he said. "I got a load of food in my motel fridge."

He insists he's not panhandling. "I'm not asking for nothing. I'm just holding a sign."

So what does he call it? He laughs.

"Making money."

LAST WORDS. I try not to end stories with quotes. Usually, you can write things better than people can say them. But sometimes what they say is so perfect, you have to use it. This man was offended when I called him a panhandler. So I asked my final question and gave him the last line. I loved finding a lighthearted ending for a story on a subject that is so often sad or derisive.

07

CAST AROUND

Gone in a Flash: A Garbage Truck Driver Walks into a Bar

Reported in a couple of hours; written the next day. Published September 11, 2007

BEFORE THE STORY

There's this dive bar I used to go to after work. It may be a cliché, but bars (and coffee shops) are great places to overhear stories and talk through things you're working on. Almost anyone will talk to you in a bar.

And if you're a regular, and the bartender knows what sorts of true tales you like, sometimes he'll serve you one with a drink. I even had a bartender friend who kept some of my business cards under the counter. When she heard a story she knew I'd want to share, she'd give the customer my card or ask if she could jot their name and number on the back to give to me.

One day, I walked into Buddy's as a group of guys were swilling Budweisers, egging on an older man, encouraging him to "tell it again." Everyone was laughing.

So I primed them with a bucket of beer bottles, pulled up a stool and begged, "Please, let me hear it." No one asked me not to use their names or quote them. But they were all secondary characters, like a Greek chorus urging the hero to recount his adventure — and reacting.

Bars are great places to overhear—and find—stories. Most people can be bribed with a bucket of beer. Photograph courtesy of unsplash.com.

I don't record interviews. I get too distracted making sure the technology is working. So all of these quotes were written verbatim. And it helped that the main subject wasn't talking to me. It wasn't an interview or even a conversation. He was just telling his friends.

The story has a great frame tale set at the bar. And all the ingredients needed for a narrative: a willing subject (character), a petty crime (action), a dark house (setting), even suspense—a knock on the door. The theme could be gullibility (or maybe that some men get distracted by boobs).

THE STORY

Allen Smith props his pool cue against the wall and hangs his head. "Stop laughing," he pleads for the fifth time this afternoon. "It's not funny."

But the guys at Buddy's bar keep crowding around Smith, slapping him on the back, pleading, "Man, tell your story again!"

"Well, it wouldn't be funny if it happened to you," says Smith, sliding onto a brown vinyl bar stool.

"Oh, yes, it would," Mike says.

"Stuff like that never happens to me," Matt says sadly.

"C'mon, man. We'd all have done the same thing."

"What red-blooded American man wouldn't?"

"Somebody buy that man another beer."

So, bribed by a Bud longneck, Smith begins: "Sunday morning. 5:30 a.m. I wake up and put on a pot of coffee. I'm going to go fishing, so I want to check the tides. So I sit back in my recliner and click on Channel 28. I guess I was kind of dozing off there, waiting for the coffee and the tides and all.

"Then I hear this knock at the door."

Allen Smith is 53. He has a round face that is almost always crinkled into a grin, sky blue eyes, brown hair cropped short beneath his ball cap. He's lived in a one-story house on Fourth Avenue N since he moved to St. Petersburg 16 years ago.

On weekdays, Smith drives trucks and heavy equipment for the city of Gulfport. Most afternoons, when he gets off work, he stops by Buddy's on 49th Street to shoot pool. Some Saturdays, he plays lead guitar and sings in a band called Bacon Fat. Last Saturday, the Saturday before the Sunday morning of this story, Bacon Fat had been playing at Buddy's. Smith had made $68. "Fun money," he calls it. "Bar tab," the bartender says.

BOUNCE BETWEEN BARS. Every place has its own personality. From coffee shops to nightclubs, you can find different kinds of regulars, depending on where you go. Most people hanging out are happy to talk. Barflies are seldom introverts and often want an audience. So bop between bars, from holes in the wall to posh places. And always have your own neighborhood bar, "where everybody knows your name."

FRAME TALES. Guys urging the garbage truck driver to tell his story again was what got me interested. So when I wrote the opening, I wanted to frame it like that: not just the story, but the scene of how the story was told—à la *The Canterbury Tales*. I wanted readers to feel like they were there, hearing it unfold over a drink, enjoying the ribbing with the other patrons. Of course, the ending had to come back to the bar, the beer, the cautionary tale. And one final laugh.

RELAX THEM WITH BEER. We know never to pay our sources or offer them anything in exchange for information. But I've found buying a round—of Starbucks or IPAs or even ice cream—often helps people relax, open up and share their stories. I never let anyone buy me anything, not even a bottle of water. And I won't buy more than two drinks for others. But even that helps create intimacy and engenders more casual conversations. Often you also get telling details: a craft beer connoisseur is a different breed than a Budweiser guy.

BE CONVERSATIONAL. When I'm covering something casual, I want to capture the way people talk, even in my own narration. When Smith retold his tale, I tried to propel the action by using colloquial phrases like "So anyway…" "Now, Smith doesn't know…" "To prove her point, or something…" Play with language. Have the confidence to mirror your speaking voice in your writing.

So anyway, that night, Smith had gotten home about 1 a.m. He had ordered a pizza. Half the pizza was still sitting on the coffee table that Sunday morning, when someone knocked on his door.

"So I get up from my chair and ask, 'Who is it?'"

"It's Kelly, from up the street," a girl answers. "I need to use your phone."

Now, Smith doesn't know anyone named Kelly. But then again, he doesn't know all his neighbors. He opens the door.

There on his porch, he says, are two of the most beautiful women he's seen (up close) in years. They're both about 5-5, about 120 pounds, in their early 20s, wearing hip-hugger jeans and tank tops. One of them has short, dark brown hair, almost black. The other's hair is shoulder-length, sandy blond. They're both barefoot.

"Our friend put us out of his car," says the dark-haired woman. "We saw your light was on. Can we use your phone to call a cab?"

Smith doesn't hesitate. Who would?

"Sure," he says, a smile crinkling his face. "Wait here. I'll go get it."

"This is where the story gets good," someone interrupts.

"Yeah," Smith answers. "Maybe for you."

So anyway, that morning, Smith turns back into the house to get the phone. But the dark-haired woman stops him. "It's okay," she says. "We're not armed."

To prove her point—or something—the woman lifts her tank top over her face. Her friend does the same.

The dark-haired woman is wearing a white sports bra underneath. Her friend isn't wearing anything. They stand there, silhouetted by the streetlight, waiting on Smith's porch while he stares from his doorway.

"The boys at the bar will never believe this," he's thinking.

After a minute, after he finally can pick his chin up off the porch, peel his eyes away and find his voice, he asks, "Is this a joke or something?"

"No," the blond reassures him sweetly. "We just need to use your phone."

"Well, keep it down out here and I'll get it," Smith says. "My wife is asleep in there. I don't want to wake her."

Still not sure he's not dreaming, Smith pads back inside, down the hall, and gently closes the master bedroom door. Then he tiptoes to the kitchen and gets his cordless phone. When he walks into the living room, the women are waiting.

"Hey, can I have a piece of that pizza?" asks the dark-haired woman.

"No, I don't think so," Smith says.

He's slightly annoyed that they let themselves in. He closes the cardboard box and hands her the phone.

"Hey, you don't have to get all upset," says the woman. "We told you, we're not armed."

This time she lifts her sports bra, too.

Smith hasn't yet gotten over the first flashing. He still can't believe this is real.

"Okay. Okay," he says. "Just use the phone and go."

A minute later, after both women are gone, he walks down the hall and opens his bedroom door. He wakes his wife, Linda. "You won't believe what just happened!" he says.

So he tells her. And she listens. And before he even gets to the part about the second showing, his wife stops him.

"You better go check and see if your wallet's still there," she says.

He had left it on the coffee table the night before, when he paid for the pizza.

It was gone.

So was his ATM card, his VISA, his Sears charge. His driver's license. Plus his fun money. "After paying for that pizza, I had $56 they took," he says. "The only other thing in that wallet was a picture of my wife."

———

About 6:15 a.m., Smith called the police. They didn't send anyone out to fingerprint the phone, or the door, or the pizza box. An officer took down details over the phone.

"He had no idea who these women are. We had no leads to follow," says St. Petersburg Police Sgt. W. Korinek. "Not that we would mind going out looking for them . . ."

Since Smith let the women into his home, the crime was a petty theft, punishable by up to a year in jail. Police say they have not heard of similar cases around St. Petersburg or surrounding cities. If there were any, Korinek says, he's sure word would have gotten around.

Back at the bar, someone prompts Smith. "Go ahead!" the guy says. "Tell 'em how you described those girls."

"Well," Smith says, obviously relishing this part, "I had to tell the cops, pretty much, I don't think I'd know those girls' faces if

TAKE INVENTORY. What's in your wallet? Purse? Backpack? Who's on your speed dial? What's your most liked Instagram post? That information tells a lot about a person, what they need, value, share. Any time you mention that someone is carrying something—or lost something—you need to get the exact details of what was in there. Knowing Smith lost a credit card wasn't surprising. But the fact that it was a Sears card said a lot about him.

EMBRACE HUMOR. I wish I was funny. It's not a talent I have. So when I hear something humorous, I often want to share it. I see my role more as a straight woman, stepping back to show the context or reaction, then letting others tell the punch line. In this section, I could've just quoted the cop saying they didn't have any leads. But when he went on to joke that they wouldn't have minded looking for those buxom girls, I continued his quote—and sandwiched it between the police-speak.

RESET THE SCENE. After Smith told his story and I talked to the cops, I had to return to the frame tale. It's easy to transition with a simple phrase like "Back at the bar . . ." With those four words, I could lead readers to the scene and continue the narrative. And that way, I got to capture Smith proudly dropping the punch line on his friends.

MAKE IT OFFICIAL. It wasn't enough to talk to the cop by phone. I needed a copy of the police report. You always get more information—and often more questions—when you can see the official document. I included details like the long case number and the suspect descriptions as a stark contrast to the casual bar story, to give it gravitas. If I had only gotten the rundown from the officer, I would never have known that part of the report said, in all caps, "(BOTH ATTRACTIVE)."

USE THE GREEK CHORUS. Having a group of people react—to a concert, accident, sporting event—gives you a way to validate the scene and include many voices, in unison or dissent. Readers didn't need to know who the other guys in the bar were, or even their names. But by including them and their comments, I made readers feel like they were part of that group, listening and laughing.

you made me look at a lineup. But one thing's for sure, in terms of IDs: Both those girls were 36 Cs."

———

St. Petersburg Police Report No. 025223 describes both suspects as white females. It includes their height and weight. Then, in all capital letters, in parentheses, it says (BOTH ATTRACTIVE).

"This is the weirdest thing that's ever happened to me," Smith says.

"Lucky dog," someone says.

"Yeah, for 56 bucks, you can't beat it!" says someone else.

Laughter flows more loudly and freely than the beer this afternoon. By the end of his tale's third telling, even Smith is starting to see the humor. After all, if you're going to be the victim of a crime. . . .

Besides, he got his wallet back. A neighbor across the street found it in her flower bed, crushing the chrysanthemums. His ATM card—and his fun money—are still missing.

"I guess it is sort of funny," he admits. "But I'm telling you so you other guys will beware, so it won't happen to you."

He finishes his beer. Looks up and grins. "I wouldn't wish it on anyone else."

08

UNRAVEL THE MYSTERY

Show your strokes,
connect the dots,
take readers with you

A Message from Roger: Long Ago, a Boy Put a Note in a Bottle

Reported in two days; written the next. Published July 10, 2003

BEFORE THE STORY

A reader called me at the newspaper. He had found this bottle, with a note inside. Could I help him track down the writer?

It sounded like some tired trope, fictional fodder from movies and sappy songs.

Or, maybe, too good to be true.

How could we ever find the author? What if we did and the person was boring? What if that bottle had just bobbed around in that same canal for months? Who cares?

I wondered: Was there even a story there?

But when you can take readers with you through the process of reporting, uncovering clues and making connections, you can get them to feel the thrill of the hunt—and enjoy the journey and anticipation as much as the potential payoff. Like resurrecting a mystery from a watery grave.

This story is one of my favorites. Fate happens.

When Don Smith showed Lisa Clay the message that washed up in a bottle behind his house, she knew it was a sign. Photographer: Chris Zuppa

THE STORY

At first, he thought it was trash.

The bottle was bobbing in a canal behind Don Smith's house in Venetian Isles, drifting toward his dock. He saw it on the Fourth of July, while he was playing with his grandchildren. He grabbed a fishing net and scooped the bottle out of the murky water.

One side was fuzzy with algae. The other was clear. Black electrical tape was wound tightly around the top. The rusty cap said "Pepsi" in an obsolete logo.

Inside, there was a note.

The paper was folded, scorched sepia by the sun. It had been ripped from a school writing tablet, the kind with dotted blue lines. Smith pulled it out and smoothed it on a table.

"To whoever finds this letter please write me a letter and let me know," the note said in shaky pencil. "Roger J. Clay, 890 Linwood Ave., Fairfield Ohio, 45014."

Don and his wife, Carol, know the place. They are from Cincinnati, about 25 miles from Fairfield. Their son Sean works in Fairfield. "What are the odds?" Don asked.

Then he saw the date. On the bottom right corner, the paper said: 12/27/84.

That bottle had been in the water for almost 19 years.

Don's daughter-in-law is a teacher. By the handwriting, she said, whoever wrote the note was probably 7 or 8 years old. Roger J. Clay would be 26 or 27 now.

"Wouldn't it be great if we could find him and let him know we found his bottle?" Carol said.

"I'll try," said Don. "But 19 years is a long, long time."

That night, after the fireworks, Don got on the Internet. He didn't find Roger J. Clay. He found this:

"Roger K. Clay, 890 Linwood Ave., Fairfield, Ohio."

A few more clicks and Don found public records showing Roger K. was 49. "Must be the kid's father," Don told his wife. "And it looks like he still lives at the same house. What are the odds?"

Don tried to find a phone number, but had no luck.

So he wrote a letter: "I found your son's message in a bottle behind my house in St. Petersburg, Florida," he wrote. "I just thought you would want to know."

SEE IT FOR YOURSELF. The man who found the bottle read me the note. But I knew I needed to see it and also where he'd found it. So I invited myself over, and we hung out by his canal. By being there, you see things others might not notice: the fuzzy algae, obsolete logo, school writing tablet, shaky pencil handwriting. Including those details helps readers form their own picture.

He mailed the letter the next morning, Saturday.

On Monday, he called the *St. Petersburg Times*.

——

Don and Carol Smith are 56 and retired. Don owned a Cincinnati business that manufactured trailers to haul mobile television studios. Carol was a Realtor.

"I couldn't believe it. Could a bottle really last that long out there? In Tampa Bay?" Don asked. "Geez, 19 years!"

Back at work, we tried to find out more about the boy who wrote the message. Caryn Baird, a *Times* researcher, tapped into electronic databases, tracked all sorts of records. But she couldn't come up with a Roger J. Clay.

Then she scanned Social Security files. There he was.

"He's dead," she said.

——

There had been an article in the paper.

Nine days after his 21st birthday, Roger J. Clay was driving home on his new Suzuki. "His motorcycle went left of center and collided head-on with a pickup," the *Columbus Dispatch* reported. "Police are still trying to determine why Clay's motorcycle went left of center."

It happened on July 10, 1998. Five years ago today.

I called Don Smith and read him the news.

He coughed. Or choked. Or something. "Oh my God. Oh my God. I knew it," he said. "That's terrible. I can't explain it. Oh my God. I just had this feeling something had happened to that kid."

Now Don was even more determined to find Roger's parents. "Imagine what that message would mean to them," he said.

So Caryn found a new address and a phone number for Roger's dad. Then she found a number for someone she thought might be his mom, at a different address. I gave the numbers to Don.

A half-hour later, he called me back.

"You're not going to believe this," he said.

Roger's dad wasn't home. So Don had called the other number, the one for Lisa M. Ferguson, who used to be married to Roger K. Clay. A woman had answered. No, Lisa wasn't home. "I'm Lisa's sister," the woman said. "Can I help?"

Don explained why he was calling.

"Oh my God!" the woman gasped. "Lisa is away," she said. Every year this time, she goes away. "She can't stand to be in Ohio around the anniversary of the accident."

SHOW YOUR STROKES. Investigative pieces often start with "The newspaper has learned…" Then the findings are laid out with bullet points. But in narratives, it's often intriguing to peek into the process and work up to the payoff. Instead of telling readers what we'd found, I showed them what we did, even introduced them to the researcher as she poked through public records.

LET 'EM HEAR IT. I could have just told readers the news myself—in a two-word sentence. But I thought it would hit harder if they heard it like I did, in a quote from the researcher, unembellished, absent of emotion: "He's dead." Including her attribution keeps readers in the scene and connects them to the discovery, not just the declaration.

WORK WONDER. Try to capture your character's excitement, enthusiasm, incredulity—or, conversely, angst—and pepper your writing with that feeling. Exclamations like "I couldn't believe it! What are the odds? You're not going to believe this!" echo through this story, help propel it, put readers in the same sense of awe.

She gave Don a cell phone number.

"Lisa is down in Florida," her sister said. "In Seminole."

———

Lisa had just come back from the pool when her cell phone rang. She and her husband, Al, were cooling off in their hotel room.

When Don told Lisa he had found a bottle, she started screaming. She knew the rest. She remembers that note. She remembers the day her son wrote it.

They were in Clearwater, celebrating Christmas with her sister. Roger was 7. His dad took him fishing on Pier 60. Roger wrote the note and took tape from the tackle box and sealed the note in the bottle and tossed it off the pier. Lisa remembers telling him he was littering.

Roger was a happy, active kid. He liked to pretend to climb the walls like Spider-Man. He liked shooting squirrels with his dad. He raced dirt bikes. He fished. And he dropped a Pepsi bottle in the water even though his mother disapproved.

Now, 19 years later, a stranger had called and given her back her son.

"Here I am, trying to escape Roger's death, and he reaches out and gives me this message, this gift," she said.

Lisa told Don she wanted to see him. She wanted to hold that bottle. She wanted to touch that note, trace Roger's childish letters with her finger.

Don wanted to see Lisa, too. He wanted to learn about Roger. They agreed to meet for dinner at 7:30 Tuesday night.

———

How does it happen? Can a message really float around in a bottle for 19 years and surface so close to where it started?

"I'm not at all surprised," said Robert Weisberg. He is a professor in the College of Marine Science at the University of South Florida, St. Petersburg. He makes models of currents, tracks tides and studies how objects travel in water.

"There would be no problem at all getting a bottle from Clearwater's Pier 60 to Tampa Bay. Water does move," he said. "There are currents out there that are driven by wind. There are tides. It certainly is reasonable for something like that to stay in circulation around this area."

The bottle could have gotten hung up in a mangrove somewhere and stayed there for 15 years, Weisberg said. It could have moved around a bit, floated down to Sanibel Island and come back up into the bay again. It could have circulated up the gulf

ASK EXPERTS. Shoring up a story with science makes it so much more authoritative, gives it context and credibility. Every university has academics who study the minutiae of ocean floors, voting rights, addiction—and they love to discuss their subjects. So whatever you're writing about, reach out to a professor or some other expert.

EXPLORE "WHAT-IFS?" Instead of asking, "Could it have?" I wanted to know "how" that bottle could have floated around Florida, what paths it might have traveled. Ask people to help you explore possibilities as well as probabilities, then paint a picture for readers, offering specific landmarks, so they can envision the journey.

toward the Panhandle, then gone to Texas and come back under the Sunshine Skyway bridge. "Once something drifts offshore, there's no telling," he said.

Vembu Subramanian, who works in USF's office of Coastal Ocean Monitoring and Prediction Systems, said the bottle could have traveled thousands of paths from Clearwater to Venetian Isles. "There could have been boats moving it. It could have bounced through all those little islands. Who knows what kinds of influences could have impacted its path all those years?"

All day Tuesday, Roger J. Clay's mother couldn't stop smiling. And crying. And smiling.

She called her daughter in Ohio. She called her brothers and sisters. She called Roger's dad, who cried so hard he had to hang up.

"I had forgotten all about that bottle. It's kind of hard to put into words, all the emotions that brings back," Roger K. Clay told me from Ohio. "I told Lisa, it was like he was trying to remind us he was still with us."

Lisa told Roger's dad she would get to see the bottle that night. She and Al got to the restaurant early. At 7:40 p.m., a man with blue eyes and salt-and-pepper hair walked up, holding a bubble-wrapped bottle. Lisa smothered him, weeping, without even introducing herself. Don hugged her back. Hard. Then they stood there, in the lobby of the restaurant, holding on and sobbing into each other's shoulders. Their spouses stood by, dabbing at their eyes.

"Isn't this unreal?" Carol Smith asked.

"He's still touching lives," Al Ferguson said. "He was an amazing kid."

Over Diet Cokes and iced teas, salads and flaky rolls, the two couples talked about Roger. How he loved to play practical jokes, rig buckets of water above his sister's bedroom door, string fishing line across the hallway. How he lettered in football three years in high school. How he played varsity baseball. How the girls all loved him. He loved country music, they said, and fishing and deer hunting.

"He was buried in his blue jeans."

Ever since he was a kid, Roger had wanted a motorcycle. He begged his mom, then—after his parents got divorced—he started in on his stepdad. They kept saying no. Too dangerous.

So the day he turned 21, Roger bought a brand new Suzuki

GSX-R750W. He drove it to his mom's house, where he still lived. She turned white. He grinned.

But his bike kept breaking down. The fuel hose kept popping off, killing the engine. Roger took the bike back to the dealership four times the first week. Five years ago today, he picked it up after it was supposed to be fixed again. He and two friends headed down the highway. Roger's fuel hose dropped off a few miles from home. The engine cut out and he crossed the center line.

"It's not natural," Lisa said. Under the table, she cradled Roger's Pepsi bottle in her lap. "You're not supposed to have to bury your baby."

Lisa slipped her wallet from her purse and pulled out a photo. Roger's high school graduation portrait. He was wearing a blue oxford and jeans.

"What a nice-looking kid," Don said. "What a shame."

"He was studying to be an FBI agent," Lisa said. "He was going to school during the day and working third shift. Everyone loved him. More than 400 people came to his funeral."

A few weeks after the funeral, she said, a notice came in the mail. Suzuki was recalling its GSX-R750W line because of a fault in the fuel system. Lisa called a lawyer. She spent five years suing Suzuki. Finally, in February, she settled out of court for an undisclosed amount.

"The money will never bring back Roger," she told her dinner companions. "But you all have."

"I dread this time of year every year. It's the worst. But now I have something wonderful to think about," Lisa said. She reached across the table, grabbed Don and Carol's hands. "You all have given me so much to be happy about. You have given me this message from Roger. He's still playing tricks on me."

When dinner was over, the two couples walked out into the dark.

"Why don't you all come visit us in Ohio?" Lisa asked the Smiths. She plans to put the bottle on her mantel, and wants them to see it.

PAN THE CAMERA. Lie on the floor. Climb on the cabinets. Look under the table, where a mom is cradling a Pepsi bottle. When I'm observing a scene, I want to be as invisible as possible, so I don't interfere. I try to stay silent, hoping people will forget I'm there. But I'm constantly watching, shifting my lens, taking notes about what people are doing, not just what they're saying.

PLAY IT FORWARD. The story could have ended three paragraphs higher, when the mother tells Don and Carol they brought back her son. But I followed them into the parking lot, where I heard the mother invite the couple to Ohio. And I had one more question: What is she going to do with the bottle?

Davion Only was tired of waiting
for adults to find him a family. So
he went to church to make a plea.
Photographer: Melissa Lyttle

09

CARVE OUT THE ELEPHANT

Edit your story so each detail supports your theme, cut extraneous information, show don't tell

Davion's Prayer: A Teenage Orphan Goes to Church to Find a Family

Reported over three days; written the next day. Published October 7, 2013

BEFORE THE STORY

How do you carve an elephant out of a bar of soap?

My former editor loves that riddle. His answer: Carve away everything that doesn't look like an elephant.

It's amazing to have a skilled editor you trust. But many writers have to rely on themselves to whittle out their story from a block of information.

Thinking of a one-word universal theme helps me start stripping down details, so I can figure out what really supports that main spine of the story and cut the rest.

I had known Davion's adoption manager for years and had told her I wanted to write about a foster kid hoping to find a family. She introduced me to Davion at his group home and told me about his past. I interviewed his mentor and counselor, hung out with him at a pancake house, then a park.

But when it came time to write this story, my editor suggested I tighten the frame to a single day at church.

I left out so many scenes and quotes. But by zooming in on that

EXPLORE THE AFTERMATH. It's important to tell subjects why you want to tell their story, and what might happen. It also helps to ask them about their worries and expectations. Davion is quiet and private. So speaking in front of strangers was going to be hard. When his caseworker told him I wanted to share his story in the newspaper, he balked. So together, we outlined possible outcomes. Con: More people would know his past. Pro: Someone might see the story and want to adopt him.

one hour, I was able to focus on what really was at stake—not only in that moment, but for this boy's whole life. He was putting all his hope into a few minutes at the pulpit, pitching himself to strangers.

THE STORY

CELEBRATE TENSION. Opening with a problem is a sure way to get readers' attention. I chose to start the story at the moment Davion decided he wanted to back out, to make readers wonder what was at stake as well as what was going to happen. By being in the car with them, I was able to overhear their conversation and use dialogue to heighten the suspense.

OBSERVE, THEN ASK. In the process of trying to paint a picture of Davion, I jotted down what he was carrying and what he was wearing. But those descriptions didn't mean anything. It was only afterward, when I asked him where he got the Bible and the black suit, that I realized everything he owned had been donated. And the real insight came when I asked if he had tied his own tie: another reminder he didn't have parents.

KNOW NAMES. Ask people about their names and nicknames: Where they came from, what they mean. Sometimes, a name says more about that person's parents. Other times, the question brings up a namesake— someone your subject aspires to be, or despises. Often names give insight into how people see themselves. Or, in the case of nicknames, how others see them. I knew Davion's name was the only thing his parents had given him. So I asked if he knew what it meant.

As soon as they pulled into the church lot, Davion changed his mind.

"Miss! Hey, Miss!" he called to his caseworker, who was driving. "I don't want to do this anymore."

In the back seat, he hugged the Bible someone had given him at the foster home. "You're going to be great," Connie Going said.

Outside St. Mark Missionary Baptist Church, she straightened his tie. Like his too-big black suit, the white tie had been donated. It zipped up around the neck, which helped. No one had ever taught Davion, 15, how to tie one.

"Are you ready?" Going asked. Hanging his head, he followed her into the sanctuary.

This had been his idea. He'd heard something about God helping people who help themselves. So here he was, on a Sunday in September, surrounded by strangers, taking his future into his sweaty hands.

Davion Navar Henry Only loves all of his names. He has memorized the meaning of each one: beloved, brown, ruler of the home, the one and only.

But he has never had a home or felt beloved. His name is the last thing his parents gave him.

He was born while his mom was in jail. He can't count all of the places he has lived.

In June, Davion sat at a library computer, unfolded his birth certificate and, for the first time, searched for his mother's name. Up came her mug shot: 6-foot-1, 270 pounds—tall, big and dark, like him. Petty theft, cocaine.

Next he saw the obituary: La-Dwina Ilene "Big Dust" Mc-Cloud, 55, of Clearwater, died June 5, 2013. Just a few weeks before.

In church, Davion scanned the crowd. More than 300 people packed the pews. Men in bright suits, grandmoms in sequined hats, moms hugging toddlers on their laps. Everyone seemed to have a family except him.

Davion sat beside Going, his caseworker from Eckerd, and struggled to follow the sermon: something about a letter Paul wrote. "He was in prison," said the Rev. Brian Brown. "Awaiting an uncertain future . . ."

Sometimes Davion felt like that, holed up at Carlton Manor with 12 teenage boys, all with problems. All those rules, cameras recording everything.

Davion wants to play football, but there's no one to drive him to practice. He wants to use the bathroom without having to ask someone to unlock the door.

More than anything, he wants someone to tell him he matters. To understand when he begs to leave the light on.

"You may be in a dark place," said the preacher. "But look for the joyful moments when you can praise God."

Picking at his fingers, Davion wondered what to say. And whether anyone would hear him.

––––––

Davion always longed for a family. His caseworker took him to picnics, put his portrait in the Heart Gallery. But he had thrown chairs, blown his grades, pushed people away.

When he learned his birth mother was dead, everything changed. He had to let go of the hope that she would come get him. Abandon his anger. Now he didn't have anyone else to blame.

"He decided he wanted to control his behavior and show everyone who he could be," Going said.

So someone would want him.

"I'll take anyone," Davion said. "Old or young, dad or mom, black, white, purple. I don't care. And I would be really appreciative. The best I could be."

All summer, he worked on swallowing his rage, dropping his defenses. He lost 40 pounds. So far in 10th grade, he has earned A's—except in geometry.

"He's come a long way," said Floyd Watkins, program manager at Davion's group home. "He's starting to put himself out there, which is hard when you've been rejected so many times."

Davion decided he couldn't wait for someone to find him. In three years, he'll be on his own.

"I know they're out there," he told his caseworker. Though he

INTERVIEW AHEAD. Whenever you're able to, interview your subject before you observe them. That way, you have a better idea of what to look and listen for. Before I went to watch Davion at church, I knew he felt trapped and controlled at the group home, that he hated asking for permission to use the bathroom and being locked behind so many doors. I knew what he wanted. And what he was scared of.

SEEK PARALLELS. The church was hot. The sermon was long. I knew I didn't need to write down everything the preacher was saying. So while I was watching Davion, looking for his reaction, I was listening for anything that might relate to his own story. In the Bible verse, Paul was in prison, "awaiting an uncertain future." Kind of like Davion. Later, when the preacher talked about a dark place, I knew Davion always begged to leave the light on at night.

WATCH BODY LANGUAGE. Sometimes the way people walk, sit or fidget is revealing. Are they hunched over? Ramrod straight? Always twirling their hair or tapping their foot? Watch for movements and gestures, then ask about them. Davion's palms were sweaty, he was picking at his fingers, he wouldn't look up—even from the pulpit. I asked what he was thinking in those moments. And got such insight that way: he was worrying no one would hear him.

DO SOMETHING. Sitting across from someone while you're interviewing them is always uncomfortable. Most people find it easier to have a conversation while they're engaged in another activity. Having coffee eases the tension. So does watching a Little League game or walking a dog. Davion gave us a tour of his group home but didn't want to talk there. He wanted pancakes. So we went to Denny's, then to a park. While I asked questions, the photographer threw a football with Davion.

WELCOME WINGMEN. I used to get annoyed if subjects wanted to bring someone with them to an interview. Now I embrace it. Sure! Bring your boyfriend, your best friend, your mom. Having another person along makes your subject feel safer and gives you the chance for dialogue and details you might not otherwise gather. Davion brought his caseworker with us to get pancakes, and we met his mentor in the park. He seemed much more comfortable having them there and opened up.

is shy, he said he wanted to talk at a church. "Maybe if someone hears my story . . ."

The preacher spoke about orphans, how Jesus lifted them up. He described an epidemic, "alarming numbers of African-American children who need us."

Then he introduced Davion, who shuffled to the pulpit. Without looking up, Davion wiped his palms on his pants, cleared his throat, and said:

"My name is Davion and I've been in foster care since I was born. . . . I know God hasn't given up on me. So I'm not giving up either."

AFTER THE STORY

Davion's story got picked up around the world. Bloggers and celebrities shared his plea and posted his picture. Barbara Walters interviewed him on *The View*.

More than 10,000 people contacted the foster agency to adopt him. An official with Florida's Department of Children and Families praised "the Davion effect" for raising awareness about other teens who need homes. The number of inquiries about adoptions, she said, increased almost threefold.

But six months after he became the face of adoption, Davion was still floundering in foster care.

He met with relatives he didn't know he had and with four families who had seen his story. Then he moved to Ohio to live with a minister and his wife, who already had three kids. "I got baptized!" Davion wrote on his new Facebook page. But when he got into a fight with one of the minister's kids, the family sent Davion back to Florida, to the state system where he had lived with strangers his whole life.

For months, he didn't talk to anyone. Then, on a sticky evening in late July—after being shuffled between four homes and four schools in a year—he dialed the only number he knew by heart, of the only adult who had been a constant in his life: the woman who had been his caseworker since he was 7. He asked her to adopt him.

Of course, Connie said yes. Over the years, she had helped more than 1,000 kids get adopted. She felt like she had failed Davion. Now she had the chance to save him. In addition to finally getting a mom, Davion got two big sisters, Connie's daughters, and a brother—his best friend from the group home, also adopted by Connie years earlier.

In December 2015, I wrote a follow-up story: "Finally, a Family for Davion."

Since then, he graduated from high school and received a scholarship to attend the Culinary Institute of America, where he's studying to become a chef.

PART

—

02

ON ASSIGNMENT

For the first decade of my career, almost all of my stories were assigned. Since I started writing features, most of the ideas have been my own.

But even after doing daily journalism for more than 30 years, I still get sent to news events, to cover hurricanes and mass shootings, protests and pandemics.

Whenever possible, I try to find someone who has been affected by the news to follow as they navigate the aftermath, hoping to make the public event personal. Every news story has at least a few follow-ups, which offer writers an opportunity to explore different people's perspectives.

Many of the stories in this part were broad assignments from an editor: Go to Orlando on the day after the Pulse nightclub shooting and find a story no one else has reported. Come up with a new way to narrate the approaching hurricane. Hang out at the strip club where President Trump's porn star partner is going to pole dance.

Four of these stories I reported and wrote in two days, to peg to the news. The longest took six months to report. And one I jumped on as soon as the tragedy happened, then had to wait five years to write.

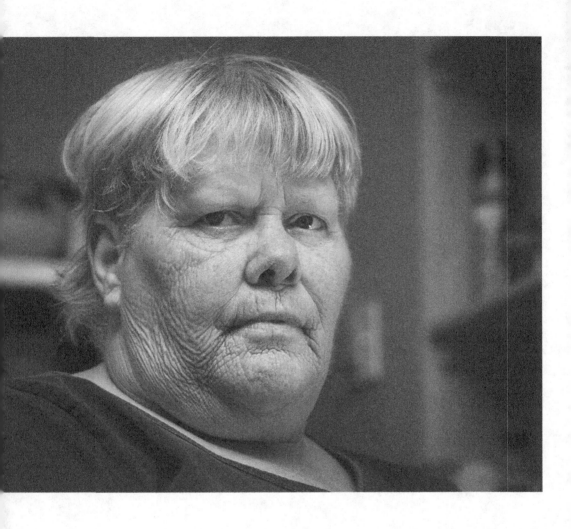

Barbara Burns never dated and had few
friends. She cared for her younger sister,
Debbie, and they did everything together.
Photographer: Martha Asencio Rhine

10

EXPLORE
NEWS BRIEFS

Go deeper, pull
police reports,
knock on doors

The Saint and the Sacrifice:
She Was Devoted to Her Sister
but Wanted Her Life Back

Reported over two weeks; written in four days. Published October 24–25, 2005

BEFORE THE STORIES

A woman had just been arrested for shooting her sister, the news brief said. She had lived with the body for more than six weeks, then fled Florida, been caught in Virginia. That was it.

So many great stories get buried in briefs, news nuggets that no one had time to report further, or had no more information about in the moment.

Keep a file of briefs from newspapers and web postings, things you can go back to and explore more deeply.

I knew there was a bigger story here. Sisters don't usually shoot each other, and who lives with their sibling's rotting body for that long? What had happened? And why?

The story hadn't been on TV or covered by any other media. I started by pulling police reports, evidence photos, autopsy records, an inventory from the cleanup crew—which was part of the investigation. Then I went to the trailer where the slaying happened and started knocking on neighbors' doors.

Crime stories usually are quick, done on deadline. But unraveling the narratives behind the news takes time—and empathy.

THE FIRST STORY: THE SAINT

There's a dog in there, the woman next door told him. At least there was a dog. One of those yipping little ones, with long hair. Wonder what happened to that dog.

No one has lived in that mobile home for months, the woman said.

Phillip McCain already knew that. For six months, no one had paid the mortgage on the double-wide near the end of Yellow Pine Street. The bank was foreclosing. McCain and his son Jason had been hired to clear out the place.

McCain unlocked the door and walked into the kitchen. It was May 4, about 1 p.m. The house was dark. All the blinds were drawn, curtains closed. The air was thick and hot. Sour.

McCain's stomach churned. What was that rancid smell? Like rotten food, only worse. As he walked into the living room, the odor got stronger.

He clicked on his flashlight, aimed the beam up and down. It looked like someone had just walked away and left everything: couch, TV, computer. The walls were papered with Star Wars posters; every shelf was full of Star Wars games, Star Wars magazines, little R2-D2s and a Yoda. Some spoiled kid must have lived here, McCain thought.

He followed the hall to the bedrooms. Two doors were open. The third was closed. As McCain approached the closed door, the stench grew.

He pushed it open, and almost retched.

Someone had tried to mask the smell. Dozens of cardboard air fresheners dangled around the room. Plug-in air fresheners bloomed from every outlet. In the master bathroom, empty spray cans of air freshener filled the trash can, the tub, the sink.

McCain and his son looked at each other. What was this?

"You don't reckon," he remembered saying to Jason, "that someone just left that dog in here to die?"

Two single beds shared the room, set close, in an L-shape. One of the beds was piled with sheets and blankets. Someone had strewn baskets of potpourri across the covers.

McCain reached to pick up the pile of bedding, but couldn't lift it.

Something was in there. Something heavy.

His son tried to help. He tugged at the fitted sheet, and the whole pile thudded to the floor. Jason started peeling back the layers.

Then he ran, screaming, out of the house.

———

The McCains had been expecting just another cleanup job. What they uncovered was the story of two desperately intertwined lives: a story of love, death and crushing obligation.

Susan Ignacio, from the Pinellas County Medical Examiner's Office, knelt in the front bedroom and began to unwrap the body.

A Star Wars comforter formed the outer layer of the shroud. She turned it back and found a brown blanket, and beneath that, a white shower curtain. Inside the shower curtain was a 2004 Star Wars calendar marked only with the times of a few TV shows, or countdowns to the shows. Its owner didn't seem to look forward to much else.

Next came a light blue comforter, then a faded Star Wars sheet. The medical examiner pulled at the sheet and found, finally:

A skull cradled on two pillows.

It looked as if the person had been sleeping, lying on the left side. The right arm was bent at the elbow, draped across the chest. The left arm was tucked beneath the pillows. The body was so badly decomposed, Pinellas County sheriff's deputies couldn't tell whether it was a man or woman, black or white, old or young.

In the front of the skull, right in the center of the forehead, was a hole where a bullet had gone in.

———

By the time Detective Ed Judy arrived about 5:30 p.m., 15 officers already were working the scene. The deputies logged everything that might be a clue: a Sony camera, a wedding veil, a blood-stained mattress and box spring.

But they had only a few facts. A call to the power company let them know that the electricity had been cut off seven months earlier. In the two months before that, the power bill had more than tripled. It seemed someone had cranked down the air conditioning as cold as it would go, and left it there.

The investigators found out something else. Through tax records, they learned that the mobile home had been occupied by two women.

Barbara and Debbie Burns.

———

SOMETIMES SUBTITLE. True-crime shows always include kicker lines like "a story of love, death and crushing obligation." So I wanted to incorporate something like that in the writing. It serves as foreshadowing and gives readers just enough drama to connect to those universal themes. Try coming up with subtitles for your stories. Even if you don't use them, they can help you focus.

NEIGHBORS KNOW. It's one of the oldest tools for detectives and reporters: knock on doors. Even when neighbors don't know each other, they notice things: how many cars were in the driveway, how many packages piled up on the porch, whether there was a pet. The fact that no one knew much about these sisters was telling. And the next-door neighbor was a gold mine. She not only described the sisters and their relationship but knew how many teeth they had.

SEE THE UNSEEN. I love writing about people in the shadows, the ones others might not care about. So when neighbors, coworkers, even a doctor described the sisters as "women you'd walk by without noticing," that intrigued me. Maybe that's why no one realized they were missing. Ask about things known and unknown.

The neighbors didn't know much about the women who lived in the white double-wide.

At door after door, deputies heard the same answer: We don't know them. Never met them. We hardly ever saw anyone go in or come out.

Only the woman next door had talked to them. "They were sisters," Shirley Greilick told detectives. "They moved in four or five years ago. Always stayed to themselves.

"The older one, Barbara, I'd just see her going in and out to her car. That was it. I never saw any company come. Never saw anyone else over there at all. We'd just say, 'Hello,' or, 'Nice weather.' That was it.

"The younger one, Debbie, you couldn't understand her real good. She'd try, but you know, I think she was retarded or something."

Debbie didn't drive, the neighbor said. Barbara had to take her everywhere she wanted to go.

The neighbor told detectives she hadn't seen Barbara in months. But it had been even longer since she had seen Debbie. Once, she had asked Barbara if her sister was sick or something.

Debbie's in California, Barbara had said. Taking care of our aunt.

The night the body was found, detectives worked until dawn trying to identify the victim.

They learned that Barbara Burns was 53, Debbie 40. A background check showed neither had ever been arrested. From picture IDs, the detectives could see that both sisters were short and stocky, with shoulder-length light brown hair. The kind of women you'd walk right by without noticing.

"They looked a lot alike," the neighbor had said, except for their smiles. Debbie had only three teeth. Barbara didn't have any.

That description helped detectives determine which sister was dead: The skull on those pillows had three rotten teeth.

Now detectives knew it was Debbie Burns who had been shot. The obvious question: Where was Barbara?

Barbara drove a gray 1994 Dodge Caravan, which she had bought at Pinellas Auto Brokers, Detective Judy found out. He called the car dealership and talked to a woman who remembered the Burns sisters.

They were very nice, the woman said. When they came in to make their car payment, they'd bring cupcakes.

But the woman hadn't seen them since last year. They had stopped paying on the van, and repo men had spent months searching for it.

Around January, the woman said, she got a call from someone at the Greyhound station in St. Petersburg. The Dodge Caravan had been abandoned behind the bus depot. Homeless people were living in it.

Barbara's credit application at the auto broker showed she had worked for 10 years at Howard Johnson's in St. Pete Beach, then at Bealls Outlet and Lowe's. Detective Judy tracked names and phone numbers of Barbara's bosses. He talked to them that day.

They all used the same words to describe her: quiet and reliable, straightforward, honest. One of the most patient people you'll ever meet.

"Barbara was very nice," said Linda Ware, who was Barbara's supervisor at Bealls. On birthdays and holidays, Linda and Barbara would go out for a drink on Treasure Island. Barbara would always bring Debbie along.

Linda said Debbie walked with a limp and had the mind of a child. She could be demanding, Linda told the detective. Whenever Barbara was having fun, Debbie would start complaining, loudly, saying she was tired, ready to go home RIGHT NOW. Like a first-grader throwing a tantrum.

Barbara was always kind to her sister, though, Linda said. Even if Barbara hadn't finished her first Coors Light, she'd help Debbie up from her chair and drive her home.

Then Linda told the detective something else. Sometime around 2000, Debbie had inherited some money. She didn't know how much.

Was money a motive for the killing, Judy wondered? It didn't seem likely: All the evidence showed the sisters were broke. Barbara had filed for bankruptcy just three years later: July 2003.

That same month, she had started working at Lowe's as a cashier for $7 an hour.

Barbara was always on time, her boss, Jason Carrier, told the detective. She never argued. She was friendly to the customers. She was voted Employee of the Month. Once, she gave a coworker a smiley face coffee cup.

After working at Lowe's for more than a year, Barbara abruptly quit. She said she had to take care of a sick relative.

SLOW DOWN. Fast-forwarding through information is effective. And trimming excess clauses or set-ups is necessary. But sometimes it helps to slow things down, work the drama. "Then Linda told the detective something else..." That sentence could have just reported what Linda said. But adding the lead-in builds suspense. Entice readers by telling them you're about to reveal something.

That was in late August 2004, eight months before her sister's body was found.

———

Two days into his investigation, Detective Judy discovered someone was still cashing Debbie's disability checks. The money was going to a bank in Virginia Beach, Va., into the account of Barbara Ann Burns.

Bank statements also showed Barbara was getting paychecks from a 7-Eleven in Virginia Beach. The detective called the convenience store. The manager said Barbara was on the schedule for the next night.

It was a big break. Now detectives knew where Barbara was and when they could find her. Barbara hadn't changed her name or tried to hide her identity.

Detective Judy and his partner flew to Virginia Beach and staked out the 7-Eleven. Barbara looked so much older, more worn out, than in her driver's license photo. Dark circles underlined her tired eyes. Her frizzy hair was streaked with gray. She kept slumping against the cash register. All night, she sold cigarettes and lottery tickets: other people's escapes and dreams.

As he watched through the window, Detective Judy kept wondering: What makes a person suddenly snap? He thought about all Barbara had done for her sister: paid the bills, bought her drinks, helped her walk, driven her places, even shared a room with her.

How could she have wrapped Debbie in blankets and left her to rot?

———

At daybreak, when Barbara's shift ended, the detectives introduced themselves. "We're from Florida," Detective Judy told Barbara. "We want to talk to you."

Barbara followed them to their car. She didn't ask why or how they found her.

She seemed to be expecting them.

On the way to the Virginia Beach police station, detectives asked Barbara about her house and family. She said she was living in a homeless shelter. She swore she had never owned a mobile home—not in Florida or anywhere else—and didn't have any family.

Again and again, she said she never had a sister.

An hour into the interview, Detective Judy showed Barbara

copies of the deed for her mobile home, her power and cable TV bills. Barbara kept saying she didn't remember signing them. She insisted she had never lived in any double-wide in St. Petersburg.

"Barbara," the detective said. "At this residence, uh, we found a body."

"A body?"

"Yes."

"Okay, I don't—I don't know. I couldn't tell you."

"Couldn't tell me?" the detective repeated.

"Well, whatever you're asking."

———

Detective Judy pulled out some pictures: Barbara, holding a long-haired Chihuahua; Debbie, hugging the same little dog.

Barbara's face fell. She stared at her lap. "Could you pick that up and look at it?" the detective asked, sliding the photo toward her. "Do you recognize her?"

"Honestly, I've never seen her," Barbara said quickly.

Detective Judy pulled out more pictures. He said he had talked to Barbara's neighbor, her bosses, people who could confirm she had a sister. Then the other detective, Misty Manning, turned to Barbara.

"While he's been talking to you, I've been just sitting here observing you," she said. "Every time you look at this picture, you tear up."

Barbara wouldn't look up. "I do," she said softly. It was a statement more than a question.

———

After almost three hours, Barbara admitted she had a sister. She told detectives how much Debbie loved soap operas and Star Wars and her little dog, Leo. How sweet Debbie was. How they'd watch movies and sometimes go to the mall together.

"I loved when she was fine," Barbara said.

"You loved when she was fine?" Detective Manning asked. "Okay."

Debbie was fine, Barbara insisted, the last time she saw her. The day she drove away. "I just, uh, got in the van and left," Barbara stammered. "I told her I needed some down time. That's what I told her, and she said okay."

She said she waved goodbye to her sister through the front bedroom window. She said she never called Debbie after that.

The detectives pressed her. You wouldn't just walk away from

AVOID ATTRIBUTION. When only two people are talking, and it's easy to figure out who's who, you don't need to keep writing "he said," "she said." Let the dialogue flow, like you would in a play. This scene came, verbatim, from the interrogation transcript.

WATCH THE VIDEO. First, the police gave me the transcript. But when I realized the interrogation had been taped, I asked for the video, too. Being able to watch the exchange was so much more helpful than just reading the words. I got to see the detectives pull out photos, show them to Barbara, watch her body language, hear the tone of her voice. So many things are filmed now. Ask for surveillance footage, body-cam video, street camera recordings, Ring doorbell downloads.

someone you loved, someone who needed you, they told Barbara. You're not that kind of a person.

"All the people we have interviewed, they said Barbara is an unbelievable person," Detective Judy told her. "I'm sorry to tell you this, but the word that was used to describe your sister, who you loved, was a bitch. And, and I apologize to use that language in front of you. She was demanding; I'm not making this up."

"Yeah, I know," Barbara said. "She was demanding."

"Okay, and they said they did not understand how you could—you were a saint."

Barbara started sobbing. "I was a saint," she echoed.

Then the saint told detectives what she had done, and why.

THE SECOND STORY: THE SACRIFICE

"Patience is my virtue," Barbara Burns says through the video screen at the Pinellas County Jail. Visitors aren't allowed into the lockdown, so she has to hold a phone and look into a camera.

"I'm very patient," she says softly. "You wouldn't think so now. But I am."

Barbara has been in jail for four months, ever since a cleanup crew found her sister's body in an abandoned mobile home in St. Petersburg. Debbie had been shot in the forehead and swaddled in Star Wars sheets.

It's late August now—a year since Debbie died.

When detectives first questioned Barbara, she insisted she never had a sister. Later, after seeing a photo of her sister with her dog, Barbara broke down and confessed.

"She kept crying. She said she wished she hadn't done it. She was sorry," Detective Ed Judy would say of the interview. "She's a really nice person, as far as murderers go. She's the nicest murderer I've ever met."

Barbara is charged with first-degree murder. Her court-appointed lawyer hasn't decided whether he'll enter a plea or take the case to trial.

He told Barbara not to talk about what happened to her sister.

But if you visit Barbara, if you sit and talk with her through the video screen, she'll tell you about herself and her sister, about their lives together, how she looked after Debbie, helped her walk, drove her everywhere she wanted to go.

"I just took it all in to the breaking point," Barbara says softly, through the jail phone. "Then I exploded."

MAKE THEM WANT MORE. Find a cliff-hanger to end each section of a story. Think of it as hooking TV viewers enough to make them want to come back after a commercial break because they can't wait to find out what happens next. This section could have ended with Barbara echoing that she's a saint. But I wanted to alert readers that they were about to learn crime details—and the motive. The fact that this story was published over two days made the suspense even greater.

TAKE THEM WITH YOU. There are different ways to invite readers to partake in the process. Using "If you . . ." transports people by asking them to imagine being there. The device can be overused but also can be effective, like holding the readers' hands or having them watch over your shoulder. Most people haven't had to visit someone in jail, but here they can come along. Foreshadow why they should.

Barbara looked after her disabled younger sister for 40 years—Debbie's whole life. People described Barbara as an angel, or a saint.

She paid a price for her goodness. Being selfless means you lose yourself. And there's a fine line between saint and martyr.

———

Barbara grew up in Maryland, just outside Washington, D.C. Her dad, John, was a printer who worked nights, drank days; her mom, Margaret, stayed home with the kids.

Barbara's parents had four kids in five years. For a long time, when she was little, her dad would drive the family to Virginia Beach every summer, Barbara said in the jail interview. She loved splashing in the surf with her brothers and sister, building castles in the sand.

Then along came Debbie, who changed everything.

Barbara was 13 when Debbie was born. Debbie was the baby, so she was spoiled from the start. Plus, it was hard to take a baby to the beach, so that ended their vacations.

Then, when Debbie was 2, she got scarlet fever. She was never right again, said her brother Bob, a truck driver who lives in Maryland. The high fever, raging for days, damaged Debbie's brain. Doctors said she would grow to have, at best, the mind of a 6-year-old. She would never be able to take care of herself.

The next year, their dad died. Their mom had to start waiting tables to pay the bills. She couldn't afford child care, so she made Barbara drop out of school to look after Debbie.

Barbara was 16, the age most girls' lives begin. Debbie was 3, still in diapers.

"That was it for Barbara. After that, she just stuck around the house all the time," Bob said. "She never had any friends or went out with anybody that I know of. Only Debbie."

Soon, the other siblings moved out. Barbara and Debbie stayed in Maryland with their mom, in the house they grew up in, sharing a room, sleeping in single beds, side by side.

"Barbara was slow, too. Not as bad as Debbie, just slow," Bob said. "My mother was always brow-beating her, telling her, 'You're not smart enough to go out alone.' Barbara didn't leave because she didn't have the confidence to leave.

"But she never complained," Bob said. "She never asked for help. It was like that was what she was supposed to do, take care of Debbie."

———

BE TRANSPARENT. Grounding readers in the here and now gives your writing authenticity. I like to signpost, now and then, where I got that information or where I did that interview. Simple asides like "said in the jail interview" serve as subtle nods to where the knowledge came from. And remind readers of a scene they already saw.

FIND FAMILY. Triangulate your reporting. I couldn't just rely on Barbara's memory or retelling of her childhood. I needed to verify her story, seek other perspectives, piece together what really happened. I reached out to all of her remaining siblings, several times. Thank goodness Bob replied and gave me his time, insight and family photos.

WHAT'S IN AN AGE? When you're comparing or contrasting ages, you can add perspective with a couple of short clauses. Barbara wasn't just 16—she was the age when most girls' lives begin. Debbie was three, still in diapers. It's almost like setting a stop sign in her path of development, thrusting adult responsibilities on a meek teen.

In 1981, when their mom got too tired and arthritic to work, Barbara and Debbie moved with her to Florida. Barbara was 30, Debbie 17. Now Barbara had two people to care for. Her mom's Social Security plus Debbie's disability checks didn't even cover the rent on their little house in South Pasadena. So Barbara had to become the breadwinner, too.

Her first job was dishwasher at the Howard Johnson's on St. Pete Beach. Barbara said she loved that job, loved having a reason to get out of the house. She would wake up an hour early and ride her bike to the beach. With her headphones on, a Garth Brooks tape blaring, she would walk the sand behind the motel, watching the sunrise, waiting for her shift to start.

Those were the only hours Barbara ever had to herself.

For more than a decade, Barbara worked at the Howard Johnson's, moving up to busing tables, then cooking. She always worked the day shift. She had to be home in time to make dinner for her mom and Debbie. She never had time for hobbies, not even much TV.

Debbie, though, had all day—every day—for whatever she wanted to do. She loved Star Wars and Snow White and soap operas, especially General Hospital. She spent hours on computer chat rooms. She adored dogs. She always went overboard, craving more of whatever she was into. She was always bombarding strangers with her stories.

"Debbie would get into these conversations that would go on and on and on, about Elvis, Star Wars, whatever," said Debra Henson. Henson worked at the Mail Boxes Etc. near where the Burnses lived. Once a week, the sisters would come in to buy a money order or mail a package.

"I guess Debbie had met someone on a chat room, and she'd send him things: T-shirts, teddy bears, little trinkets and stuff," Henson said. "She said she was going to marry him, but you never knew what to believe."

Barbara didn't talk much, Henson said, except to urge Debbie along. "She was always nice to Debbie, she wouldn't fuss at her, even when she wanted to leave and Debbie kept talking. She was always totally patient," Henson said. "Debbie limped, a bad back or something. And Barbara was always helping her get around."

When they walked out of the shop, Henson said, the sisters usually were holding hands.

GO TO THEIR HAPPY PLACE. I love asking people when they were the happiest, where and why. Especially when you're talking about something tragic, seek the good times and places. Learn what helps people escape, what they long for, where they vacation. At night, when they're falling asleep, what do they picture? For Barbara, the beach was her bliss.

CHANNEL THE CHARACTER. Imagine if you were the person you're writing about. What would it be like to be in their head? Their world? What would they say? How would they say it? In this section, I tried to inhabit Debbie, use words she would use, embody the child-like enthusiasm and insistence everyone said she exhibited.

In the fall of 2000, everything changed. Barbara and Debbie's mom died, leaving the sisters alone.

Within days, they got a call from a lawyer. Their brother John had just died of diabetes and left his entire estate—about $350,000—to Debbie, to make sure she was cared for.

"That's the last time I talked to either one of those two, when I told them there was money coming their way," their brother Bob said. "I got nothing. Our sister Jo, nothing. Barbara and Debbie, they were just gone after that."

Bob said he called them seven or eight times and left messages. Then the number was disconnected.

"For a person who never had money, to get a boatload of it," Bob said, "well, you might go a little crazy."

Debbie had always been excitable. People said she acted like a little kid, upbeat one minute, brooding the next. She could be demanding.

She knew just what she wanted to do, now that she was rich. She wanted to travel, see places she'd seen on TV. And collect Star Wars stuff. Lots of Star Wars stuff. Oh, and buy a pinball machine and a foosball table and a dart board and a skateboard . . .

On a computer chat room, Debbie read about a General Hospital fan club convention that was coming up. In California. Barbara booked two plane tickets and a hotel room and the sisters flew across the country.

Australia was another adventure, Barbara said from jail. The leading man on General Hospital was supposed to be from Down Under, so of course that's where Debbie wanted to go. Barbara got the brochures, made the reservations and the sisters flew to the other side of the world.

———

In October 2001, home from their travels, they put a down payment on a double-wide near the end of Yellow Pine Street in the Tyrone area of St. Petersburg. They signed a loan for $81,126: their first house.

The mobile home has three bedrooms. But Debbie was scared of the dark, scared of being alone, scared of everything. So Barbara stayed in the front room with her. She pushed her single bed close to Debbie's, their heads almost touching.

Every night, Barbara said, she fell asleep listening to her sister breathe.

———

SAVOR SILENCE. Capturing noise is easy. Conveying quiet is hard but so effective. I knew, from the cleaning crews' photos, that the sisters' beds were head to head. I couldn't imagine living like that as an adult, especially when they each could have had their own bedrooms. When I asked Barbara about that, she shared that her sister was a heavy breather. And always fell asleep before she did.

CAPTURE DESPERATION. As the tension increases, the pace of the writing should increase, building toward a climax, keeping readers on edge. Here, I tried to convey Barbara's perspective, her growing despair, her sister's increasing demands. Long sentences with lots of clauses help propel the desperation, jealousy and isolation.

The money trickled away, sand through a sieve. In less than three years, the Burns sisters blew through the $350,000.

Barbara declared bankruptcy. She had to go back to work. She started working as a cashier at Lowe's, taking extra shifts, trying to meet the mortgage.

Debbie was home alone all the time, so Barbara bought her a dog. It was a tiny Chihuahua with long, silky brown hair like a guinea pig, pointy ears like a gremlin and a triangular pink nose that made it look like a teddy bear. Debbie loved that dog. Barbara, too. They called him Leo.

Even working holidays and overtime, Barbara couldn't make the $766 monthly payment on their double-wide. In 2003, the bank started calling. Barbara said she was trying.

Before she knew what it was like to have money, she said, she didn't miss it. But once she and Debbie got the inheritance—once they got used to eating out, traveling, buying whatever they wanted—they got used to an easier lifestyle. That made everything so much harder when the money ran out.

Especially when Barbara was working so hard, taking extra hours, and still couldn't keep up.

Especially when her sister was sitting home all day watching soap operas, ordering pay-per-view movies, playing with her Yoda doll, complaining that Barbara was home late, and demanding: Where's dinner?

After a while, Barbara got tired of it. But there was no one to help, no one even to talk to. No end in sight.

———

Much later, when the detectives tracked her down, Barbara had no trouble remembering the exact date of the shooting. Aug. 15, 2004—Debbie's 40th birthday.

She had taken her sister out to dinner at Macaroni Grill the night before, she told them. They had started arguing about money. Debbie wanted more and more things, and she got angry when Barbara said they couldn't afford them. Debbie couldn't understand why not, since her brother had left her all that money.

All the way home, they fought, all the way through that night's TV news. A little after 11 p.m., Debbie fell asleep. Barbara lay in the bed beside her.

A few hours later, before it got light, Barbara got up. She told detectives she walked to the dresser, opened the third drawer from the top and took out a Smith & Wesson .38-caliber revolver. She had bought it years ago at a pawn shop to ward off intruders.

She pulled out a box of bullets and loaded one into the steel blue gun.

The shot was fired from 2 feet away from Debbie's forehead, detectives said.

Barbara tucked the gun back beneath some clothes in her dresser. The detectives found it much later, among things the cleanup crew had taken out of the double-wide.

How can you take care of your sister for 40 years, love her, raise her, put up with her, protect her, fold your whole life into hers, then suddenly do away with your only companion?

Experts say sister killings are extremely rare. And it's unusual for caregivers to murder their patients. Barbara Burns was the rarest case of all: a sister and a lifelong caregiver.

For other caregivers, duties eventually end. Parents die. Children grow up. You may end up looking after your spouse your whole life, but when you get married you know that's a possibility.

It can be even harder to take care of someone when you didn't choose it. Things can work out if you have other people to help you and you have a life of your own, says Dr. Kathleen Heide, a criminology professor at the University of South Florida.

"But if the two individuals do not have other healthy relationships and good boundaries in place," Heide says, "the relationship can become increasingly taxing for both parties."

Even the most devoted person can run out of patience, Heide says. "Issues can be minor," she says. Over the years, the buildup of little things can lead to suppressed rage. "The triggering incident for the explosion of a torrent of homicidal rage can be quite trivial."

Debbie wanted to order more premium cable channels and Barbara couldn't make her understand they were broke.

A few hours after shooting her sister, Barbara told the detectives, she went to work at Lowe's. When she got back to the mobile home that night, she moved her mattress out of the front bedroom. For the first time in 40 years, she slept by herself.

Later, Barbara returned to Debbie's body, which still lay on the bed. She wrapped Debbie in blankets, then a shower curtain. She added comforters, threw in a Star Wars calendar.

For the next six weeks, she stayed in that double-wide, living

WAX PHILOSOPHICAL. Step back from your story and ask big-picture questions. What does it mean? Why did that happen? Is there a take-away? Jot down your queries, relish incredulities and existential angst: sometimes those expand the minutia to the mega. Then try to answer your own questions by quoting statistics, interviewing experts and asking the people who lived through the event.

with her dead sister. She kept adding air fresheners and baskets of potpourri to mask the smell. She turned down the air conditioning as low as it would go.

She knew she didn't have long. Soon, the bank would come to reclaim the double-wide.

One day last fall, Barbara's neighbor saw her digging in the front yard, a hole at least 3 feet long and just as wide. Barbara had lined four bags of concrete mix along the driveway. The neighbor had never seen Barbara working in the yard, so she asked what she was doing.

"She said she was going to put a piece of concrete out there to put her chair on. And I thought, 'Oh my gosh, her whole front is already concrete!'" Shirley Greilick said. "But I never asked anything more about it."

Barbara quit her job at Lowe's, telling her boss she was going to California to care for a sick aunt. On Oct. 1, she packed two suitcases, ditched her van at the bus station and rode the Greyhound to Virginia Beach. No one noticed she was gone. Nobody missed Debbie, either. For the next seven months, no one asked about the Burns sisters—not until the crew came to clean out their abandoned mobile home.

In Virginia Beach, Barbara moved into a homeless shelter within walking distance of a 7-Eleven. Now that she didn't have to cook dinner for anyone, she worked nights.

In the jail interview, Barbara remembered how she spent her free time. Every morning when her shift ended, she would walk to the beach and watch the sunrise, a new day. She loved being back on the same sand she used to chase her brothers on when she was a girl, and had a life.

"I'm finishing high school here. They're helping me," Barbara says through the video camera at the jail.

She spends her days, now, talking to the other inmates, eating meals someone else cooks, watching TV she never had time for before.

She's making friends here, she says. Everyone treats her real nice. When you've already served a life sentence, the county jail might not seem so bad.

One more question, Barbara, before the guards cut us off: Whatever happened to that little dog you and Debbie loved so much?

"Oh, Leo!" Barbara says, and her face lights up for an instant. "He was real sweet. When I left, I had to put him in the shelter."

Barbara sounds sad now. She says she hopes someone nice took him home. She didn't want to drop him off there, but she says she didn't have a choice. Did she?

She couldn't just leave a little dog like that all alone, to die.

AFTER THE STORIES

After 12 years in prison, Barbara was released in February 2018. Since then, she has been trying to build a life. And forgive herself.

"I'm a very loving, caring person. I'd give anyone the shirt off my back," she told me in 2020, when I wrote a follow-up story ("She cared for her sister her whole life. Then she killed her"). She still swears she blacked out the night of the murder, that she doesn't remember shooting her sister.

She lives in a halfway house now, in a two-story stucco building in an industrial area of St. Petersburg, only a few miles from the home where she lived with her sister's body. She shares an apartment with two women. For the first time in 69 years, she has her own room.

She scrapes by on Social Security, goes to AA meetings, rides the bus to Walmart, hangs out with other residents at "Celebrate Recovery."

In November 2020, Investigation Discovery featured Barbara's story in an episode of *Twisted Sisters*.

EMBRACE IRONY. Come back to the beginning. If the dog made you care in the opening, made the murderer cry in the middle, connected the neighbor and the cleaner, it's only fitting that he own the last scene. Leo seemed to be the most important character to the sisters. And though Barbara lived with her sister's corpse for six weeks, then drove away, she couldn't just leave a little dog.

While President Donald Trump was paying off porn star Stormy Daniels, she rode the pole at a Tampa nightclub on a tour dubbed "Make America Horny Again." Photographer: Luis Santana

11

IGNORE IMPORTANT PEOPLE

See who is in their shadows, search for stakeholders, who else cares, don't punt—swivel

Stormy Daniels: The President's Porn Star

Reported in one day and long night; written the next morning.
Published February 17, 2018

BEFORE THE STORY

The strip club owner promised backstage access while the porn star got ready. Reporters would be able to interview her, he said, then see her show. Afterward, they could watch her do lap dances—and see what the president had seen.

News had just broken that Donald Trump's lawyer had paid Stormy Daniels $130,000 to not talk about their affair. But now, she was talking. And kicking off a national tour titled "Make America Horny Again."

My editor's idea was to narrate that night, talk to Stormy while she put on her pasties, ask about the president's performance.

But long after she was scheduled to take the stage, the bouncer said she had changed her mind. She wouldn't do interviews.

A dozen other journalists packed up their cameras and left. But I knew there was a hole on the front page, waiting for our story. I knew folks across Tampa Bay had heard she was coming and would want to know what had happened. So what do you do when your subject shuts you down?

Find someone else. Another person with a stake in what's going on.

I talked to at least 20 men waiting for the show. None would give me their names. I talked to strippers, bartenders and the bouncer. They were all too busy making money. Finally, I zeroed in on the only person who seemed to be there alone.

This wasn't the story I set out to get.

But it has the best punch line I've ever written.

THE STORY

ADD INSIGHT. The whole scene inside the strip club was new to me, and I tried to remain objective, writing down everything—just the facts. But I kept staring at that photo of the president, beaming beside the porn star, and I became fixated on her face. "She looks bored."

KNOW TOO MUCH. Since I thought I was going to interview Stormy, I wanted to know all I could ahead of time. I spent hours reading tabloid stories, searching websites, watching porn. I didn't get to ask her about *Good Will Humping*. But I got some saucy film titles in the story. And I got to include a list—as a sidebar—of things most folks didn't know about her: She was editor of her high school newspaper, president of her 4-H club, and she hopes when she gets to heaven, God says, "Nice tits."

NOT MUCH NEWS. By the time I wrote this story, everyone who wanted to know the details of the president's dalliance with the porn star already did. I spent a lot of time asking people in the audience what they cared about. Most were just there to be close to such a salacious celebrity. So I condensed the context of the news into a single sentence, giving it equal weight to Stormy's personal life and career, trying to stay in the mindset of the folks at that club.

In the center of the nightclub, between the cigar case and bustling bar, a giant screen blankets the back wall. Usually, ads for drink specials and coming attractions scroll across.

But Friday night, a life-size picture of President Donald Trump peered at the stripper pole.

Then there he was, puckering beside a porn star. In another shot, he's squeezing the blonde's shoulders, beaming at her big boobs. She looks bored.

"Stormy Daniels," read a huge headline. "Make America Horny Again."

Shows at Thee Dollhouse typically start after midnight, but the owner had scheduled an early-bird performance, so young professionals could come right after work. So retirees could enjoy a lap dance before bed.

"As soon as I saw the news, I knew this was going to blow up," said Warren Collazo, co-owner of the Tampa strip club. "Stormy was here three years ago, she used to live here, she's a great girl who's had a great career. Why not jump on that bandwagon? So I called her agent and said: 'Let's get her booked. I'll get some hats made.'"

Most of the 70 people at the matinee didn't know Stormy Daniels' real name is Stephanie Gregory Clifford. That she's 38 years old, 36DD and raising a young daughter. They didn't care that she has starred in more than 150 adult films like *Good Will Humping* and *Porking with Pride*, had won dozens of porn awards, had a cameo in *The 40-Year-Old Virgin*.

They had never heard of her until last month, when news broke that the president's lawyer had paid her $130,000, reportedly so she'd keep quiet about meeting Trump at a celebrity golf tournament in 2006 and having "textbook generic" sex with him—while Trump's wife was caring for their infant son.

They just wanted to watch the president's alleged mistress crawl across the stage in a G-string.

———

"Get your dollar bills ready!" the DJ shouted at 6:15 p.m. "We've got the first lady of the United States right here tonight. She'll give you a lap dance just like she did the president."

A North Dakota man and his brother-in-law, who were staying at the Ramada next door, had seen the marquee and ditched their wives. "We couldn't miss this." A bartender and his pal had read about the show in the newspaper. "My girlfriend wants me to send her a selfie with Stormy." A lesbian couple who hates Trump, who had gone to Washington, D.C., for the women's march, who had never been to a strip club, came because "this is just so bizarre, we couldn't resist."

Mike Remmert, 74, voted for Trump, "because he's not a politician." He didn't care if the president had sex with the porn star. "More power to him if he did!"

Remmert has been a regular at Thee Dollhouse for more than a decade. Dancers call him "the Candyman," because he brings them bags of Starlight mints. He lives alone, works at Walmart, saves his paychecks for Crown Royal and Cokes and cover charges. He paid $20 to get in Friday, $80 more for four red mesh ballcaps: "Making the Dollhouse Great Again." He pulled one over his sparse white hair and gave the others to his favorite girls.

"I knew Stormy before all this stuff broke," he said proudly. "I met her here years ago. She signed a picture for me." He had bought a couple of her DVDs that night but said he never watched them.

He wanted to ask if she remembered him. He wanted to tell her a joke.

"We're just three songs away from the main event," the DJ called at 6:40 p.m. "Get ready to welcome the most famous woman on the planet."

Stormy was supposed to give interviews, talk to reporters in her dressing room, pose for pictures. But 40 minutes after she was scheduled to go on, the club manager said she was refusing to take any questions or even address the audience. And she was banning photographs.

The TV news crews left.

NO NAMES. You don't always have to identify people by name. When you're trying to paint a broad-brush view of a scene, it's okay to scan a crowd and describe individuals by what they're wearing, where they came from, or who they say they are. The "North Dakota man and his brother-in-law who were staying at the Ramada" and the "lesbian couple who hate Trump" refused to share their names. But they gave me enough information to give readers an idea of who was there.

SUM THEM UP. You only need a few precise details to give readers a glimpse of your main characters. Mike had been a regular at the strip club for more than 10 years, and he had a nickname. I love when people have nicknames—their backstories tell you so much about how others see them. And ask the follow-up questions: He still works... where? Why? How much does he make? That way, when he pays for a lap dance, you know how many hours he had to work for that.

WHAT'S AT STAKE? The best question to carry any narrative is "Why?" Once you know why the main character cares, that thread can drive the story—and keep your readers wondering. Instead of just asking, "Why are you here?" I often ask, "What are you hoping for?" or "What are you worried about?" Mike made it easy: "He wanted to ask if she remembered him. He wanted to tell her a joke."

"I'm embarrassed. Very disappointed. Angry," said the owner, who was paying her $1,000 per show. "If I had known she was going to shut everyone out, I'd never have booked her."

————

The patrons didn't seem to care. They ordered another round from buxom waitresses, paid tattooed dancers to straddle them on barstools, stuffed singles into lace panties. In the front row, center-stage, Remmert nursed his drink, grinning, rehearsing his joke in his head.

"You've read about her in the news. You've seen her on Jimmy Kimmel. Porn star to the president!" the DJ finally called. "Batten down the hatches. Things are about to get Stormy!"

VERB CHECK. Action words can make your story. After I finish writing, I go through and circle each verb—and see if I can come up with something better: "Lights **spun**. Fog plumes **erupted**. A song **throbbed** through the giant speakers as Stormy **snaked** toward the crowd."

Blue lights spun overhead. Fog plumes erupted from the floor. Big Spender throbbed through the giant speakers as Stormy snaked toward the crowd in a scarlet evening gown, threading a white boa around her ample bosom. She rubbed her butt into the chest of a middle-aged man, "motorboated" a 30-something guy's face between her breasts. Then she sauntered to Remmert, removed his new ballcap and kissed his bald spot. He tried to hold her. But she wriggled away to mount the stage.

The next song was performed by President Kennedy's paramour, Marilyn Monroe. Stormy peeled off long, satin gloves, then the long skirt. *"There may come a time when a lass needs a lawyer..."* Off came her top. *"But diamonds are a girl's best friend."*

Men rained wads of dollar bills onto the stage. Women pressed through the men to smack her butt. Remmert's eyes widened as Stormy sank into a split. On the screen above her, her alleged lover leered.

Five songs in, it was over. Stormy pranced off in her platform heels. A bouncer swept money into a silver bucket.

"You don't have to be the president of the United States to enjoy the hotness tonight!" yelled the DJ. "America really is beautiful."

Some people seemed disappointed. "That was it?" Others were thrilled. "So that's what Trump saw!" The dancers, many half her age, weren't impressed. "Boring," one said of her routine. "It felt dated," said another. "Being a porn star doesn't make you a good stripper. She didn't even work the pole."

————

A half-hour later, Stormy emerged in a midnight blue halter dress and set up court in the VIP lounge. For $20, you could buy an autographed picture, a DVD or a T-shirt: "Got MILF?" Remmert was first in line. He paid a bouncer to take a picture with his phone. And when Stormy let him hold her breasts, he got so excited he forgot to tell her his joke.

No one in the loud, dark club was paying attention to the latest headlines about Russians being indicted and a Playboy Playmate who may have been another Trump mistress.

Remmert couldn't stay for Stormy's second set or see her shows the next night. He had to get up early for his Walmart shift, and he didn't have $200 for a lap dance. But he had one more $20 bill, enough to buy another minute with his muse.

"She's smart, charging for each time you talk to her," he said. "She may even be a better businessman than Trump."

He went to the back of the line, waited for 20 people. "You again?" Stormy asked. She remembered!

"I have a joke," he said. "Have you ever smelled mothballs?"

She looked confused. Was he referring to himself? To Trump? Slowly, the porn star said, "Yesss . . ."

Remmert laughed. "Well, how did you get them to spread their little legs?"

AT LEAST TRY. From the moment I heard the joke, I knew I wanted that to be my ending. And I knew the managing editor would worry it was too offensive. So instead of just writing it into the story and blindsiding her, my boss called her at home and told her the joke. She laughed.

ANOTHER STORY. Good stories often lead to other stories, so always keep your eyes open for interesting angles and opportunities. When I went backstage to talk to the strippers, I met the middle-aged woman running the dressing room and discovered another story. For years, she has been "house mom" to the young women working the pole. There's my next Mother's Day story!

Matt Casler, *right*, came out to
his mom after the Pulse nightclub
shooting. By then his sister Sara,
left, had been openly gay for years.
Photographer: Cherie Diez

12

FIND A GUIDE

Pulse Nightclub: Aftermath of the Orlando Shooting Tests a Young Man's Courage

Reported in two days; written in one. Published June 19, 2016

BEFORE THE STORY

Writing about mass shootings, surrounded by a pack of other journalists, is sometimes a horrible necessity of my job. So when I was sent to cover the aftermath of the massacre at a gay nightclub in Orlando, I set out to find a unique perspective that hadn't been reported by every other news outlet.

Other reporters flocked to the crime scene, the police station and the hospital. I started at a Starbucks near the makeshift memorial that was being erected.

When you're covering a scene with hundreds of people, instead of diving into the center of the crowd, scan the edges. Someone is often standing alone, watching from a safe distance, thinking.

I wasn't sent to the Pulse nightclub to cover the news. I was there to put a face on the tragedy. I zoomed in on just one. Often it's easier to make readers care about a single person than a larger group.

I wanted a guide to what was going on.

My son was in a Facebook group for Florida kids going to Northwestern University and told me about a young man who lived near the shooting. So I messaged him, asked if I could buy him a coffee.

As he talked about how the deaths were affecting him, I knew I wanted to share his story. I wrote other Pulse stories about a victim, a witness, a drag queen. But this was the most surprising way in — and showed the ripples of that tragedy.

THE STORY

MAKE CONNECTIONS. Show how an event fits into history, how it affects a town, a family, an individual. Go from big picture to personal, tightening the frame. In this opening section, I put Pulse in context with other mass shootings: the most victims. I connect Matt's siblings to the bar by having them describe it. Then we zero in on Matt, how he was a victim of this tragedy, too: he'd wanted to go there, a rite of passage. Now, he was afraid.

Matt Casler didn't recognize his neighborhood as he drove home last Sunday morning. Cop cars lined every corner. Barricades blocked the streets. Sirens screamed.

A few hours after the deadliest shooting in U.S. history, it had been turned into a war zone.

He steered past armed troopers, beneath hovering helicopters. Dizzy and disoriented, the 18-year-old kept checking his phone: 20 dead so far, and the count would climb.

Pulse nightclub is on a residential road two blocks east of Matt's home, far from the Disney castles and downtown skyscrapers, surrounded by townhomes and chain stores: Starbucks, Chipotle, Pizza Hut.

Normally, the neighborhood is quiet.

Now his hometown would be on that list, ahead of Columbine, Aurora, Sandy Hook.

How could that happen? Just because they were gay?

Matt's brother and sister had hung out at that bar. They'd promised to take him there this summer, before he left for college—his first foray into a new world. They had told him how open everyone was there, how warm and accepting. How people of all ages escaped to those strobe-lit rooms to watch drag shows, dance to the DJ and surround themselves with folks who made them feel like family.

It had seemed like a safe haven. Now that it was gone, would people feel like they had to hide?

A couple of months earlier, before graduating as valedictorian of his high school, Matt finally summoned the courage to tell his mom he was gay. But he wasn't ready to tell the world.

The whole drive home, he worried about who had died.

And how he would he ever feel safe enough to be himself.

He was a toddler when his parents divorced. His dad, a photographer, moved out but saw him often. Matt and his older brother and sister, who are twins, grew up in a tall house with an energetic mutt and their mom, who is a pediatrician.

She took them to church and art museums, to the symphony and library. She told her children they could be whoever they wanted to be.

"I want them to help others, and be happy," said Alix Casler, 54. "I just told them to be the best people they can be."

Matt's sister, Sara, came out to her parents at 16. Her mom was fine. Sara has hardly talked to her dad since.

Sara's twin, Nick, told his mom the next year.

Matt was 12 when he started noticing boys. But he was too scared to approach any.

At Boone High, he had 2,900 classmates. Only 15 had come out. Matt immersed himself in AP classes and was accepted at Northwestern University. He was named Florida's Student Journalist of the Year.

He dated a couple of girls, went to homecoming twice. For junior prom, he brought his camera instead of a date. Last month, he went to a journalism convention instead of his senior prom, where his classmates voted him king. "No one knew I was gay."

Telling them just felt awkward. He wasn't ready to brave his classmates' taunts, endure their questions or accept that label. Before he could tell others, he had to be more sure of himself.

He controlled what he could, he said, concentrating on achievements and image, staving off emotions. Trying to convince himself he didn't need to get close to anyone, so his sexuality didn't matter.

In April, Matt's mom took him to Toronto. They were in the elevator of the CN Tower, riding up 115 stories, with two young men who were holding hands. Matt could tell they were in love.

"That," he thought, "is what I want."

———

No one at Matt's house could sleep Sunday night. He texted his brother, who is in medical school at Florida State University. He talked to his mom, who said, "There is so much more good in the world than bad."

Matt and Sara slumped on the couch with their dog, in front of the TV, while CNN started scrolling victims' names across the screen.

SEEK TURNING POINTS. Find out when things changed, when someone realized something, how they knew. I started when Matt's parents got divorced, when his world shifted. Then his siblings came out. Soon he knew he was gay. Sum up people's lives through milestones, moments that shaped him. Later in the story, I ask when he decided to go to the vigil. And why. Another turning point.

USE ONLY GOOD QUOTES. I used to let subjects ramble and would fill my stories with long paragraphs of quotes. Now I mostly paraphrase what people say, write the information I need, not all their words. Learn to listen for good quotes, ones that show something about how the person talks or sees the world. There aren't many quotes in this story, but the ones in there are strong. And move the attribution to the middle, to slow important things down: "That," he thought, "is what I want."

A travel agent. A worker from Universal's Harry Potter ride. A young drag queen, who had a young son.

Sara's girlfriend lost a friend in the massacre. Another still was missing.

Like millions of others, Sara and Matt kept thinking: That could have been me.

ASK WHAT THEY KNEW. If you're going to incorporate a chunk of history into a story, do it through your subject's lens. What do they know? How much do they understand? Matt knew a lot of gay history. But even if your subject doesn't, you can always fill in the blanks by pointing out what they don't know, and drawing attention to what isn't taught in school: He didn't know about . . .

Few high schools teach gay history. While struggles for women's rights and African-American equality have been added to curriculums, accounts of the LGBT movement seldom are.

Matt knew the highlights: The 1969 Stonewall Riots in New York City, when gays finally stood up to police. Arson at a New Orleans gay bar in 1973, which killed 32 people. Harvey Milk, the first openly gay elected official in California, who was murdered in 1978. And Matthew Shepard, who was tortured and left to die in Wyoming, in 1998, the same year Matt was born.

"I know being gay used to be considered a mental disorder," he said. "And I know it used to be illegal."

Instead of causing people to retreat further into the closet, past attacks on the gay community brought people out.

At the time of the Stonewall Riots, there were about 50 gay groups in the country. A year later, there were at least 1,500, said activist Frank Kameny, who organized gays to picket the White House in 1965. Two years after the riots, Kameny said, the number of gay groups had grown to 2,500.

Milk knew someone would shoot him and hoped his death would help others. "If a bullet should enter my brain, let that bullet destroy every closet door in the country," he said.

"Sometimes it takes a crisis to get people to come out," said Dr. Judith Glassgold, 59, an executive at the American Psychological Association. "Human connections can provide solace and a sense of safety."

Matt and his sister had talked about how glad they are to be growing up now, when being gay is next to normal. Gay people are being elected to Congress, hosting talk shows, playing professional sports. They can even get married.

"All these people fought for us for all those years," Matt said. "We don't remember their pain."

He and so many young people thought the violence was behind them.

But Sunday's attack shattered Matt's dream of going to Pulse—or any other gathering of gay people.

"I wouldn't put myself in that possibility of danger," he said. He had never felt such fear.

———

Monday morning, Matt's neighborhood was still on lockdown. He steered past stone-faced troopers and gawking residents. He had a summer internship at the marketing company contracted by Orlando Regional Medical Center. Usually, he spent the days sifting through the hospital's social media feeds.

But now the hospital was full of shooting victims. Matt found himself fielding online pleas from desperate people. Has my son been brought in? How's my partner? One woman emailed a detailed description of her daughter's outfit, and who she had been with at Pulse.

"I felt this enormous sense of shame," he said. "All those people who had gone out that night, they weren't afraid."

Still, he refused to go to the Monday night vigil. He didn't want to be out there, surrounded by thousands of gay people. What if protesters showed up? What if another shooter took aim? What if someone from school saw him?

"Orlando PD is saying don't do it," Matt told his sister. "There's not enough police to protect everyone."

Sara scowled. "Now is not the time to stay inside," she said.

No thanks, Matt said. He was going to shoot pictures of Pulse, of the broken building and blocked-off roads. He wanted to document the aftermath through a long lens.

———

Maybe it was the news teams that had planted tents so anchors could have shade to blot their makeup. Maybe it was the TV reporters who kept pontificating about politics and guns instead of talking about the victims. Maybe it was the way they joked and laughed, as if no one had died.

Did being detached mean being insensitive?

Mostly, Matt said, it was the security guard who confronted him while he was photographing the fresh scars on his neighborhood.

"Hey!" the guard yelled. "You don't belong here."

"I don't belong?" Matt snapped. "I live here."

As the sun slipped behind the hospital, Matt turned back toward the nightclub for a few final photos. The towering satellite dishes, the hedge of microphones, the new normal. All the sidewalks wrapped in sunshine-colored police tape.

Matt was walking back to his car when it hit him:

EMPLOY SUBTLE IMAGERY. Trying to write similes or create symbolism can be tricky. Often those passages feel forced or overdone—and need to be edited out. But when the imagery is appropriate, and subtle, it can be effective. I especially like being able to use words that reference the subject matter to make a more abstract observation. Matt wanted to see the scene of the tragedy "though a long lens." Later, he "hid behind his camera," literally and figuratively, "trying to focus."

Thousands of people from all over Florida had flocked to a downtown park to raise candles. News crews from across the world had come to watch.

And here he was, scouring the streets stained with yesterday's headlines, afraid to embrace either of his identities.

He is gay. He wants to be a journalist. Both will force him to confront realities that make him afraid.

"If this is what I want to do, I should start now," he told himself.

He didn't have to talk to anyone. He just had to be there.

It was dark when Matt approached the park, except for a few flames flickering on the ground. People had set candles on cardboard signs, planted them beside pinwheels and around pictures of lost loved ones.

Matt walked against the thinning crowd, folks of every race and age. Wearing cowboy hats and do rags, silk ties and homemade tattoos, nun costumes, military caps, Republican T-shirts. Everyone seemed to be with someone.

Matt hid behind his camera, trying to focus.

He moved on through the makeshift monuments, photographed a twirling toddler and a girl playing guitar. When he saw a sobbing young woman, about his age, he stopped to frame the shot. Then put down his camera.

Usually, Matt wasn't a hugger. But he draped his arm around the girl. When she hugged him back, he started to cry. Others came, and enveloped them both. They held each other up.

He had planned to go to Pulse this summer with his siblings, to finally dip his toe into the new world he hoped to enter.

Instead, he dived into a sea of strangers. And they embraced him.

Monday night, from the window of his third-floor bedroom, Matt could see a halo from the police strobes. People still were suffering in the hospital. Families were starting to plan funerals.

He flipped through his photos and tagged the most emotional: people hurting, hugging and singing. Wide shots to show the swath of the scene. Tight zooms on shimmering tears.

People should see this, he thought. They should feel it. He uploaded an album to his Facebook, 80 pictures, and started to type. He was ready for everyone to know.

IGNORE THE EVENT. Other reporters were there to cover the vigil. I followed Matt as he photographed the nightclub, blocks away from the park where thousands of people were lighting candles. I felt like I was missing something. But you have to stay with your subject, see what they're doing, how they're thinking and feeling. The event becomes the backdrop to your scene. By the time Matt changed his mind and headed to the vigil, it was almost over.

CELEBRATE SMALL VICTORIES. Sometimes the biggest breakthroughs come in small moments. Be alert for even little changes worth celebrating, or mourning, things people have been hoping for or needing. Like many photographers, Matt used his camera as a shield, protecting him from the world. So when I saw him put it down to hug a stranger, that seemed like a victory.

FRIEND EVERYONE. What people put on social media shows how they want the world to see them. So ask everyone you write about if you can friend them on Facebook or encourage them to send you a request. I don't reach out to them for a connection without their permission. But even before you contact them, you can check out their Twitter, Instagram, LinkedIn, and other social media accounts. You can find out so much about people by scrolling through their feeds and "about" pages. And as you're writing about them, you can follow their public persona while you're getting the inside scoop. Matt was prolific on his page, which helped me immensely.

Last night, I trudged back to my car from the Pulse Shooting Vigil with my camera in my right hand, its grip sticky with sweat and its backside covered in tears. I went to the event as a journalist, to try to showcase the pain my city was feeling, but I found myself swept up in the sadness.

I cried with people who I had never met over loved ones whose names I did not know. I hugged strangers who sat alone in the grass, tears flowing down their faces. I witnessed a mass outpouring of hurt.

But this pain is not a display of weakness. This pain is not surrender. This attack on the LGBT+ community, my community, proves its resilience and strength. We stood in defiance of fear to show our love and fortitude to the whole world. Forty-nine people may now have passed, but we stand united still, with the world at our backs.

WAIT FOR IT. I could have ended this story after the last section, when Matt embraces the crowd. But late that night, when I saw his post, I cried. This was his coming out. After such an emotionally exhausting day, he had finally decided to share his secret. His strength and pride overcame his shame and fear. I called him about 11 p.m. and asked if I could share his words with the world. Sometimes, when you wait awhile, you get a better ending.

"Hurricane Hunk" Jim Cantore films a live shot for the Weather Channel from the Florida Panhandle. Off-screen, the popular meteorologist was dealing with a personal storm. Photographer: Lane DeGregory

13

LISTEN TO THE QUIET

The sound of silence,
what doesn't happen,
questions not answered

The Storm Chaser: Riding out a Hurricane with the Weatherman

Reported in one day, with a follow-up call; written the next day.
Published August 28, 2005

BEFORE THE STORY

Hurricanes kept pounding Florida that summer, so everyone was watching Weather Channel meteorologist Jim Cantore. "The hurricane hunk" some dubbed him. He seemed strong and unflappable even in gale-force winds.

So when I learned he was coming to the state's panhandle, a long drive but quick flight away, I booked the last plane out of Tampa and met him on the beach, then asked if I could shadow him through the storm.

Between broadcasts, I watched Hooters waitresses bring him wings, tourists ask for autographs before they fled. After his last shoot, he invited me to join him and his videographer for a beer in their hotel—the only one open. I was staying there, too.

He opened three bottles, then called his wife from the other side of the room. In the quiet, the cameraman and I heard him crying.

I would have never thought to ask the weatherman about his personal storm.

THE STORY

He walks down the beach, holding his microphone, his Teva sandals slapping the rain-pocked sand. Wind tugs the brim of his Storm Stories ball cap. White foam skips across the waves.

The sky is bruised. Dark clouds sweep in from the south.

"Ten seconds," he hears through the wire in his left ear. Enough time to adjust the black T-shirt over his gym-built biceps. "Four seconds." He sets his jaw, turns his back to the storm. "Two." He stares into the camera. "One. And . . ."

"You can look behind me here and see the rain bands coming in," he tells a million television viewers, arcing his right arm along the shore, so they can see. "This thing is still a long way away from us. But once it makes that turn, it could start to speed up. We'll continue to track Hurricane Ivan as it heads closer. And we'll keep you posted."

He nods gravely.

"For now, I'm meteorologist Jim Cantore, reporting live from Panama City Beach, for the Weather Channel."

Cantore and his crew have been following Ivan across Florida for days. The weatherman is sick of waiting, tired of working 18-hour shifts, ready to get off the road.

He's worrying about a much bigger storm back home.

He feels as if he has been chasing hurricanes all summer. First Charley, in Fort Myers. Then Frances, in Melbourne and Palm Bay. He has endured days without air conditioning, hot food or a shower. Countless nights trying to sleep on sandy sheets, in dumpy motels. Five weekends with his family washed away.

He has never heard of a hurricane season like this one.

He has never been away from his wife and kids for so long.

He met Tamra 18 years ago, on his first day at the Weather Channel. She's petite and blond, six years older than he is. She was in management then, selling the fledgling station to cable companies across the country.

Her job was to get Jim Cantore into as many homes as possible, make him a household name.

In 1990, she became Mrs. Jim Cantore. Together, they helped build the station. He gave weather something new, a macho face. "We both traveled a lot. We got to the point where we were passing each other in the airport. After we had kids, it got real hard," Tamra says.

Daughter Christina is 11. Ben is 9. When Ben was 18 months old, the Cantore family's world began crumbling.

Ben wasn't walking. His wife's arms were shaking, but not from carrying the big boy. When Tamra went to the doctor, he focused on her first.

"I haven't let this out before. I don't know why I'm telling you now," Cantore says. He's leaning against the headboard in Room 116 of the Days Inn, trying to wind down during a break between broadcasts. "Maybe because I'm so exhausted and emotionally drained. Maybe because I'm feeling so guilty I can't be there for them. Maybe it's just time." He turns his head away. Swallows.

"My wife has Parkinson's."

———

"I shuffle, sometimes. I get tired and have to lie down," Cantore's wife says from their home in Atlanta. "When it's real bad, it gets embarrassing—Jim has to cut my meat and feed me."

Tamra Cantore has the same type of early-onset Parkinson's as actor Michael J. Fox. There is no cure.

"My kids have never known me when I didn't shake, shuffle around and seem so stiff," she says matter-of-factly over the phone. "Some days, I'm not strong enough to open a jar of peanut butter. It's not as bad as what some people have to put up with. It's just what I've been dealt."

Tamra isn't the only one who is sick.

When she took Ben with her to her doctor's office, the doc wondered why the boy wasn't walking. At a year-and-a-half, Ben should have been running and spewing two-word sentences. But the boy could barely stand. He didn't speak.

After months of anxiety, testing tests and visits to specialists, the Cantores got the diagnosis: Both their children have a hereditary mental impairment. Their X chromosome is broken. They have Fragile X. Tamra is a silent carrier. Being a girl, Christina has a backup X, so she's better off than her brother. Her symptoms resemble social anxiety and ADHD.

Ben's condition often is mistaken for autism. "It's like having 10 kids to take care of instead of two," Tamra says. "It just gets overwhelming sometimes."

When Cantore is gone, a friend stays with Tamra to help. When Cantore is home, he drives his kids to doctors' appoint-

EMPATHIZE. Ask how people are doing, feeling, coping, and try to relate. I can't imagine chasing hurricanes all season, or having my spouse suffer from Parkinson's disease. But I know what it's like trying to raise two kids when their dad is on the road playing drums with his band, and Cantore and I talked about that—him leaving his family behind, me being left behind with mine.

LET IT UNSPOOL. Instead of sharing his son's diagnosis outright, I wanted to involve the readers in the discovery of what was wrong, so that they would experience the process like the parents. What did Cantore and his wife notice? When did they know? How did they react? Readers have better buy-in when they're along for the reveal.

ments, therapy sessions and tutors. He does laundry, buys groceries and makes the meals.

On weekends, he packs his family in the SUV and drives 90 minutes north to the mountains, to the little log cabin he bought on the river. He and Tamra lash inner tubes together and float down the cool stream with the kids, drifting away from wild weather, adoring fans and debilitating diseases.

But Cantore hasn't seen the cabin for five weekends straight. He hasn't been around to cut his wife's steak or watch his daughter dance or let Ben beat him at PlayStation.

By 9:15 p.m., the rain is spraying sideways. Lightning stabs the sea. Cantore pulls on his coat.

"Four, three," the voice counts down in his left ear. He squints into the camera, wipes his eyes. "Two, one, and . . . "

"The good news is that any potential landfall won't come here until Wednesday," he tells viewers. "That means you'll have plenty of time to prepare."

When the camera cuts to a commercial, Cantore watches the radar bleeding red. He's worried about Ivan's future track. Will it end up at his doorstep in Atlanta?

He might not be there to bail the basement. He might not be there to comfort his wife, to feed her if she's having a bad day. He won't be able to calm his kids.

"Hey, Cantore! Up here! We love you, man!" a big-bellied fan shouts from the hotel's fifth floor.

Cantore looks up and waves. "Who's winning the Broncos game?" he calls.

"We don't know," big-belly yells. "We've been watching you!"

Tan and toned. Broad-shouldered. Sicilian. Passionate. Personable.

Smart enough to know his science. One-of-the-guys enough to break it down. He fills out his black T-shirts better than Sly Stallone.

Who knew a meteorologist could be so cool?

Jim Cantore turned 40 this year. He plays on his church softball team, jogs and lifts weights. He cheers the Green Bay Packers. Goes skiing in Colorado. Loves toasted almonds and Bruce Springsteen and *An Officer and a Gentleman*.

His eyes are hazel, his jaw square. He started shaving his head when his hairline headed north.

SHORTHAND AND STACCATO. Physical descriptions can be tedious. I often write, then delete those sections. In this story, I was profiling someone most people already knew of, so I wanted to offer something to make readers feel like they understood him more intimately. Instead of writing whole sentences, try spitting out details in fragments. Ask corny questions about favorite foods, teams and movies.

On-camera, before a storm, his deep voice takes on a calm, warning tone: Don't panic, folks. But be prepared. I'll show you what's happening so you can get out of harm's way.

Everywhere he goes, people ask for advice. Should we be boarding up yet, Jim? Is it better to be in the west wall of the eye or the east? Women mob him for autographs, and teenage girls giggle. Men want to buy him beers. When one family saw him on TV, broadcasting from Panama City Beach, they made a 90-minute pilgrimage to meet him. Restaurants send him free pizza.

Even as a kid, Cantore loved extreme weather. On cold nights in Vermont, he'd make his mom leave on the barn light so he could see when snow started dusting their farm. He'd wake at 2 a.m. to shovel the steps. "I'd always take off my shirt so I could feel the flakes hitting my back," he says. "The other kids would call me to see when we'd get off school."

He joined the Weather Channel in 1986, four years after the station started—a few months after he graduated from Lyndon State College in Vermont. He has been stalking storms longer than anyone else on cable television.

Early this month, while Hurricane Frances was battering Florida, the Weather Channel was the country's most-watched cable news station, earning the highest ratings in its history. Cantore was on live eight to 12 hours a day.

When he's not in the field, Cantore hosts *Storm Stories*, the Weather Channel's first narrative series. From 9 to 11 weeknights, he also anchors *Evening Edition*. He has been interviewed by Tom Brokaw, Larry King, Brian Williams. He's one of five storm chasers who dive into the worst weather. The producer tries to put Cantore where the hurricane is going to hit.

"He doesn't fake anything," says producer Simon Temperton, who has worked with Cantore for 12 years. Their first assignment together was Hurricane Andrew. "His excitement about the weather is real—and it's contagious."

With everything he's dealing with at home, Cantore's cravings for wild weather have intensified these past few years.

The only way he can escape one storm is to immerse himself in another.

———

Days before Ivan arrives at the Florida Panhandle, the sky above the Days Inn is still swollen. But sunlight is filtering through the clouds.

"How far did you say this place was?" the producer asks from the driver's seat of the rented van.

"Just a couple miles up the beach," Cantore says. "Stop complaining. Everyone loves dolphins."

He's heading to Gulf World, an outdoor aquarium where rescued dolphins are rehabilitated. He and his crew plan a feature about trainers trying to protect the animals from the storm. While his cameraman films stingrays and sharks, Cantore interviews the keepers.

"We have a program here where children can swim with the dolphins. They have to be 5 years old and comfortable in the water," Gulf World operations director Cheryl Joyner tells Cantore. A boy about Ben's age stands on the side of the pool, throwing fish to the dolphins.

Cantore would love to do something like that with his own boy. There are so many things he would like to do with Ben.

"I'd always dreamed of taking my boy to watch the Yankees," says Cantore, who wanted to play pro ball even more than chase storms. "But Ben freaks out in crowds."

YOU NEVER KNOW. When Cantore told me they were heading to the aquarium the next day, I asked if I could go with them. I had no idea what would happen, or if I'd want to include that scene in my story, but I figured it would give us more time to talk. When Cantore saw that boy feeding the dolphin, his face fell. And he started opening up about everything he'd wanted to do with his son.

"All right, folks. Here's the deal: This thing is coming. It's going to be making big waves in the gulf here soon. This is a tremendously dangerous hurricane, people. If it stays a 5, we'll be underwater even on the second story of this motel."

He nods gravely.

"For now, I'm meteorologist Jim Cantore, reporting live from Panama City Beach, for the Weather Channel."

He's on the balcony of the Days Inn, outside Room 116. He opens the door. Cords and computers and cameras are piled on the tables, in case the floor floods. Almond Joy wrappers and empty Red Bull cans litter the dresser. The air smells like sweaty bodies and salt spray. The Weather Channel blares on TV.

"Mind if I turn this down?" Cantore asks his producer, who is slumped in a chair, scribbling notes. "I've got to call my wife."

He wants to catch his kids before they go to sleep.

"Salmon? You had salmon alfredo for dinner? That sounds yummy," he tells his daughter from the cluttered motel room. "No, I haven't had dinner yet." He eyes cold pizza on the dresser. "Did you see me on TV? Or are cartoons on?"

Ben seldom talks on the phone. If he does, it's just, "Hi, Dad. Okay, bye." But tonight, Ben tells his mom he has to talk to Daddy.

BREATHE DEEP. Smell is the most transportive sense. Writers always see and hear things, but often forget to feel, taste and smell. The briny beach air, mixed with man sweat, was prevalent in that cluttered motel room and took me back to college spring break. If you can't be there in person to inhale, ask your subject what they smelled.

When he hears his boy's voice, Cantore smiles. He asks about school and PlayStation and the Yankees. Then Ben has a question. Cantore's face falls. For a few seconds, he's silent. Then he swallows and tries to steady his voice.

"When will I be home? Well . . . I'm still waiting for this storm. I'm going to be home . . . well, I hope on Friday, Buddy." There's a pause. Cantore slams his eyes closed. "Yep, Friday," he says again. "That's four more days."

Later that night—actually, early the next morning—after the overnight reports have been taped and the autographs have been signed and the cords rolled away, Cantore clicks on ESPN to check the Packers score. He pops open a can of Miller Lite.

The TV flickers blue shadows across his tired face. The sports scores slide across the screen.

"For years, I kept wanting to do something to fix things for Tammy and the kids," he says. "But I couldn't. So I didn't want to talk about it."

He clicks to the Weather Channel. There he is, smiling with the dolphins. There he is, windblown on the balcony.

"I guess, after a while, you have to admit you can't control it," Cantore says, watching the radar. "I guess you have to just do the best you can to accept it and live with it."

Kind of like the weather.

IT'S NOT OVER. The best quotes often come when you've put away your pen, and the subject thinks the interview is over and lets his guard down. Keep reporting as long as you're in the room. When Cantore turned on the TV, I got up to leave. I didn't care about the Packers' score. But when he switched channels to see himself, I sat back down. And got that great simile as an ending.

After her IndyCar champion husband
Dan Wheldon died in a crash, Susie
Wheldon had to decide whether to let
their young sons race. At the track, she
helps Sebastian, 7, put on his helmet.
Photographer: John Pendygraft

14

WAIT FOR IT

Fast-Forward: IndyCar Champion's Widow Faces a Dilemma with Their Young Sons

Reported in three days; written in two. Published March 12, 2017

BEFORE THE STORY

When a beloved IndyCar driver died in a fiery crash on a Las Vegas speedway, in front of thousands of fans, all I could think about was his wife and two young sons. They lived in St. Petersburg, only a few miles from me.

Susie Wheldon is blonde, beautiful, energetic and outgoing. She was always at her husband's races and managed his public relations as well as his home. Their boys were a toddler and a baby when their dad was killed.

I wondered: What would their lives be like, after losing their celebrity husband and dad?

I reached out to Susie, through social media and several emails. I left voicemails, wrote letters, sent samples of my stories to her home. Every year, around the anniversary of Dan's death, I'd try to connect. "Whenever you're ready," I kept saying. "I'd love to know how you're doing."

Five years passed. Then, one day, she emailed. She'd kept the business card I'd mailed her all those years ago. She was about to start a new chapter in her life. She was finally ready to talk.

Sometimes stories off the news are stronger when you wait, so people have perspective, so some healing can happen before re-opening the wound.

Having so much time pass after the crash made this story stronger. I'm so glad I pushed enough for Susie to remember and, eventually, contact me.

THE STORY

At the edge of the racetrack, on a wide pad of asphalt, Susie Wheldon stooped to help her small son.

Sebastian, 7, already had wriggled into his Puma fire suit. Susie slid the chest protector over his head, to keep his lungs from being crushed. She strapped on the neck brace, to protect his spine. She tied his tiny racing shoes.

"Ready to go?" asked his coach.

The boy nodded, and climbed into his new Kid Kart. As soon as he pulled the helmet over his spiky blonde hair, his usual grin melted. He scrunched his freckled nose and set his jaw. "Getting his game face on," Susie called it.

He lowered the visor. She bent and kissed the spot in front of his mouth. Just like she had done before every race with his dad, her Dan.

Her husband was 33, a two-time Indy 500 champion, when he died in a crash at the Las Vegas Motor Speedway. Five years later, Susie, 38, has built a new home, started a new business and struggled to be a single mom to two boisterous boys. Letting her son race, she said, is the hardest thing she has had to do.

On a dreary winter Sunday at the Ocala Gran Prix, she watched her first-grader plant his feet on both sides of a gas tank. Between his knees sloshed a gallon of fuel. The go-cart doesn't have a seat belt; if it flips going 60 mph, the coach said, it's better for the driver to be ejected than to roll with the wreckage.

"Good luck!" Susie said, trying to smile. She waited until her son revved the engine, then stepped aside.

When Susie met Dan, they were 23. She had just graduated from a small Christian college and taken a job at an advertising agency. He had just signed with Michael Andretti's team and was named the IndyCar Series' Rookie of the Year.

They were introduced at a photo shoot for Jim Beam whiskey.

PREDICT PERIL. It makes sense to narrate how this mom dresses her young son on the racetrack. But if you want to really engage readers, ask why he wears each piece of protective equipment, explain the why of all the precautions: so the boy's lungs won't be crushed, so his spine won't snap ... This story is about danger, so I wanted to show what was at stake early and as dramatically as possible.

TRY A NUT. Most news stories have "nut grafs," a single paragraph (or more) that sums up what the story is about or why the writer is telling it. Narratives tend not to have them, letting the story unfold. But sometimes—especially if the story is from a news event that readers might remember—it helps to sum up the before and explain why you're revisiting the story now.

IN THE BEGINNING. Always ask how people met. When, why, where a relationship started, how it shifted and grew. That gives great context to the characters and offers readers a chance to connect with their own stories. Asking about childhood hopes, dreams, fears and fantasies also enhances profiles. What's your first memory? What did you want to be when you grew up?

"Cocky. Self-confident. Outgoing, but not really arrogant," she called the toothy young driver. "He was wearing this long black peacoat and had this mussed blonde hair and great English accent. I noticed he was handsome. But I was so busy trying to fake that I knew what I was doing, I never saw him as my future husband."

———

Dan Wheldon had grown up in a small town north of London. His dad, a plumber, raced go-carts and put Dan in the driver's seat when he was 4. By 10, Dan was British Junior Kart champion. After high school, he moved to America to drive Indy cars.

He and Susie worked together for two years. She set up photo shoots, staging him with the Jim Beam logo, traveling to races. She was cheering at the finish line when he won his first race in Japan, screaming beside the track in 2005, when he won St. Petersburg's first grand prix.

Later that year, after winning the Indianapolis 500, she said, "That was the first time I really felt him hug me." The celebration was epic. Susie had to stay sober, to make sure Dan got to his 6 a.m. interview with "Good Morning America." At 5:30 a.m., she pulled him out of the still raging party, propped him in a chair, put a microphone in his hand—and woke him when he fell asleep during commercials.

When Dan decided to move to St. Petersburg a few months later, he asked Susie to come work for him as his personal assistant. So she followed him to Florida, helped him build a house on Snell Isle and manage his new-found stardom.

Sometimes, she made reservations for his dinner dates and bought gifts for other women. She swore she wasn't jealous. "I loved my job," she said. "I didn't want to do anything to screw that up."

There wasn't one single moment when everything shifted, Susie said. "I just felt it happening. He started being much more tender toward me."

Just before Christmas in 2007, Dan called Susie out to the dock behind his home. "Something's wrong with the jet ski," he said. He held out a ring and dropped to one knee.

They married three months later; a year after that, baby Sebastian was born.

"Dan fell in love with fatherhood," Susie said. "He changed diapers, took his boy everywhere."

Sebastian was 18 months old, barely toddling, when Dan first sat him in his lap in a go-cart and sped around a track. "He

HIS CAREER—HER CONNECTIONS. I knew I had to fast-forward through Dan's career, because this story was about Susie. So I tried to relate his headlines from her perspective, where she was, what she was doing while he was in the spotlight. How she was helping behind the scenes, juggling motherhood and management.

would have had him driving at 2," Susie said, "if his feet could've reached the pedals."

Susie never felt frightened, she said. In almost a decade of watching Dan drive around a 2.5-mile track, topping speeds of 200 mph, she never thought about her husband being in danger.

"But Dan did," she said. "He'd bring it up when we were dating. 'You might find you don't want to be with a race car driver,' he'd say. 'This life can be scary.'"

Everyone in the racing community knew someone who had been killed on a track. One of their friends, who had young kids, had been paralyzed. Susie just didn't dwell on those possibilities.

Dan was so experienced. He had flipped cars, been crushed in pileups.

But he always came out smiling that oversized grin.

———

No one thought Dan had a chance to win the Indy 500 again in the summer of 2011. "He hadn't raced for a while," Susie said.

She took Sebastian to the track, along with a new addition to their family, 3-month-old Oliver.

She watched from the pit stall, where she could hear her husband on his headset, through the radio.

After four hours of driving, with two laps to go, Dan was still behind. Then, in the last turn, someone crashed. And Dan pulled ahead. Susie held her breath. "I thought he would run out of fuel."

When Dan won, he wept. He was the first driver ever to win the Indy 500 while only leading the last lap. Susie brought the boys to Victory Lane where Dan scooped up Sebastian and carried him to the finish line. Together, they knelt and kissed the fabled bricks.

He left his own party after only an hour that night. "He wanted to have a quiet dinner at the hotel with just us," Susie said. "He was at such a different point in his life."

Marino Franchitti, who raced carts against Dan in England, marveled at the change in his chum. He told racing writer Andy Hallbery, "It was like someone flipped a switch when he found what he was looking for in life with Susie and the boys."

That summer, Mattel issued a Hot Wheels model of Dan's Indy Car. He became the voice of a driver on TV's animated *Hotwheels Battleforce 5*. And he was able to be home more often, finally relax. He kept a Lamborghini in the garage, but drove his Honda Fit to the gym. He would get groceries with Susie and the boys, go get their hair cut.

"There was just this sense of contentment around us," Susie said. "Everything was so right and happy."

Their next trip was in October, to watch him race in Las Vegas. She has never spoken about it, until now.

Oliver was 7 months old. Susie had never left him. But the night before the race, Dan had to attend a dinner for one of his sponsors. So she left the boys at the hotel with their nanny and for the first time in a year, they had a date.

Afterwards, Dan spotted a tattoo parlor. On a whim, he and Susie had each other's initials inscribed inside their wrists. "Dan had never gotten a tattoo," she said. "I don't know why all of a sudden he wanted to that night, but he was so excited about it, he called his dad to tell him."

They went to bed around 11 p.m., each with a wrist wrapped in gauze.

The next morning, at the Las Vegas Motor Speedway, Susie settled the boys with their nanny in a suite, then went down to the track.

Dan already had wriggled into his fire suit.

Susie walked over to his car and bent to kiss him before he put on his helmet. After he lowered the visor, she kissed the spot in front of his mouth. Just like she had done before every race.

She waited until her husband revved the engine, then stepped aside.

She watched from the pit box, listened on the radio.

Dan started at the back of the pack that day, last of the 34 drivers. After 10 laps, he had climbed 10 spots.

Then a driver in an outside lane tried to cut toward the center. In an instant, cars were flying, rolling, bursting into flames. Dan was driving so fast he would have crossed a football field in less than a second. There was no way to stop, nowhere to steer to avoid smashing into the pileup—15 cars crumpled in charred wreckage.

On the radio, Susie heard only silence.

Chaos. Blackness. Confusion.

For months, Susie couldn't get out of bed. While others took her boys to play, she sat alone in that big house Dan had built, surrounded by his trophies, mourning that their children would never know him, except through the stories of others.

Hundreds of fans and drivers wrote letters. They wanted to honor Dan, find ways to keep his name alive. So Susie would drag

OWN THE UNVEILING. If you're the first person to tell a story, own that, especially when it's about a celebrity some people think they already know. Saying someone has never spoken about a tragedy adds to the anticipation of that revelation and leaves readers wanting more.

TAKE IN TATTOOS. Always ask about people's piercings and, especially, tattoos. Where did you get it? When? Why? What does it mean? That's usually important. When I asked Susie about her tattoo, their whole last night together spilled out. It started out so joyous.

RELISH REPETITION. The second half of this section echoes the opening scene, from him wriggling into his fire suit and lowering his visor, to her kissing him on his helmet. When I asked Susie about that routine at the go-kart track, she said it was the same sequence she went through with Dan. The repetition in the writing is intentional and, I hope, reinforces her love, pain and fear.

SAVE THE HARD PARTS. When you know you have to ask someone to revisit tragedy, don't start with that. Start with good times and establish intimacy before you dredge up sorrow. The videographer I was working with put a microphone on Susie in her store and started by asking, "Tell us about the day Dan died." Before she said a word, Susie started crying. So I asked her about how they met, happier times, and saved the sadness until I knew a bit about them and their boys. The aftermath came last.

herself into the shower and steel her way through public appearances.

She took the boys to the next Indianapolis 500, where 300,000 fans donned Dan's signature white sunglasses. She took the boys to a go-cart track in England, where Dan's boyhood buddies told stories of his pranks. She took them to a Top Kart race in Indiana, where a team owner presented Sebastian with his own go-cart. The boy, barely 4, begged his mom to let him "drive like Daddy."

Susie wanted to go to those events, to show her boys how beloved their dad was. "But I felt like I had to share Dan with so many people, I couldn't figure out where I fit in anymore," she said. "Every time someone told a story about Dan, it was like ripping off a Band-aid."

That whole first year, she kept thinking Dan was going to come home, just walk through that door and scoop her into his arms. "It wasn't until I had to go to the Social Security office and sign that form that said: Marriage terminated by death. That's what made it real."

Jenn St. Cin, who is Susie's closest friend, tried to help her through the aftermath. "She's been to the darkest place of anyone I've known," said Jenn. "I've never seen the physical pain of grief like that. She couldn't breathe. Literally. She would call me five times a day saying, 'I'm not going to make it.'"

After three years, Dan's jeans were still in his closet, his hair gel still on the bathroom sink.

Finally, Jenn convinced Susie to get help. "She needed some therapy," Jenn said.

Susie knew she needed to start healing, so she could be there for her boys. She had to figure out who she was without Dan.

To move on, Susie decided, she had to move. There was too much of him in that house. The Realtor convinced her to pack Dan's trophies. Jenn helped her sort through his closet.

Susie rented a house in the Old Northeast and put the two cars he had won at the Indy 500s into storage. When her boys are old enough, Sebastian will get the 2005 convertible Corvette, which was the car that set the pace and positioned racers for the first race; Oliver will inherit the 2011 Camaro.

Once she had resettled, Susie set about designing her dream house. Dan had left her a comfortable inheritance, and she wanted plenty of room for her boys to play. Working with an architect, she created a modern two-story surrounding an in-ground pool, with a walk-in closet that would have made Dan proud.

They moved in October 2015. A brick from the Indianapolis Motor Speedway is embedded into the front steps. Trophies from Dan's Indy 500 wins watch over the boys' desks. His handsome face grins in every room. But this house is hers.

For a while, Susie drove to Calvary Catholic cemetery to talk to him. But she never really felt him there. When she needs to be close now, she rises before dawn, careful not to wake her boys, and tells the nanny she'll be back.

She runs down the waterfront, past the Vinoy where she and Dan were married, past the sailboats, piers and parks, about 2.5 miles—all the way to a monument dedicated to him on Turn 10, "Dan Wheldon Way." She presses her forehead against the cool stone and watches the sun rise above Tampa Bay.

Susie tries not to dwell on questions of what if or why. "There would never be a good enough reason," she said. "I don't really have a clear answer to tell my kids when they ask, 'What happens after you die?'"

In the fall, Oliver started kindergarten. And Susie decided she needed her boys to see her working. Her life is finally starting to feel stable now. A new normal.

She opened a boutique on Central Avenue, near M.L. King Jr. Street, with double doors and wide windows. Inside, trendy jeans and T-shirts hang on long racks. The back wall is covered with a mural of a giant lion sporting a heart-shaped pendant with the initials DW—Dan Wheldon, the Lionheart.

Susie rented the space last fall. She called a friend whose clothing company had sponsored Dan, called another who worked at Nordstrom. She painted baseboards, set up dressing rooms, ordered high-end streetwear for men and women. She named the shop after Dan's favorite band, Verve.

She scheduled the grand opening for March 9, the first day of St. Petersburg's Grand Prix, so that her friends in the racing community could share in her next chapter.

She has taken off her wedding ring, but still wears Dan's silver cross. She hasn't dated. She still cries, sometimes at the strangest times. Like Sebastian's first school conference. Oliver's soccer game.

The hole, she said, hurts most at the track. Dan should be there, watching his son race. He would tell Susie not to worry. Everything was going to be alright.

How can she ever believe that again?

PRIVATE AS PUBLIC. One of the most intimate moments in this story smacks into one of the most public. Ask people how they're coping after something awful, how they escape, rage, make sense of what happened. Susie was trying to start over, put her past behind her. She had stopped going to the cemetery. Instead, she ran through the predawn darkness, past places she and Dan had enjoyed, to a marker the city erected, engraved with his name. Where her forehead met the cool stone.

SPOTLIGHT

Beyond the specific Tips & Takeaways embedded in the individual stories, here is some more in-depth advice about reporting stories.

REPORTING

Preparing: Even after 30 years of reporting, I still write down a long list of questions specific to that story before an interview.

I want to know what I need to know before I meet the person and to make sure I don't forget to ask anything while I'm talking to them. Thinking about the questions ahead of time, and having them written down to refer to, gives me clarity and confidence.

You don't have to dive into the interview right away or read the questions off the page. Make a connection first, strike up a conversation, explain your intentions and ask if they have any questions for you. Then begin wherever feels natural or like an easy in, follow your curiosity and ad lib when needed. Then go back to your list and make sure you addressed everything you wanted to.

I also keep a set of 30 generic questions to ask anyone.

Try these, especially for people you're profiling:

1. Tell me the story of your life.
2. What's your earliest memory?
3. Describe your family, house, pets . . . and how you fit into the dynamics . . .
4. Recreate some family traditions, holidays—best and worst . . .
5. What did you want to be? Did you picture yourself married? Children?
6. Were you popular in school? What activities did you do?
7. Who were your heroes . . . and why? Who are they now?
8. What was your first experience with death?

9. How did you meet your girlfriend, spouse, best friend?
10. Tell me about the most difficult decision you ever had to make.
11. What do you dream about?
12. Who knows you best? Who do you confide in?
13. Do you believe in God? Go to church? What do you pray for?
14. Are you politically involved? How active? Why?
15. What's in your wallet... or purse... car... refrigerator?
16. What do you worry about most for yourself? Your family? The world?
17. What do you want most with what's left of your life?
18. What are you searching for, questions you still have?
19. What do you regret and why?
20. If you could relive any moment, what would it be? Would you change it?
21. What one word best describes you?
22. What do people misunderstand or assume about you?
23. Tell me something about you that few people know.
24. What bugs you most about yourself? Others?
25. Do you want your children to be like you when they grow up? Why or why not?
26. What are you most proud of?
27. What do you think happens to us after we die?
28. Why are you here, on this earth, at this time?
29. Who will come to your funeral?
30. What do you want to be remembered for?

Interviewing: To get a subject to let you in, they have to trust you. Before you start interviewing them, have a brief conversation. Share a bit about yourself; make a connection; talk about dogs, kids, cars, sports; ask if they have any questions for you. Then let them start the interview by telling their own story. Where do they want to start? That gives the subject a sense of control and helps put them at ease.

Taking notes: Reporting for a narrative is different from reporting for information. In addition to getting the backstory and news, you need scenes and settings, specific details, a big-picture perspective. I always use legal pads, because I don't want to have to keep flipping those skinny reporter notebook pages—and because I like to diagram my notepad and use different sections for different parts of the reporting.

In the top left corner, I note the date and time, so I can tell how much time has passed as I flip the pages: "Oh, it took five hours to

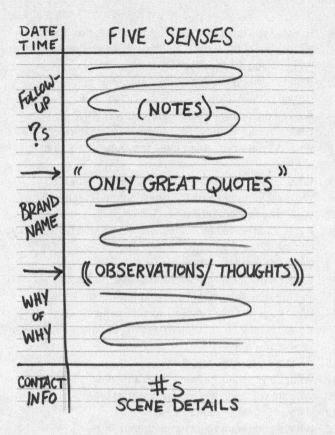

seat the jury." In the top margin, I write what I see, smell, taste — or if something is tactile, how it feels: "The cold metal of the chain-link fence."

Down the left margin, I mark arrows when someone tells me something and I want to go back and ask follow-up questions: "What kind of dog?" "What brand of beer?" That way, I don't interrupt while they're telling their story, and I won't forget to ask at the end of the interview. I just go back and find those arrows. At the bottom of the page, I put numbers so I can find them easily: "How many years have you been married?"

The main notes go in the center of the notepad. I don't try to write down everything people say, mostly paraphrasing the information. But when I hear a great quote, I write it down verbatim and surround it in big marks, so I can go back and find it easily. I also jot down observations and thoughts and put them in double parentheses: ((Was that guy lying to me?))

15

GO BACK

The Long Fall of Phoebe Jonchuck: Her Dad Threw Her off a Bridge

Reported over six months; written over three weeks. Published January 7, 2016

BEFORE THE STORY

This story wasn't my idea. The publisher made me write it. He wanted me to recount the horrific story of a man who had thrown his 5-year-old daughter off a bridge, into Tampa Bay.

Nearly six months had passed since the tragedy. Coworkers already had written dozens of stories about it. Across the country, at least 70 publications had carried the news.

I couldn't figure out what I could do differently or what I could add to the story. I like writing emotional stories and don't mind sad ones, but I want there to be some hope that something could change, get better, or at least be looked at a little differently. I couldn't find any hope in this story. I asked the publisher why he was so passionate about this idea.

"We owe it to our readers, to Phoebe," he said. "No one knows who she was, except the girl whose dad dropped her to her death.

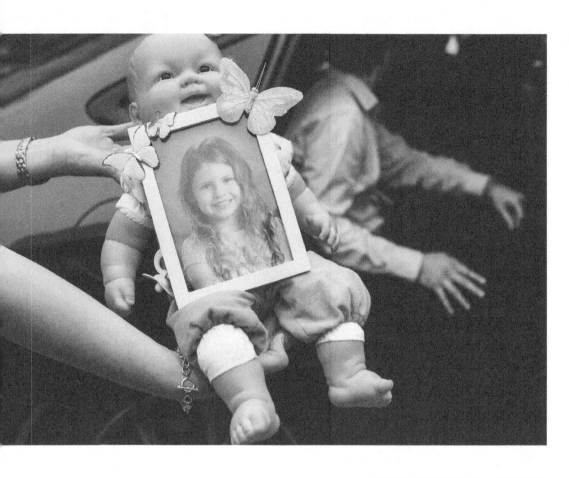

Phoebe Jonchuck loved butterflies and the color purple. Her kindergarten photo rests on a doll her grandmother gave her. Photographer: Eve Edelheit

I want you to talk to everyone who came in contact with her, learn how she lived, paint a picture of what led to this awful event."

The news was old — but people were still talking about it, wondering, theorizing.

The publisher gave me six months to report the story, a long time by newspaper standards. He wanted to run it on the anniversary of Phoebe's death.

So I made a list of 100 people and started knocking on doors. Since so much time had passed, many folks who wouldn't talk at first agreed to let me in.

THE STORY

Part 1: The Good Father

On the night Phoebe's dad scooped her from her bed, the moon was high outside her window. The house was quiet. He carried her out the door, into the dark.

It was blustery and cold, especially for Florida. He didn't zip her into a jacket or wrap her in a blanket. All the 5-year-old had on were shorts and her green cat T-shirt.

Her dad was tall and thick, with wild hair, wearing a hoodie and plaid pajama bottoms. He eased Phoebe into the back of his PT Cruiser and strapped her into her pink booster seat.

Down the highway they raced, crossing Tampa Bay, reaching 80, 90, 100 mph.

In St. Petersburg, a police car pulled behind and followed, lights off. At the crest of the span leading to the Sunshine Skyway bridge, the PT Cruiser stopped, and Phoebe's dad got out.

"Get back in the car!" the cop yelled. "Let me see your hands!"

Phoebe's dad walked between the cars and shouted at the officer, "You have no free will!"

Then he went around to her door, opened it and bent inside. He lifted her out and carried her to the edge of the bridge.

Salt spray stung her skin. The wind whipped her bare legs. Her cheek rested on his sweatshirt as he cradled her against his chest.

Phoebe's dad held her out over the guardrail, six stories above the black waves.

And let go.

START JUST BEFORE THE CLIMAX. We debated where to begin this story. One editor suggested we start with the splash. But I wanted readers to be on that long, wild ride from the moment Jonchuck lifted his sleeping daughter from her bed in the middle of the night. What parent does that? To me, that was the beginning of the end. Try opening stories with those last few minutes, hours or days before everything goes wrong—or right.

That was a year ago, in the first minutes of Jan. 8, 2015.

John Nicholas Jonchuck Jr., 26, is in a state mental institution. Psychiatrists say he is not fit to stand trial.

He must be crazy to have killed his own child. It's the only thing that makes sense.

But few who knew him believe it.

Family and friends say he's a con artist. A manipulative, vindictive, violent man who alienated people who cared about him. Who forged checks and faked falls and believed in demons, but not in God.

He was a schemer who used the courts for profit and revenge. He was a paranoid, angry meth addict who had been arrested for battery and domestic violence seven times. He had been involuntarily committed, by his family's count, 27 times.

And yet, in its report on Phoebe's death, the Florida Department of Children and Families concluded, "There was nothing in the preceding several years that could have reasonably been interpreted as predictive of such an event."

It's true, no one imagined John Jonchuck Jr. would murder his daughter. He was a good father, friends said, who taught Phoebe how to count trees, painted her tiny toenails pink and loved sharing Slurpees that stained their lips blue. She was the light in his dark, stoned eyes.

But whether he was crazy or conniving, plenty of people believed John would hurt someone. Most likely his mom, whom he hated. Or Phoebe's mother, whom he still loved.

Phoebe clung to her dad as he drifted from address to address. She slipped through one safety net after another:

Her family, who knew how violent John could be.

The state, which had known about John since he was 5.

The dozen people who saw him that last day, holding her hand, ranting about exorcism and an ominous, biblical plan.

So many people could have stopped him.

No one did.

———

Go looking for answers about John Jonchuck, and you'll find scores of people who were fed up. You'll read police reports spanning generations: theft, drugs, domestic violence. You'll comb through court cases, listen to calls to the child protection hotline, uncover a lifetime of lies, rage and revenge.

You'll meet people who were too numb to recognize the dan-

REPORT ENOUGH TO BE AUTHORITATIVE. After interviewing more than 50 people, reviewing court records, police reports, child abuse investigations, lawsuits, running background checks and going to a dozen places Jonchuck had lived, I felt pretty confident describing him and his character. I chose to put the attribution at the start of that section, quoting "friends and family" without naming an individual. That comes later. Here, I wanted to give readers a glimpse of the guy they were about to explore.

SEEK GOOD IN EVIL. It's easy to write about bad people, to stack evidence against them. But you need to get the good, too: the Dr. Jekyll side of Mr. Hyde. Ask about good memories, better times, how the person fooled people. Sharing tiny details like Jonchuck painting Phoebe's toenails and buying her blue Slurpees illuminated their relationship and humanized him.

ger or too scared to stand up to his temper. People who wonder what clues they missed or ignored.

From the beginning, there were so many signs.

He was a child who kicked the dog, stuck screwdrivers into electrical outlets, got thrown out of a dozen preschools.

"He was a monster," said his uncle, Bryan Morris, 51.

"Born evil," said Tim Maynard, 55, Bryan's partner for more than two decades.

John's father, John Jonchuck Sr., was a hard-drinking construction worker who got arrested for beating John's mom and lost his license after too many DUIs. He moved away when John was 3.

John's mother worked at Dunkin' Donuts, got caught stealing and with cocaine. She left John when he was 5.

Uncle Bryan and Uncle Tim took in the boy. They gave him a gold necklace with a tiny cross.

When John threw fits, a counselor suggested wrapping him in a sheet like a straitjacket. Tim tried. "He stomped my feet until he destroyed my new Bass loafers."

They paid for a psychiatrist, who prescribed Ritalin and Adderall. Neither seemed to help.

Then, one day, John's dad showed up, yelling, "I'm not going to let two fags raise my child!"

"Which was fine with us fags," said Tim. "We were done with him."

———

John was 12 the first time cops folded him into the back of a police car.

He was still living with his dad and stepmom in a duplex by a Tampa scrapyard.

Child protection officers visited his dad four times. Those reports are long closed. John's friends saw bruises on his face, which he tried to hide with sunglasses.

Tampa police records show that on May 15, 2002, John's dad told him to clean his room.

"And he went off! Attacked me with full soda cans, pulled my hair," his dad told police. "Then he grabbed a one-foot knife and ran out."

John admitted making a motion to stab his dad with the butcher knife. He said his dad was hitting him.

Hates his dad, wrote the officer. *Hopes he goes to hell.*

The police report concludes: *No treatment necessary.*

At Pierce Middle School in Tampa, John was the loudest, funniest, smartest—the only guy who could grow a mustache.

He was a great actor, his classmates said, who made puppets and performed plays in the cafeteria.

"He never wanted to be at home," said Amanda Serrano, 26, who has known John since sixth grade. "So he'd come over to my house a lot."

In eighth grade, John told everyone he was gay. People made fun of him, but he seemed to like the attention.

He dropped out of high school the next year and, soon after, climbed onto the roof of his dad's duplex and slit his wrist with a knife.

His family committed him. That was the first time.

When John got out of the hospital, Bryan and Tim took him in again.

He was taking online classes, earning his GED. But one night, when John was supposed to be studying, his uncles caught him playing a video game on his computer. They tried to take the laptop. John hurled it over a balcony, smashing it to bits.

Another time, when John was mad at Tim, he coated the wooden staircase with thick wax. When Tim headed downstairs, he tumbled to the bottom and broke three ribs.

John watched. And laughed.

———

He moved out at 17. Started smoking spice, then crystal meth.

"He started working at a strip club," said Amanda. "He made a lot of money doing stuff with older guys."

John never got arrested for drugs. But every few hours, he had to get high.

Amanda and five others described his favorite buzz—from a brand of synthetic marijuana called WTF, which gas stations sold in shiny $20 packages.

Cheaper and stronger than pot, spice has been linked to bizarre violence: Two Michigan men beat a family with baseball bats. A Texas man strangled and ate a spaniel. Other users screamed they were possessed or being chased by demons.

When John smoked it, the spice sometimes helped him relax. Other times, it made him mean.

Crystal methamphetamine also makes people paranoid and violent. John smoked meth so often, his fingertips were charred from holding the little glass pipe.

John was high when he met Michelle Kerr. A friend introduced them when he was 18.

He couldn't stop staring.

"You're so beautiful," he told her. Again and again.

A buxom woman with blond hair, freckles and wide blue eyes, Michelle was 23. She had a young son and daughter.

John and Michelle sang Avril Lavigne songs and put on their makeup, side by side, in her mirror, then went dancing at gay clubs.

One night, they were slouched on Michelle's sofa when he said, "Maybe I'm not gay."

She laughed.

"Maybe I'm not gay," he said, "because I'm in love with you."

She thought he was handsome, in a young Jay Leno kind of way—6-foot-2, 200 pounds, same thick pompadour and prominent chin.

She told him about her life. She managed an insurance agency. She had been charged with neglecting her son when he was 5, after the babysitter didn't pick him up from the bus stop. She still had custody of him, but her daughter lived with relatives.

Michelle's dad had left when she was in kindergarten. When Michelle was 16, her mom swallowed a pile of pills and killed herself. Michelle kept her mom's tiny wedding ring.

John told Michelle that his dad had beat him and he hated his mom, who had abandoned him. He said he was bipolar but taking his meds.

"He was charming," Michelle said. "Then the devil came out."

The first time she saw it was on Valentine's Day, when he got jealous and slit her tires.

Even after that, she let him move in. They enrolled at Hillsborough Community College, where she took graphic arts classes and he studied to become a paralegal.

He asked her to marry him. Four times, she refused. "He'd be as sweet as anything, then go all Dr.-Jekyll-and-Mr.-Hyde."

One afternoon, Michelle was talking to a neighbor in the yard when John called her into the kitchen, upset she had been outside so long. He held up her mother's little wedding ring, the only piece of her mom Michelle had left.

"Watch this!" John yelled. He hurled the ring out the window, into the overgrown yard.

GO GET 'EM. You have to know what you need and keep pushing until you get it. I knew I had to talk to Phoebe's birth mother. But she'd moved so much, I had trouble tracking her down. On the last police report she had filed, she listed the name of her new boyfriend and his cell number, so I called him. He said he was working at a bar and couldn't talk. I asked which bar—and drove straight there. And there she was, drinking Long Island iced teas!

She stayed with him. Because she was pregnant.

Their daughter arrived early, on a bright August morning in 2009. John named her Phoebe, after his Chihuahua.

She was a beautiful child, with green eyes, honey-colored curls and her father's round face. Seldom fussy, easily soothed, she loved being sung to and having someone rub her arm until she fell asleep. John changed diapers, warmed bottles, surprised everyone with his tenderness.

"When Phoebe was born, that changed him," said his uncle Bryan. "He stepped up more than he ever had."

John's mom came back into his life to see her granddaughter and was proud that her son was such a good dad.

When Michelle went back to work after maternity leave, John wanted to stay home with "Pheebs." But Michelle's left leg started seizing up. Soon, she couldn't walk. Doctors diagnosed her with multiple sclerosis, and she went on disability.

John tried telemarketing, dabbled in insurance. Mostly, he sponged off Michelle's disability income and concocted a series of easy-money schemes.

"He'd take people's Social Security numbers and credit cards," she said. He bought a machine that printed forged checks.

He faked a fall at the Cheesecake Factory, Michelle said, then sued the chain for $250,000. He told everyone he would never have to work again.

———

Phoebe was 10 months old when Hillsborough sheriff's deputies first came to Apartment 207 on Royal Sand Circle. Her dad had thrown her mom onto the floor and punched her legs. John completed a court-ordered domestic violence program, and Michelle dropped the charges.

Two years later, neighbors called the cops saying John was choking Michelle. Phoebe, who was 2, hid in her parents' room and locked the door. John had to kick it down to get her out. A DCF report from April 14, 2012, concluded: *Family violence threatens child.*

Five days later, an updated report dismissed the concerns because John and Michelle were in counseling.

Signs of present danger is low.

DCF didn't know the couple kept skipping appointments.

———

Just inside the door of From Here to There Day Care, a small blue plastic chair sat alone beneath the coat hooks.

Phoebe's chair.

She started coming to Linda Mattos' school when she was still in diapers. John always dropped her off, because Michelle was too sick to drive. Every morning, Phoebe would wait on that chair for 30, 45 minutes, until she was ready to interact with other kids.

"Well, look at that," Linda would say. "Phoebe is finally coming out of her turtle shell."

Phoebe was almost nonverbal, said Linda, 50. She would just stand still and stare. She liked apple juice and Cheetos, sparkly pink sneakers and books about dogs.

Linda set up playdates for Phoebe and treated her to Chuck E. Cheese's. Despite all the chaos around Phoebe, she seemed happy. Her smile stopped strangers in Walmart.

Linda's son Nick, 16, took Phoebe to their backyard pool and tried to teach her to swim. But Phoebe was terrified of water; she wouldn't even take a bath.

"John would tell her, 'Phoebe, it's okay!'" Nick said. "But she was always so scared."

To get her into the shallow end, Nick had to put pirate floaties around Phoebe's arms, a Neverland doughnut around her waist, then ease her into a blow-up boat.

Even then, she had to hold on to him.

———

Phoebe came from a long line of motherless children. Her great-grandmother had abandoned her grandmother. Her grandmother had abandoned her dad.

None of them knew what a good parent was, or how to be one.

But when Phoebe was still a toddler, John's mom decided she finally had a reason to stay sober. Michele Jonchuck, 52, went to rehab and came back with a new purpose. Phoebe called her MawMaw.

She sometimes lived with them as they shuttled through a series of apartments. John couldn't forgive her. The slightest suggestion about how to raise Phoebe unhinged him.

"You didn't raise me!" he screamed. "Why do you want to raise my daughter?"

Every few months, he would fly into a rage at his mom or Michelle. He would punch holes in walls, shatter windows. They would get evicted or run out of rent money.

"Things were so weird and demented for so long," Michelle said.

SEE SIGNS. Finding themes and meaning helps elevate writing. Look for details that foreshadow incidents, make connections or show broader context. When I learned that Phoebe was afraid of the water and the dark, I knew I needed to show the teen trying to teach her to swim and her dad leaving cartoons on at night.

DETAILS IN DOCUMENTS. Most of this section comes directly from documents. Before I set out to interview anyone, I scoured courthouse files in two counties and three cities. I looked at civil, criminal and traffic cases, went through lawsuits and restraining orders. Having months to report allowed me to really dig deep. Phoebe's mother and grandmother gave me other documents I never would have had access to. Always search official reports—and ask everyone for paperwork.

John thought every place they lived was possessed by bad spirits, she said. She told him he was the demon.

In the years after DCF determined *Signs of present danger is low,* the cops kept getting called.

Phoebe watched her dad grab MawMaw by the feet and drag her down a staircase. She watched him punch MawMaw in the face.

Phoebe saw her dad pour hot coffee on her mom, throw a concrete block at her, try to strangle her with Christmas lights. She saw him chase her into a closet, then stab a knife into the door.

She was in the back yard when she saw her dad shove her mom into the sand, punch her face three times. Then he chased her mom into the bathroom and cracked her head against the tub.

John went to jail for that one. As usual, Michelle dropped the charges, but she was done with John. She moved out.

When he got out of jail, he turned on her and told a judge she had pulled a box cutter on him.

A child protection investigator wrote: *Mr. Jonchuck was observed to have six straight cuts on his interior right wrist that appeared to be self-inflicted.*

Nevertheless, John managed to get Phoebe, Phoebe's share of her mom's benefits and a restraining order against Phoebe's mom. Michelle never got the notification about the court hearing, so she didn't contest the injunction. She couldn't afford a lawyer.

No one ever officially granted John custody of Phoebe. But because of the injunction, Michelle didn't see her daughter for more than a year.

There are implications for child safety. This is due to the family's history of prior reports . . . and to the father's history of child abuse and neglect, DCF concluded on June 7, 2013.

A month later, after John had been arrested for DUI and Michelle for theft, the agency noted they were no longer a couple and issued an update:

The father interacts with Phoebe in a caring manner. The case is being closed with verified findings for family violence threatens child.

It's unclear what the agency did about the threat except provide pamphlets on pool safety and respite care.

All the calls to cops and DCF—none of them saved Phoebe. None of them helped John, who had been a toddler when DCF came into his life.

During Phoebe's five years, investigators looked at each incident but missed the big picture. Phoebe never had a consistent caseworker who understood that her dad was beating her mother and grandmother, that he was using drugs and hallucinating, that he was dragging her all over town with her clothes in a garbage bag.

Michelle begged John to let her see Phoebe. But he kept moving and changing his phone number, and she was too sick to fight.

When an investigator visited Phoebe at daycare, *She stated she misses mommy.*

Under what circumstances should a parent lose custody of his child?

When he has no stable address? When he abuses drugs? When he attacks people? When he doesn't take medication to control his mental illness? When he keeps getting arrested for domestic violence? When people keep calling the abuse hotline, worrying about the child?

It's hard to imagine what more John Jonchuck Jr. needed to do to get the attention of the state.

DCF has been overwhelmed and understaffed for years. At Florida's abuse hotline, counselors answer about 300,000 calls a year and dismiss 20 percent. They turn the rest over to investigators, who juggle 25 cases at a time.

The agency's goal is to keep families together. But over the past decade, almost 500 children that investigators already had checked on died in their parents' care. Most of those parents abused drugs or alcohol. Many of them, including Phoebe's, had signed a state-sanctioned "safety plan."

Child protection investigators visited Phoebe five times and saw signs of danger. Each time, they left her with her dad.

John adored his daughter, everyone agrees. Phoebe told him all the time, "I love you, Daddy."

John taught her the alphabet, how to hold a crayon and write her name. He brushed her long hair, which had never been cut. He let her win at tic-tac-toe. When she cried, he gave her candy. At night, he let her fall asleep to *Blue's Clues* because Phoebe was afraid of the dark.

They never lived by themselves—just daddy and daughter. John always needed company, and rent money. Phoebe gave John his best role: Single Dad. With her by his side, he got sympathy and second chances.

He wanted desperately to be accepted and understood. But when he felt challenged or rejected, or most of all, abandoned, he would lash out and seek vengeance on those closest to him.

During the last year of Phoebe's life, John dragged her to stay with at least eight different family members and friends. Five single moms told the same story: They would never have let John move in, but they couldn't bear to leave Phoebe without a home.

At Linda Mattos' house, John highlighted her hair and did her taxes. She took him to church, where he played on his phone.

At Amanda Serrano's house, he made spaghetti while Phoebe watched *Toddlers in Tiaras*. Amanda told him to stop getting high around his daughter.

"He looked at me with these nasty eyes, these devil eyes. Not like the John I knew," she said. "That was when he smoked that meth."

At Melody Dishman's house, he trashed the guest room, piling potato chip bags as high as the mattress. One evening, when Phoebe wanted a fruit cup before dinner, John got so angry he grabbed her by the arm and dragged her to her room. Melody scolded him and worried. What else would set him off?

That's the only time any of them saw him get rough with Phoebe, but there were plenty of times he scared them.

One morning, after John had been smoking meth all night, he was driving Amanda and her brother when the two men started fighting. All of a sudden, John floored the accelerator, speeding 100 mph down the interstate. Amanda started crying, screaming, "Slow down!"

"It was like he blacked out," she said.

Each time a roommate kicked him out, he called the cops on them for revenge.

He left behind dirty clothes, piles of trash, broken furniture.

All he took with him was Phoebe.

For a while, John's uncles took in Phoebe while he slept at a friend's house. She loved their big Victorian home with Reese's cups in crystal dishes and koi in the backyard pond.

Bryan and Tim worried about Phoebe's safety with John. They even printed paperwork to adopt her.

But just as John's dad had done 20 years earlier, John screamed, "I'm not going to let two fags raise my kid!"

Phoebe turned 5 on her second day of kindergarten. John brought cupcakes for the class. When he turned to go, Phoebe grabbed his leg and wailed.

COMPARE MEMORIES. When you're trying to recreate the past and get a sense of a person, use some of the same questions for everyone you interview. I reached out to more than a dozen of Jonchuck's roommates and asked each of them if they'd ever seen him get angry with Phoebe. This incident was the only one anyone mentioned. So I could write with certainty, "That's the only time any of them saw him get rough with Phoebe, but there were plenty of times he scared them."

Cleveland Elementary teacher Micha Olivier had never seen a child with such separation anxiety. "She just didn't want to leave her daddy's side."

After a month of Phoebe's fits, John snapped in front of the teacher, "Why does it have to be this way?"

The next day, MawMaw started bringing Phoebe, and drop-offs got easier. MawMaw rearranged her schedule at the deli and always was first in the car line.

That fall of 2014 was the most stable period of Phoebe's life.

She moved in with MawMaw while her dad crashed with friends. Phoebe learned how to gargle and say her prayers. She slept beside MawMaw in her double bed, clutching her life-size baby doll, Lucy. In the morning, she woke to MawMaw singing, *You Are My Sunshine.*

In school, Phoebe made friends who sat with her at the table by the window. She learned to cut shapes and sound out words. She opened up and started telling jokes. She told her teachers she was going to be a dancer. Or a doctor.

"She was never on my radar as someone to worry about," said Micha, 38. The teacher has taught kids who acted out sexually, a girl whose face had been slashed with a belt buckle, another burned by a bug zapper.

Phoebe never showed any signs of neglect or abuse. The teacher knew her mom wasn't around, but said her dad and MawMaw adored her. "Phoebe was always clean," Micha said. She said, "Please," and, "Thank you," and knew how to share.

"She was loved," Micha said. "She never missed a day of school."

At MawMaw's house, Phoebe hogged the bed and smiled in her sleep.

Then, one night, she woke screaming. Shaking, she told Maw-Maw, "I dreamed someone was taking me from you."

The wait was too long at Cracker Barrel, so they went to Denny's for Thanksgiving—turkey and stuffing for $9.49. John had finally agreed to let Phoebe's mom see her for the holiday.

Looking back, it was probably the beginning of the end.

Phoebe's mom brought her new boyfriend, a weekend wrestler. She told John they had moved in together. Phoebe seemed to like the new guy.

After dessert, she begged, could she stay with her mommy?

John refused. It was hard enough seeing Michelle with a new man. He wasn't about to share his daughter.

ASK FOR HELP. Everyone you talk to can lead you to someone else. Ask each person you interview: Who else? Can you help connect me? We started with the kindergarten teacher because school was almost out. At the school, she showed us Phoebe's desk and told us about a garden the kids were dedicating for her. We went to that ceremony, where the teacher introduced us to Phoebe's grandmother, who introduced her uncles. And each of Jonchuck's friends led us to another.

DID YOU EVER? Evidence files included calls and accusations Jonchuck had made about Phoebe's mom, trying to get a judge to terminate her custody. So, of course, I asked her if she'd ever called the child abuse hotline on him. She and her boyfriend both had. Those records aren't open to the public except through a Freedom of Information Act request . . . at least in Florida.

For a man who so feared abandonment and rejection, the next month delivered a series of blows. John got two new jobs and lost them. He reached out to old friends, who wouldn't take his calls. Michelle was in love with someone else, talking about getting married. And she wanted Phoebe back in her life.

John called the child abuse hotline, bad-mouthing Phoebe's mom. Two people called the hotline about him.

He started sending strange texts to his friend Melody on Dec. 14. She had no idea why.

"He was harassing me, calling me a whore, telling me I was a demon who needed God, that he was coming to kill me," she said. She called police, who told her to get a restraining order. "I knew that wouldn't work with John."

A few days later, John got a notice about his lawsuit against the Cheesecake Factory, the one that was going to make him rich. For the case to continue, he had to submit X-rays.

He also got a letter from Social Security asking him to account for Phoebe's benefits, giving him 15 days to respond or lose the $600 a month.

Phoebe kept asking to see her mom. So they all spent Christmas Eve at Michelle's house: John and MawMaw, Michelle and her boyfriend and teenage son, and Phoebe. John brought Sonny's BBQ. To everyone's surprise, he said a blessing.

"I thought maybe all my prayers were answered," said MawMaw. "He finally knew there was a God."

"He became fixated with the Bible," said his stepmom, Mickey Jonchuck, 58. She had a huge family Bible, a century old and written in Swedish, which John started carrying around.

On Christmas Day, John texted Michelle saying she didn't have to worry about him keeping Phoebe from her any more.

John and MawMaw watched Phoebe open her presents— Play-Doh, a scrapbook kit, bottles of bubbles, a Sparkle Girlz doll.

Then John blew up at MawMaw, yelling, "I never got toys like this!"

John hadn't worked full-time in months. He had staffed the drive-through window at Burger King for a while, cooked for a day in a Jamaican cafe. The week after Christmas, with Amanda's help, he got a job at a telemarketing company.

"He looked the part—clean-shaven, dressed very nice," said his boss, Scott Hedger, 35, who ran CCS Dial. "In one breath, you could have the most educated conversation in the world with this guy, and I'd be thinking I could take him to a board meeting. Then he'd flip, and the devil would appear."

Scott fired him for cursing, hired him back when he begged. "He could compose himself completely," said Scott, "when he had the motivation to do so."

As the new year approached, texts between John and Phoebe's mom erupted into nasty name-calling—trollop, fat ass, scorned woman, garbage slut—then turned to threats about filing for full custody.

> Court house tomorrow for phoebe
> MICHELLE KERR

> Beat you there
> JOHN JONCHUCK

> I want nothing to do with u ever again
> MICHELLE KERR

> no one wants anything from you
> we want the baby safe thats all
> JOHN JONCHUCK

TEXTS TALK. Many texts between Phoebe's parents were in the police files, downloaded from Jonchuck's phone. Those were all fair game to quote. Because they were now part of the public record, I didn't need permission to reprint the messages from both people. Others were in Phoebe's mom's, grandmother's and uncles' phones. Always ask if you can see people's exchanges and include them in the story. Texts make the dialogue more immediate and intimate.

Phoebe's mom called the DCF hotline Dec. 29, saying John had no stable address and that, years ago, he had smacked Phoebe in the face. The DCF counselor forgot to get John's address, so no one ever investigated.

The next day, John called to say Phoebe's mom was insane and using drugs. DCF went to her house, and she passed their drug test.

On New Year's Eve, John petitioned for another injunction against Phoebe's mom, saying her new boyfriend was dangerous. *There are amos, knives and swords in the home.* The judge denied John's request.

That night, Phoebe sat in MawMaw's lap, watching her great-uncles set off fireworks. She ate two whole steaks, medium rare, and fell asleep before midnight.

During the first week of January, John texted a half-dozen people asking for something he had never seemed to care about: forgiveness.

I am very sorry for being such a d—head. And saying mean and horrible things I was an addict, he texted his uncles.

Please don't give up on me.

No one responded. John had used up all their goodwill.

He spent Sunday at his mom's house, mulched her yard, played Old Maid with Phoebe. His mom kept talking about how much she wished she could keep Phoebe. That night, John burst into his mom's room and yanked Phoebe out of bed.

"You're not taking my kid!" he yelled.

Stunned, John's mom watched him carry Phoebe out the door. He took her to his dad and stepmom's house.

"If I'd tried to take her," she said later, "he would've beaten me up."

————

When Phoebe's seat in kindergarten was empty that Monday, the teacher hoped she wasn't sick.

When Phoebe didn't show up the next two days, Micha wondered if she should call.

At his dad's house, John became even more obsessed with his stepmom's big Swedish Bible. He spread salt around the doorways to keep out bad spirits. He told his stepmom Phoebe was a demon.

At work, John kept quoting Bible verses, talking about Abraham and Isaac and sacrificing a lamb.

His boss didn't know the Old Testament tale about God commanding Abraham to kill his son, then sparing the boy. So Scott didn't think John's ramblings were any more than that.

"Either he was mentally unstable or on drugs," Scott said. "I couldn't tell which."

Scott and Amanda even talked about trying to get John help. "But he can't check in somewhere," Scott told Amanda. "Or he'll lose his daughter."

That evening, John told Scott, "I'm going to be fine."

Then he said something no one understood until later:

"I've got to walk the pyramid," John proclaimed to his coworkers. "I just hope when I get to the top, I don't have to do it. I hope I don't have to make that sacrifice.

"I hope someone stops me."

Part 2: The Last Day

At the lawyer's office, Phoebe curled up in a green chair by the window.

It had been a strange morning. This was the third day she had

READ THE BIBLE. Whenever there's a reference to a religious text, or famous poem, or even a song, look it up. It might not mean anything, but at least you'll know. Sometimes it helps to include at least a snippet for readers to make their own inferences. Jonchuck railed about the Bible a lot and left one open in his car that fateful night. The verses he referenced all were eerily prescient.

ANTICIPATE ENDINGS. I'm always searching for questions, cliff-hangers, intriguing quotes to wrap up sections. Short stories often still need breaks. But when you're writing a longer story or a project, it helps to set stakes and build suspense within each section, as well as the overall story. When Jonchuck's former boss told me that quote, I knew it would be a climax to end an important portion of the story.

missed kindergarten. Her father was jumpy and upset, still wearing his pajama pants.

He had brought her here first thing, then disappeared upstairs with a lawyer. The paralegal was nice. She gave Phoebe a cup of crayons and a blue piece of paper.

Phoebe drew a house—a rectangle on the bottom, triangle on top. Phoebe was always drawing houses. In five years, she had lived in 15 different ones. She gave the house a yellow roof. A green door.

Upstairs, attorney Genevieve Torres had the custody petition ready. All her client had to do was sign. But he was talking fast, waving his hands. Not making sense.

John had brought a big, black satchel, which he laid on the table between them. He pulled out a heavy, ancient, leatherbound Bible.

Read this, he said. The lawyer looked at the yellowed pages, but they were printed in some foreign language.

You're the Creator, he said. You can read any language.

Genevieve started to get scared. No one can hear me up here, she thought, unless I scream.

John was babbling about wanting to be baptized; in an hour, he had an appointment with a priest. The more the lawyer tried to steer him back to his case, the angrier he got.

After a few minutes, he said, "Don't worry about filing the paperwork. None of this is going to matter tomorrow."

All kinds of scenarios spun through her mind.

Was he going to move? Take Phoebe to Mexico? Was he going to hurt Phoebe's mom?

Genevieve decided she had to get John out of there. Then she would call police, so they could intercept him at the church. She helped him zip the Bible back into its bag, and ushered him downstairs to the door.

Can Phoebe stay with you? John asked her. Just while I go to the church?

Genevieve hesitated. Phoebe didn't know her. She didn't want Phoebe to be scared. And she didn't want John to come back shouting that she had kidnapped his daughter.

She saw Phoebe coloring. Her own daughter was the same age. Surely Phoebe would be safe at the church, with a priest, until the cops got there. She told John he would have to take his daughter.

Phoebe didn't want to go yet. She wanted to finish her picture.

FEEL THEIR FEELS. I couldn't talk to Phoebe, to know what she was feeling that last day. But after interviewing the lawyer and paralegal, I got a pretty good perspective on what she was doing, how she was acting before that. Try imagining the world through your subject's eyes: What would it be like to be a 5-year-old watching Daddy rant, landing in a lawyer's office, coloring houses you'd never had?

MAKE IT PERSONAL. The lawyer had a daughter the same age as Phoebe. When I found that out, I understood better why she was so emotional about not letting Phoebe stay with her. When I asked her about picking up her own daughter after school that day, she broke down. Connecting personal lives to professional actions strengthens emotional ties—and gives readers more insight.

She drew a stick figure girl, with long, orange hair. On top of her hair, she drew a green circle. Like a halo.

She had 13 hours left to live.

———

More than a dozen people saw Phoebe that last day—priests, deputies, well-meaning strangers.

They saw her dad acting strange. They worried. Some intervened. Others just did their duty. Counselors screened calls. Investigators filed reports. They consulted the Florida statutes, the DCF child maltreatment index.

But systems are impersonal, protocols are inflexible, and it's scary to act on your instincts.

How could so many people know something was so wrong, and still, a little girl died?

———

Genevieve, 35, had never called the cops on anyone. She knew if she reported John she would be violating her attorney-client privilege.

But she had to do something.

As soon as John left, she told the paralegal, "Call 9-1-1."

On the phone, the lawyer's voice shook, then broke. "He's crazy," she sobbed. "And he has a minor child with him."

"Did he want to harm himself?" asked the dispatcher.

"No," Genevieve said. "He kept saying I was God. I don't know if he was on drugs or what.

"I should've kept the child."

———

Just before 11 a.m., Phoebe followed her dad through the dim sanctuary of St. Paul Catholic Church in Tampa.

In the next four hours, he would drag her to two more churches.

A secretary took Phoebe to the preschool while John talked to the Rev. William Swengros. John told the priest he needed to be baptized.

"I am the pope," John said. Then he corrected himself, "I know I am not."

He said he was possessed and asked the priest to perform an exorcism.

There's a process to being baptized, the priest told him. He gave John some forms and a number to call.

When John came out of the priest's office, two Hillsborough County sheriff's deputies were waiting. One had been trained to evaluate people with mental illness.

Was John a danger to himself or anyone else? the deputies asked the priest.

No, the priest said.

He told deputies John had been acting paranoid, saying everyone was out to get him. He didn't mention the exorcism until police interviewed him again the next day, when it was too late. He didn't tell them John had asked how many people had jumped off the Skyway. Why did he wait to tell police? He wouldn't talk for this story.

That day at the church, John was clean-shaven, noted Deputies Jessica Hallberg-Calebro and Aaron Rizzo. He did not seem drunk or high, they wrote. John told them he had new clarity in his life.

Do you think your lawyer is God? they asked him.

No, he said, but God spoke to me.

He said he hadn't heard voices or been diagnosed with schizophrenia, but at one time, he had been on 37 different medications. Currently, he wasn't taking any.

The report says: He did not exhibit any signs of mental illness.

Are you upset about having to file for custody of your daughter? one deputy asked. John said no. He and Phoebe were living with his dad and stepmom. They were happy there.

He left the church holding Phoebe's hand.

The little girl appeared happy, wrote the deputy. And waved at me when she was leaving with her dad.

John drove Phoebe 5 miles south to St. Lawrence Catholic Church.

The Rev. Cesar Petilla won't say what happened there, citing confidentiality. He later told police John was "asking for something over his expertise."

Next, John picked up his stepmom and drove her and Phoebe back to the first church—St. Paul. About 1 p.m., he barged in and demanded again to be baptized. Right away. When the priest again refused, John said he would find another church.

Lake Magdalene United Methodist Church was three minutes away. Phoebe was skipping as she came through the door. Receptionist Valerie Mallory gave her a lollipop, and Phoebe sat on a sofa beside John's stepmom. Neither said a word.

I just found out I'm related to the pope, John told Valerie, but the Catholic Church won't baptize me. He put his heavy Swedish Bible on her desk.

Valerie could see he had issues, but didn't think he would

hurt anyone. She told him he would have to meet the pastor, who wasn't there.

She gave him the minister's email address, which seemed to pacify him. Then John grabbed his Bible and said, "Okay, let's go."

"It was almost like he came in one way," Valerie remembered later, "and in a snap, he was calm."

———

Genevieve waited anxiously for the phone to ring, for the Sheriff's Office to tell her John had been committed.

When the call came, she was livid.

"How is that even possible?" she asked. "What else do they need?"

The deputy said John didn't appear to be a danger to himself or to Phoebe. John was on his way back to the lawyer's office, the deputy said, to pay the filing fee.

That didn't make sense. If he wasn't going to file the custody papers, why would he bring her money?

He must have realized she was the one who had called the cops on him. Was he coming back to hurt her?

Instead, about 2 p.m., John started calling her office. Eight times in the next hour. He kept saying Phoebe wasn't really his daughter.

While the paralegal fielded John's calls, the lawyer dialed the DCF hotline. If police wouldn't help, surely child investigators would. For 18 minutes, the lawyer spilled her facts and fears.

"He's delusional and he has a child with him," Genevieve said. She told the counselor about the Bible, that John said she was God, that he was saying Phoebe wasn't his child.

"I just can't believe he didn't meet the standard for being Baker Acted," she said.

While she was on the phone, John called again. He told the paralegal everything was fine. He was at his dad's house.

"The stepmother is there now, at least there's another adult. But still. I just . . . ," the lawyer told DCF. "He's out of his mind."

"Okay," said the counselor, who had been on the job for six months. She put the lawyer on hold, then told her, "Okay, based on the information you provided, unfortunately it doesn't rise to the level of Florida statutes for us to be able to accept the report at this time."

The lawyer gasped.

"Based on what you've told me," the counselor continued, "it sounds like they at least have some support next door with his parents, so . . ."

The lawyer kept trying. "I just wanted to make sure you all knew he's not in his right mind and he has a 5-year-old with him."

"Right," said the counselor.

The lawyer's voice trailed off, "I just wanted you to know."

At 3:25 p.m., the hotline worker shelved the report.

———

After such a strange day, that evening was quiet. John took a nap at his dad's house while his stepmom fed Phoebe.

John's mom stopped by after dinner, but didn't notice the sea salt he had strewn around the doorways.

Over the last week, he had been acting weird, even for John. He had been sleeping with the Swedish Bible. He told his stepmom his daughter was a demon.

No one seemed concerned.

Everyone crashed on the couches, watching cartoons.

At 8 p.m., MawMaw got up.

"Time to go," she told Phoebe. Her backpack was ready for the next morning. She could sleep over with MawMaw, who would take her to kindergarten.

Phoebe wanted to stay with her dad.

John promised he would take her to school the next day.

MawMaw didn't want to make him mad, so she left by herself.

A half-hour later, John called her saying he didn't feel well. Could he bring Phoebe over?

Just go to bed, MawMaw said. Let Phoebe sleep.

———

Something set John off.

Around 9:30 p.m., he started texting his friend Noemi, telling her they were meant to be together, talking about scripture and sea salt.

Noemi Bresnahan was older than him, 40, and had a son Phoebe's age. John had stayed with them for a while.

He told her he had asked a priest how many people had jumped off the Skyway bridge.

Noemi freaked out. She didn't respond.

———

When John's dad and stepmom heard the door shut about 10 p.m., they thought John was taking Phoebe to his mom's house. They heard the car drive away.

QUICK CUTS. A lot happens in this short section. It covers about five hours, packed with action and asides, decisions that, if they were considered differently, might have saved Phoebe. Why didn't Jonchuck's mom notice the sea salt? Why wasn't anyone worried about the big Bible? What if MawMaw had let her son bring Phoebe over? By fast-forwarding through these scenes in sharp, staccato language, I wanted to heighten readers' concerns about the imminent, increasing danger.

They didn't know he hadn't buttoned his daughter into a jacket on that chilly January night. Or that she was wearing the gold cross necklace John's uncles had given him as a boy. They didn't see that he had packed Phoebe's Christmas presents into trash bags and stuffed them into the trunk of his car.

They went back to bed.

FILL IN THE GAPS. Make a detailed timeline of events and people's lives. You might not use every entry, but to write a really rich narrative, you need to know. I couldn't figure out what happened between when Jonchuck left his parents' house and when he dropped Phoebe into Tampa Bay. One of the women who'd taken in Jonchuck and Phoebe mentioned another woman, who said he had scared her that night. After a couple of days, I reached her—and realized she'd been the last stop before he sped to the bridge.

Phoebe stood behind her dad, shivering and barefoot, while he pounded on Noemi's door at the Oakwood Apartments in Tampa.

Noemi hid in her bedroom. She didn't see Phoebe with John. Later, she said she thought John had come to kill her and her son. She wouldn't say why.

John paced in the parking lot, back and forth, holding Phoebe's hand. A neighbor saw them and worried about the little girl with no shoes, but didn't call the police. A witness reported a white PT Cruiser barreling 100 mph down the interstate, past the West Shore exit, heading south.

Where was he going? Why did he take Phoebe with him?

He drove into St. Petersburg, past all the beach exits, then jammed his brakes.

An off-duty cop saw the smoke from the tires. St. Petersburg Police Sgt. William "Drew" Vickers, 37, was on his way home. He tailed the car as it raced toward the Skyway.

The officer didn't turn on his lights or siren. But he called in the license plate.

"There's a white PT Cruiser southbound on 275 at a high rate of speed," he radioed just after midnight.

Suddenly, his tone changed. He sounded confused.

"It's slowing down...."

START OVER. The story began just before the climax, a good place to consider when picking an opening scene. Then it flashes back to Jonchuck's childhood. Here, near the end, I return readers to the beginning, reminding them of the initial action while adding context and details, inviting them to revisit that riveting scene now that they know so much more.

The PT Cruiser veered right, then, at the top of the Dick Misener Bridge, stopped on the shoulder.

A bulky man with dark, disheveled hair climbed out of the driver's side, wearing plaid pajamas, carrying a big black book.

"Get back in the car!" the officer yelled. The man kept coming, walking in front of the cop. He was a car-length away.

He yelled, "You have no free will!"

Then he walked to the rear passenger door of his car and ducked inside. The sergeant raised his Glock and shouted, "Let me see your hands!"

Instead of pulling a weapon, the man emerged holding a child. The girl's face was pressed into his shoulder. Long curls spilled across her back.

Along the span, yellow-green lights blinked. Cars blurred by. Palm trees bowed in the wind.

More than 62 feet below, whitecaps licked the dark water.

The officer saw the man walk toward the guardrail. He saw the child stretch against him, like she was waking up.

She must have wondered where she was, and why she was so cold.

She nestled against her father as he held her there, between the dark and the water—the two things she dreaded most.

Without losing eye contact with the cop, with the officer's gun still pointed at him, the man carried the girl to the edge of the bridge, and hoisted her over the concrete wall.

The officer heard a faint scream.

Then a splash.

Part 3: One of Ours

He didn't look down.

After dropping his daughter off the bridge, John didn't lean over the rail to watch her small body hit the water. He didn't react when she screamed.

He turned away. He walked to his car.

"He . . . he just dropped his kid over the railing into the water!" Sgt. Vickers yelled into his radio. "He's fleeing south to the toll plaza."

The officer's voice grew louder, more urgent. "Give me rescue! I'm right on the interstate. The kid's in the water!"

He ran to the railing, stared at the expanse of black water below.

With his flashlight, he traced the pilings, searching for a \sign.

Way down there, waves slapped the concrete, rocked the channel markers. A couple of boats bobbed by. But he couldn't see anything that looked like a child.

"I'm going to try to go down the ladder here," the officer radioed. "Can we get someone out there to light up the water?"

The ladder was metal, encased in an open cage that clung to the side of the span. The rungs were slippery.

"Be careful on the ladder," someone said on the radio. "It's a 25-mph north wind out there and the current's coming from the east, which would push 'em up by the old Holiday Inn."

Sgt. Vickers climbed down.

Above him, other police cars were lining up on the Dick Misener Bridge, red and blue lights flashing. Below him, Tampa Bay seemed to stretch forever.

He kept calling for the child, "Yell and let me know you're okay!"

All he heard was the roaring traffic and the rushing wind.

When he got to the bottom, the officer shone his beam in wide arcs, threading through the mangroves and mist.

Please let me see her, he kept praying. Please let her be okay.

John barreled through the toll booth, over the Skyway bridge, into Manatee County. A pack of cop cars roared up behind him, lights blaring. On Interstate 75, John made a wide U-turn and sped up the highway—in the wrong direction. He almost hit another officer head-on.

A police helicopter hovered, its spotlight dancing in the dark. More than a dozen officers from three counties joined the chase. Over the radio, someone shouted, "Shut the interstate down!"

Deputies threw stop sticks onto I-75. John plowed over them, blowing a tire.

TIME STAMP. Whether you're writing about an accident, a hurricane, even a wedding, try to provide time stamps along the way. How long before the police arrive? The storm hits? The bride walks down the aisle? Watching the clock tick makes the action seem more urgent. As the rescue unfurled, I wanted to know how long Phoebe had been in the water.

"Let me see your hands," said an officer. "Get out of the vehicle."

John just sat there, clutching the steering wheel.

"Get out of the vehicle!"

When John still wouldn't move, the officer raised his baton, smashed the driver's side window, grabbed John by the arm and yanked him through the broken glass.

His daughter had been in the water for 13 minutes.

———

On the bow of the boat, bobbing beneath the bridge, Alice Elliott sang songs in her head so she wouldn't have to think about what they were searching for.

She was 21. She had helped boaters who had run out of gas, paddlers who had flipped their canoes. She had never been on a real rescue.

She had been studying in her dorm room when the call came. She hoped it was a false alarm.

Eckerd College has the only student-run marine rescue program in the country, and its docks are less than a mile from the

Sunshine Skyway bridge. When the Coast Guard called for assistance, Alice and four other students had piled into a 26-foot-boat and motored through the frigid wind.

All they knew was someone had thrown a child off the bridge.

As soon as they turned out of the channel, they saw spotlights streaming from the span, beams from other boats, flashlights flickering along the shore. A helicopter whirred. From their radio, updates crackled. Someone thought they saw something. It was only a seagull.

The longer it took, the more anxious Alice got. Even if the child survived the fall, in that cold water there was little chance she still would be alive. Alice said a silent prayer, Please don't let us find her. Please don't let us be the ones.

A student dispatcher plugged tide patterns and currents into a computer. The rescue crew steered the boat toward a piling and aimed their hand-held lights in expanding circles. They watched the choppy, 2-foot waves, looking for breaks in the patterns. Crab pots and pelicans kept giving them hope, then letting them down.

They had been on the water for more than an hour when Ryan Morgan, 20, noticed something near the southern end of the span, in shallower water, near a shoal.

"Contact!" he yelled, pointing off the port side. "Contact!"

He couldn't think of anything else to say.

They pulled closer, concentrating their lights, and saw a small, pale face, half-submerged in the dark current, framed by long, matted hair in the shape of a halo.

The girl had drifted under the bridge, then southeast almost a mile. She had been in the water more than an hour and a half.

She didn't look real, Alice thought. She looked like a doll.

Alice and Ryan reached over the side of the boat and lifted the child by her shoulders. She was cold, and heavier than they expected, her body beginning to bloat. Alice carried her to the stern, talking to her the whole time, hoping to revive her. She didn't want the girl to be scared.

The girl's cat T-shirt was bunched up, and they saw bruises on her back. Ryan started CPR. He had never done it on a real person, only on a practice dummy. As he inhaled, he could taste the saltwater.

When a deputy handcuffed John to a chair, he demanded an attorney.

RETRACE THE ROUTE. To transport readers to a scene, go there yourself. Or at least mine Google Earth. If you can, get in the car and drive to each place your subject had been to, especially in this case where it was his last day. See what they saw along the way, learn how long it took to get from one stop to the next. We even got the college rescue crew to take us out in the boat they'd used to find Phoebe. We went at night, to report what their ride was like as they approached the bridge, fanning their flashlights through the dark.

He wore flip-flops and an orange T-shirt; his hair was mussed, his cheek sliced by the broken car window. He looked like John Belushi on a bender. He told one officer he was God. Another he was the pope. He ate Ritz crackers, burped, asked if he could leave. He wanted his Bible. He said the whole thing was a conspiracy. When they left him alone, he cried for them to come back.

Tell me everything, an officer said.

John started with Thanksgiving at Denny's—the first time he had seen Phoebe's mom in almost a year.

Then he shut down.

While John yawned and stretched and pulled his hoodie over his head, deputies searched his car: crumbled packs of Seneca Menthol 100s, a half-eaten piece of cherry cobbler, Dolce & Gabbana Light Blue cologne.

In the back, they saw Phoebe's Christmas presents.

On the passenger seat, they found a large black satchel and an antique Swedish Bible. Below it, on the floor, a Gideon Bible was open to the Old Testament, Nehemiah 9:11:

You divided the sea before them, so that they passed through it on dry ground, but you hurled their pursuers into the depths, like a stone into mighty waters.

In the interrogation room, John told the deputy that for the last few weeks he had been feeling different.

I asked him how and he replied that he had always felt different, the deputy wrote.

They talked about the baptism he had wanted, about John's new job. Then John looked at the deputy and asked, "Is Phoebe okay?"

"Phoebe?" the deputy asked. "Who is that?"

John paused and looked down. "Phoebe was my daughter," he said. "Phoebe Jade Jonchuck."

At the end of the report, the deputy wrote an addendum:

I observed there to be no remorse or regret for what he allegedly did. The only time he showed any emotion was when he asked me if Phoebe was all right. When he asked me that, he put his head down into his hand and began to shake his head back and forth.

Despite his strange statements, despite his rumpled appearance and religious rantings—even after a cop saw him drop his daughter off the bridge—no one drug tested John.

Not the Manatee County sheriff's deputies. "If he shows signs of being impaired, you would test him," said spokesman Dave Bristow. "But it wasn't our case. We only assisted St. Pete police."

Not the St. Petersburg police who made the official arrest. "There were no indications of drug or alcohol impairment," said spokesman Michael Puetz.

Even when John got to the Pinellas County Jail, no one checked to see if he was drunk or high. Instead, a deputy filled out an affidavit, which included three boxes:

· Indication of Drug Influence
· Indication of Mental Health Issues
· Indication of Alcohol Influence

On each one, the deputy checked NO.

———

A few hours later, at the state Capitol in Tallahassee, Florida's new leader of the Department of Children and Families was introducing himself to the Legislature.

Mike Carroll told a Senate committee he was hiring more child protective investigators to reduce caseloads. He was launching a website to chronicle every child fatality.

We have a responsibility, he said, to stop those deaths.

A few minutes later, he was walking across the courtyard when a staffer pulled him aside and told him: Someone just threw a child off a bridge.

Carroll froze. He asked, "Was it one of ours?"

Guilt rippled through the community in deep, expanding rings, buoyed by regret, remorse and what-ifs.

Across Tampa Bay, people started tributes to the 5-year-old girl whose face was all over the news: white crosses on the bridge, Facebook pages, 5K fundraisers. Skinny's Bar sponsored a Poker Run. An American Legion post planted a tree. The Eckerd students who found her took up a collection to sponsor a Southeastern Guide Dog; a yellow Lab puppy now answers to her name.

Unlike other tragedies, where the child victim was invisible until the end, so many people had taken in Phoebe, tried to help, and loved her. Even strangers felt responsible. They all wondered what they had missed—and what they should have done.

The cop on the bridge: What if he had left work a little earlier, or later, and not seen that PT Cruiser? Would John still have pulled over? If he had shot at him, would he have hit Phoebe?

The lawyer who called 911: She should have kept Phoebe.

ASK ABOUT REGRETS. People won't always admit they did something wrong. But if you ask them to get introspective, and think about what they wish they hadn't done, or hadn't happened, you can open up portals of grief and guilt. That allows you to explore their feelings and realizations more deeply. Almost everyone in this story bore some burden of feeling that they had, somehow, contributed to Phoebe's death.

She said that again and again. But when John came back for his daughter, what would have happened? When the system ignores you, what else can you do?

The kindergarten teacher: Why didn't she call to check on Phoebe? Why did she wait?

All those single moms who let John and Phoebe stay with them: What if they hadn't kicked out John?

His uncles, who had asked to adopt Phoebe: Why didn't they push?

Phoebe's mom wished she had fought harder to see her daughter. She regretted thinking that, because she could barely walk, taking care of Phoebe would be easier for John. She wished she had pressed charges all those times John hurt her. Sent him to jail.

MawMaw insisted it was her fault. If she hadn't abandoned John, if she hadn't doted on Phoebe, maybe he wouldn't have been so jealous.

"What if I killed her," she sobbed, "because I loved her too much?"

What about John's stepmom, who was with him on that last day? Or his dad, who heard him leave that night? What about the two priests who sent him away? Or the deputies who let him go? None of them would say what happened.

At Phoebe's funeral, everyone wore pink and purple—her favorite colors.

———

Phoebe's fall from the top of the bridge to the water lasted less than two seconds.

An autopsy found frothy fluid in her lungs. Bruises the size of cantaloupes on her back. Bruises on her jaw and lip. Scrapes near her ear and ankle. A thin layer of blood on her brain.

The autopsy ruled she drowned.

But that doesn't explain why she died.

Over the past five years, 215 children in Florida have been killed by "inflicted trauma"—beating, shaking, intentional drowning. One-fourth of them were kids that DCF knew about—like Phoebe. Almost half of those kids had a parent who also had been reported to DCF as a child—like Phoebe's dad.

Phoebe's case included so many flags: a non-traditional family, where problems go back generations; unstable housing and income; domestic violence; substance abuse; mental health issues.

The lawyer's call to the hotline should have triggered an investigation, said DCF Secretary Carroll. At the time, an apparent mental breakdown was not an approved reason to open a case.

The day after Phoebe died, the department added new questions for hotline counselors: Is the caregiver delusional? Hallucinating? Manic? If any of the answers are yes, the new rules say, an investigator has to visit that child within four hours. Since then, Carroll said, more than 900 calls have been forwarded to investigators for concerns over mental health, and at least one baby has been saved.

"We've got to figure out what issue we are missing with the family," Carroll said. "Someone was concerned enough to keep calling us out there. We never effectively dealt with the larger issues."

Seven times, someone called about Phoebe. The frequency of reports created a boy-who-cried-wolf bias, the department concluded. Investigators dismissed some calls as custody squabbles.

"The primary stressor" that led to Phoebe's death, said the 15-page report, was that her dad was worried about losing full custody.

There was no evidence that he was experiencing significant mental health issues or might be at risk for severe decompensation.

"Can you hear me?" the judge asked.

John stood beside the bailiff, a few hours after his arrest. He was handcuffed, staring at the floor.

"You are John Jonchuck?" asked Pinellas-Pasco Circuit Judge Michael Andrews.

"That's the name that I was given."

When the judge asked if he would like a court-appointed attorney, John said, "I want to leave it in the hands of God."

"Okay," said the judge. "So you want to represent yourself?"

"I want to leave it in the hands of God."

"Pretty sure God is not going to be representing you in this case," the judge said. "Would you like someone standing next to you as you're standing trial?"

"Yes," said John.

"An attorney?" asked the judge.

"That is pure and good," John said. "Not evil."

There was supposed to be a bounce house. One of those big fairy princess castles with pink turrets and a long, blow-up slide. And dozens of 6-year-olds squealing in the yard.

MawMaw had the birthday party all planned. Phoebe would get so excited, ask how long she had to wait. Could all her friends come? Would there be cake?

Instead of celebrating on that sunny August morning, Phoebe's family took balloons to the cemetery.

"I wanted to do for you what I never did for anyone," MawMaw wept.

Lake Carroll Cemetery had donated the land near a sprawling live oak. It wasn't really a plot. The coffin, the size of a cooler, slid into a slice of grass between Phoebe's great-great-grandparents' graves.

People had planted petunias and periwinkles, ceramic fairies and spinning pinwheels. Her classmates had pressed shiny glass pebbles into stepping stones. Someone had left a crystal angel, with a solar sensor that made it glow.

So Phoebe wouldn't be in the dark.

Her kindergarten teacher joined MawMaw and John's uncles as they hugged and sang, "You are my sunshine. . . ."

They talked about the girl who would never get to take dance lessons, lose a tooth, or grow big enough to ride a real roller-coaster.

It would be easy to believe the reason John killed his daughter was because he was mentally ill. But most people live with bi-polar disorder or schizophrenia and don't kill their kids.

It could have been the drugs: the 37 medications he said he had been prescribed, or the fact that he hadn't been taking any. Or the decade he had been smoking spice and meth, hallucinating and roaring into rages.

Drug and alcohol abuse are far more powerful risk factors for violence than other psychiatric illnesses, psychiatrist Richard Friedman wrote in the *New England Journal of Medicine* in 2006. Quoting a National Institute of Mental Health study, he said people who have no mental disorders, but abuse drugs or alcohol, are almost seven times more likely to act violently than those who don't. Mentally ill people who abuse drugs or alcohol are even more likely to harm others.

Since John was never drug tested, that factor is unknown. But his friends and family harbor their own theories about why he did it.

Some think he planned the murder weeks in advance, planting clues, daring someone to notice.

He had told Melody Dishman that if he ever got into big trouble, he would claim insanity.

"In his mind, he was about to lose Phoebe," Melody said. "And if he couldn't have her, no one could."

"Do I think he's crazy?" asked Amanda Serrano. "No."

"I don't think he's insane," said daycare owner Linda Mattos.

"I don't think he snapped," said another former roommate, Angie North. When she heard the news, the first thing she thought was: Did he do it for the publicity?

John could have drowned his daughter in the bathtub. Angie said, "He wanted someone to see him."

He knew exactly what he was doing, said John's uncle Bryan. It was the worst way he could think of to hurt his mom and Phoebe's mom. "John's smart enough to build an insanity case ahead of time."

He always had a master plan, Phoebe's mom said. "He knows the system."

The only person close to John who thinks he actually might be crazy is the person who needs to believe it most: his mom. If he really was insane, she thinks, it wasn't his fault.

But even she's not sure.

————

In jail, deputies put him on suicide watch in a solitary cell.

For weeks, according to records, he refused to shower, change his scrubs, or take his meds. He wouldn't talk to anyone, not even his lawyer or the doctor. He ripped apart his mattress and shoved pieces through the food slot in the door. He banged walls, chanting, "God is good, the devil is evil." He refused to eat. He begged officers to shoot him.

In February, court psychiatrists sent John to the North Florida Evaluation and Treatment Center in Gainesville to try to get him competent for trial. In September, doctors said he still wasn't ready.

For John to be considered competent, he has to convince a psychiatrist that he understands basic concepts of the court system. What's a judge? Who's the bailiff? What are the charges against him?

John had studied to be a paralegal and had filed many lawsuits and injunctions. So he knows the court system.

Unless he has lost his mind.

John's mental status will be reviewed every six months, said

Public Defender Bob Dillinger. Prosecutors have vowed to seek the death penalty.

His next hearing is Feb. 23.

After five years, the public defender said, if John still isn't competent—and is not considered a danger to himself or others—theoretically, he could go free.

––––––

No one writes or visits John.

He has his own room, with a metal door and a tiny window. Each month, he meets with a psychiatrist. Sometimes, he goes to group therapy or makes crafts in the day room.

A couple of times a week, usually late at night, he phones his mom. She's the only person who will take his calls.

He tells her he's sorry. He can't believe what he did. He begs her to come see him.

She wishes she knew what was going through his mind that night on the bridge. She has asked him.

"I didn't get a straight answer," she said. "He just says he didn't mean to. He says he knows what he did to his baby—his best friend—and he hates himself for doing it."

A few weeks ago, just before Christmas, John's mom finally drove to Gainesville. She brought fudge. "He looked good," she said. "He's been taking his meds."

John had asked her to bring him Phoebe's picture.

The school one, from kindergarten, where her long curls tumble across her shoulders, her green eyes are bright and she's flashing her little gap-toothed grin.

Instead, John's mom gave him the program from Phoebe's funeral.

When she had to leave, he hugged her hard.

He asked, "Do you still love me?"

––––––––––

AFTER THE STORY

The publisher was right. Readers across the country shared this story and reached out to express their outrage and anger that so many people had failed Phoebe.

It was a terrible story to have to write, but after a *Times* editorial ran, pointing out how the social services system had let her slip through the cracks, the state Department of Children and Families changed the way operators have to answer the child abuse hotlines. Now, they add a question about whether the caregiver is exhibiting any signs of mental illness. I hope that change might save some child.

Four years passed before Jonchuck finally went on trial.

Prosecutors said he acted out of vengeance, killing Phoebe so her mother could never get custody and because he was bitter that his own mother loved the little girl with affection she never showed for him.

His lawyers argued that he was insane at the time of the killing, driven by imagined voices and delusions, unaware that what he was doing was wrong.

Jonchuck never took the stand. But throughout the trial, he kept telling his lawyers that he was hallucinating, hearing voices. Two psychologists evaluated him and determined he was competent to go to court.

I covered the month-long trial, along with two of my colleagues. We wrote this in April 2019: "John Jonchuck guilty of first-degree murder." He was sentenced to life in prison. He was not facing the death penalty.

After the trial, his mother and uncle both said if he was not insane, he should "rot in hell" for what he did to Phoebe.

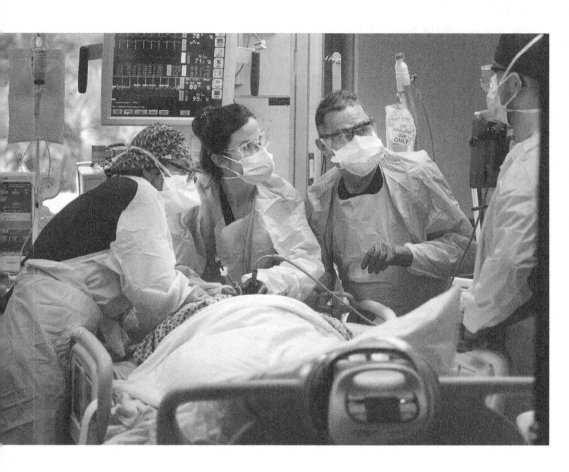

Medical workers in a COVID-19
intensive care unit try to stabilize a
patient after a resurgence in cases
in 2021. Most of the people who died
that summer were unvaccinated.
Photographer: John Pendygraft

16

FIND THE
HELPERS

Who's still working?
Zoom in, do a "day in the
life," navigate risks and
limitations, be creative

Twelve Hours in an Intensive Care Unit: During the Pandemic

Reported in one day; written in two. Published September 5, 2021

BEFORE THE STORY

How do you cover a pandemic? When everyone in the world is writing about the same thing, how do you find something different? When everything is shut down, and terror and tragedy loom around every turn, what can you do to show another angle, something more intimate?

More practically, when no one is out in restaurants, parks or bars, how do you find characters to cover? Especially when you're stuck working from home.

During the coronavirus shutdown of 2020, journalists were considered essential workers, so we got to — had to — keep doing our jobs. Some of my colleagues were terrified to venture into the world and risk their lives, so they did their reporting remotely, by video or phone.

I knew the risks, but I wanted to be out in the field watching people trying to navigate this pandemic, especially those still out doing their jobs. This was historic. I wanted to document it. I asked if I could tag along, masked and distanced. Instead of tackling broad subjects like unemployment, hunger, faith and loss, I looked for a face to put on each of those issues and focused tightly on one person or event.

I followed an out-of-work waitress, a volunteer delivering food to children, a preacher in an empty church, an old lady running a liquor store, a virtual clown, a hospice chaplain, a man staging a Facebook Live funeral.

One of the first places I reached out to were hospitals, hoping to shadow a doctor or nurse trying to save an onslaught of patients. But none would let me in. For 18 months, I kept asking, hitting up more than a dozen institutions every few weeks.

Finally, six months after vaccine distribution began, when the second surge of more severe cases began to swell, a local hospital agreed to let me witness a shift in the COVID intensive care unit. And the nursing supervisor let us into her hard, hectic life.

Any time you're in a health care setting, you have to agree to restrictions: You can't identify patients without their consent, can't reveal certain details about their medical conditions.

With COVID, we had to concede to even more stringent rules: We had to wear hospital-issued masks. We were supervised the whole time, with separate handlers for me and the photographer. We couldn't talk to patients or families or quote what we overheard them saying. We couldn't go into the patients' rooms, only watch through the glass walls. We couldn't identify patients by name, hometown, or anything else. We had to fight to be able to include their gender and ages. Finally, we convinced the public relations supervisor to let us include room numbers, as long as we didn't specify what date we were there.

THE STORY

PRONOUNS OVER PEOPLE. When you're introducing someone who can stand in for many others, try opening with a generic he or she instead of a name. The story isn't a profile of this person. She's just the conduit to show how much has changed and how much more essential nurses have become. Her name doesn't appear until the third paragraph. By then, hopefully, readers have entered her world.

She gets to the hospital 20 minutes before her shift, walks through the lobby carrying a smoothie, hoping—but not believing—that today might be better than the day before.

When she steps off the elevator on the second floor, she turns left, toward what used to be the Intensive Care Unit. Since mid-July, it's become the COVID-19 ICU.

Jennifer Tellone has started calling it "The War Zone."

In the small office she shares at Morton Plant Hospital in Clearwater, Jen lifts her mask to sip her drink. She hasn't even put down her purse when another nurse rushes in.

The patient in Room 84 can't breathe. She needs to be intubated—right away. "Want me to put in for a chest X-ray?" Jen asks, pulling an N95 mask over her surgical one.

"They're on their way."

"Is there anything you need me to do?"

"Ask for fentanyl."

Through the glass wall, Jen sees the patient on her back, gasping, arms flailing. Nurses wearing plastic gowns and respirators are struggling to sedate her. Others are pumping air into her mouth with a plastic bulb. Tubes snake from her wrists and chest. Above her head, monitors blink green, red and blue lifelines. Outside the door is a cart labeled: "For Code Use Only."

The patient is 63 years old, someone reads from a chart. She had been hospitalized two weeks earlier and rushed to the ICU that morning.

"Where's her family?" asks Jen.

"Her son is here," says another nurse.

Jen nods, then sighs. "This is how yesterday started."

Yesterday was the worst day on her ward. Ever. Three COVID-19 patients died—two before 8 a.m.

They were 44, 50 and 64 years old.

Jen had to tell their families.

A man collapsed on the floor beside her, wailing when his wife passed.

A woman begged Jen to save her husband, sobbing, "How do I tell our 6-year-old daughter, 'Daddy's not coming home?'"

Jen is a trauma nurse, mom to two teenagers. She rarely cries.

Yesterday, for the first time in forever, she broke down.

Her husband told her, "Whenever you're ready to step away, I'll support you."

Today, she woke in the dark, pulled on her blue scrubs, tied her hair into a ponytail and came back for a 12-hour shift. She'll try to save the sickest COVID-19 patients, knowing that no matter what she does, most of them won't make it—and that so many more are waiting for those beds.

———

Jen made a career in intensive care because she likes treating a variety of life-threatening conditions, helping the worst patients get better and go home. She's been a nurse on this wing for 20 years and is now a manager.

When the pandemic hit in March 2020, she helped set up the

MEET AND GREET. Before you meet someone for an interview, or to watch them work, gather as much background as possible. Search for professional and personal posts, ask to talk by phone or FaceTime first. I knew I couldn't interrupt Jen while she worked. So I requested a video interview before we met. That's how I learned about yesterday and what the stakes were for today.

hospital's first COVID-19 ward, implementing new protocols. Everyone was terrified, anxious for their patients and themselves.

But by this spring, doctors had figured out new treatments. They had better medicine, new machines. People were getting vaccinated. Nurses began scheduling vacations, wondering when they might be able to stop wearing respirators.

Jen's unit has 18 beds. In June, there were only an average of three COVID-19 cases each day.

Then, two weeks into July, cases started spiking. In one month, infections increased 10-fold. To make room, BayCare had to suspend elective surgeries in its 14 hospitals across Tampa Bay.

About 40 percent of the beds in those facilities now are filled with COVID-19 cases. On this day, near the end of August, BayCare's hospitals have 1,164 cases—462 more than during the peak in July 2020, before there was a vaccine.

Across the country—around the world—the same scenes are playing out. Emergency rooms are overwhelmed. Ambulances are being turned away. More people are dying each day: An average of 250, just in Florida.

The delta variant is spreading faster, striking harder, hitting younger people, even kids.

SANDWICH ATTRIBUTION. Vary where you put "she said" or "asked," sometimes starting with that, sometimes ending with it. I often put it in the middle of a quote, especially if it adds dramatic tension. Breaking up the nurse's two questions near the end of this section slows readers down and adds emphasis to both thoughts—which also serve to set the theme from her perspective.

The saddest part, Jen says, is this didn't have to happen. Most of her patients, and the ones suffering the most, haven't been vaccinated.

"How did we get here?" asks Jen, who got vaccinated as soon as she could. "What's wrong with people who still don't believe?"

For her and her staff, last summer's fear and anxiety have morphed into frustration and anger.

Some patients beg Jen for the vaccine, though it's too late. Others continue to insist COVID-19 is a hoax—while they're dying.

Her job is to try to save them, not judge.

But people are suffering so much more, she says, languishing two or three weeks in intensive care before they eventually go on a ventilator. Once that happens, 95 percent die.

If everyone could see what she sees, she says, the horror and hopelessness her nurses live with every day, the anguish the patients' families endure, maybe they'd believe.

6:35 a.m.

After the woman in Room 84 is sedated and someone sends her son home, after a nurse rolls away the emergency cart, after Jen checks on an 80-year-old man from an assisted living facility, she sinks into a chair at the nurses' station and opens a three-ring binder.

The night nurse manager peers over the pages with her, reports on each patient.

"This one with the belly bleed is unresponsive," says the nurse. "Too fragile to move." Jen nods. The nurse turns the page. "This girl in 93, doctors were trying to hold off for her, but . . ."

Jen doesn't look up. Now that the patients are staying longer, the nurses get to know them, and their families.

Jen knows the 36-year-old woman has two young children, that she's been holding on for two weeks, that yesterday she had respiratory failure and turned blue. "She's going to need to be intubated," the nurse says. The beginning of the end.

The ward is shaped like a U, with nine rooms on each side. The front walls are glass, so staff can see into them without opening the doors. The ventilation system has negative pressure, so contaminated air recirculates into the ducts.

Most of the patients are motionless, sunken into medical comas. The few who are still conscious sometimes moan.

TVs are not on here. There's no music. No visitors, until the end. But nurses constantly call out to each other, phones ring, the halls buzz and beep. And too often, a siren screams throughout the hospital, blue lights spin from the ceiling, signaling someone has coded—if not already died.

Nurses have little time to put things in perspective or process the pain. There's a massage chair in the break room, piles of granola bars and cheese sticks. But they often skip meals.

A poster by the medicine room proclaims: Here's to another day of outward smiles and inward screams.

8:00 a.m.

The man in Room 89 is deteriorating. His lungs blew out from pumping so much oxygen into them. Doctors put him on steroids, and he's been on a ventilator for two weeks.

To relieve pressure on his lungs, he needs to be flipped over,

FEED THE FRENZY. From the moment we entered the ICU, the speed, urgency and constancy of the nurses' duties was exhausting. To capture that, I started this section with lots of long clauses looking back on things Jen had just endured. Stringing together lots of action propels readers into a similar pace, forcing them through a quick sequence that ends, finally, with her sinking into a chair.

NOTICE NOTES. When someone tapes words on their refrigerator, cubicle or laptop, they offer insight. I always write down what's on the walls, desks or, in this case, the bulletin board. That poster conveyed the dichotomy of the nurses' demeanor—pep talk vs. reality check—and showed how they had to steel themselves to get through another day.

TIME STAMP. One of the easiest and best ways to frame a story is to follow someone through their day. In pre-pandemic times, I might have asked the nurse to let me meet her at her home before she left for work. But in this case, just being there when she got to work and staying until she left was enough. By including the time before the later sections, I hoped to show readers how much happened in such short spans, and how far she was into her shift. You also can focus on a single hour, week or month. But I love the simplicity of breakfast to bed.

onto his stomach, the respiratory therapist says. The patient is hooked to a tangle of tubes and a half-dozen monitors. He's a big man. Most of the people in this ward are obese.

He's 50 years old—the same age as Jen.

"I'm coming," she calls, pulling on blue gloves and her N95 mask. "Hey, we need another pair of hands."

Six people work together to roll sheets beneath the patient and thread tubes out of the way. Jen stands by his head as a co-worker pulls out the ventilator, watching the numbers dropping on the monitor. Two more nurses are "bagging" the man, manually pumping air into his lungs until they can reconnect the machine.

Once he's turned, Jen re-hooks his lines, smooths a clean sheet over his back, checks to see if his vital signs improve.

They don't. Ten minutes later, he's worse than when he was on his back. Jen shakes her head and tells the nurse beside her, "He's not going to make it out of here."

8:30 a.m.

Rounds are supposed to start at 8 a.m. But with so many emergencies, they often begin late.

The team gathers in the hall, a dozen people: Nurses, therapists, doctors. A pharmacist. A chaplain. A social worker. A dietician. A couple of interns. They each push a cart with at least one laptop on it, checking information, typing into charts.

Jen carries two phones and a beeper and wears an Apple watch to check email. Sometimes, nurses on other floors need her. Sometimes, she needs help, with X-rays, prescriptions, tests and specialists.

"It's a little crazy in here," a nurse tells the primary doctor on duty.

"Not as bad as yesterday," he says. Not yet.

Outside each room, a nurse reads through a chart, updating the team on the patient's condition. They talk about family members: Who is making medical decisions? If they can't find a relative, they go through the patient's phone.

They start rounds at Room 81, where the man's stomach is bleeding. "He's not doing well," the nurse says.

They're about to head to the next room when Jen interjects, "The woman in 84 is really looking bad."

So the team heads across the hall. "After you get a PICC line in, try to prone her," the doctor says, meaning they should roll her onto her stomach.

"Who is her health care surrogate?" asks Jen. "We need someone legally to make some decisions."

In Room 86: A 46-year-old man got so aggressive he had to be sedated.

Room 91: This man has been in the ICU for a week. "Very anxious," says a nurse.

On the way to the next room, Jen's cell rings. "Yes, we just got a new one. No, we don't have a bed," she tells a nurse on another floor.

Room 92: Jen says of this woman, "There's not much more we can do."

Room 95: This woman has pneumonia, almost coded yesterday.

Room 97: The man was hypothermic overnight.

On other floors, seven more COVID-19 patients are waiting to get into the ICU.

A doctor, who had been on duty the day before, walks up to Jen on his way through the ward. "Hey, are you okay?" he asks. "I was thinking about you last night."

Jen swallows and nods without meeting his eyes.

10:50 a.m.

After hours on her feet, Jen finally gets to sit. At the nurses' station, she reads lab reports, answers calls, talks to families.

Someone brings Publix subs to the ward, so she takes a few bites in the break room before her beeper goes off again.

A man who had been intubated on a ward upstairs has gone downhill. His family has decided to withdraw care. Instead of coming to the ICU, he will be going to the morgue.

"He was here with us before," Jen tells a nurse. "We transferred him out. But . . ."

By the time most patients come to the ICU, their bodies are exhausted from struggling so hard to breathe. Their hearts are deprived of oxygen, so their blood pressure plummets. They're in pain and panicking.

Nurses try to make them comfortable and update their loved ones.

MINIMIZE THE MEDICAL. It was frustrating not knowing what the nurses were talking about, not being able to interrupt and ask, or even get clarification afterward because there was no time. I spent the first half of the day being overwhelmed by all I didn't understand. But by the time they started running through rounds, I started to embrace the generic descriptions. Instead of trying to convey what the health care workers knew, I shifted to pay attention to what the families would want to know.

When you can't see the patient, you don't know how bad things are. You don't realize, or admit, Jen says, when it's time to let go.

The nurses don't want to prolong anyone's suffering, Jen says. "But we do it until the family is ready to stop."

When death seems imminent, one visitor is allowed in the room. If there's no relative or friend, a nurse holds the person's hand. "No one dies alone here," Jen says.

Some patients have Do Not Resuscitate orders: If they stop breathing, or their heart gives out, they don't want CPR. But those orders don't necessarily include ventilators, Jen says. Over the last couple of years—mostly since COVID-19—health care officials have required a new classification: Do Not Intubate.

Most people don't know they need that, Jen says.

Just before noon, she ducks into Room 85. The man from assisted living is doing so much better he can be transferred to another floor. He's the oldest person on her ward, the only one who got the vaccine.

2:35 p.m.

Blue lights flash overhead. A siren howls.

Jen and her team rush to Room 84. Around the patient, two doctors and five nurses are pumping medications through IVs, trying to keep oxygen circulating to her organs.

A machine, the size of a shoebox, is strapped across the woman's chest. The "Lucas 3" device is new, a product of the pandemic, and does chest compressions so nurses don't have to.

Each time it pushes, the woman's body convulses, arms and legs jerking.

LISTEN IN. I wasn't allowed to talk to the man whose mother was dying. But even one-sided conversations can reveal a lot. So I jotted down everything the nurse said on that call. I wanted the scene to feel intimate, as if readers were eavesdropping in the hall. I couldn't hear anything the man said, but later, through the glass wall, we all heard him wail.

"Everybody knew it was going to come to this," a nurse says from the hall.

Still, they try. And try again.

When the woman came in this morning, she had begged a nurse to do anything. Anything! Her son said the same thing: No matter what, don't let her go.

"You gotta call him again," Jen says.

Another nurse picks up her phone, dials the number on the whiteboard by the door. "Your mom has coded again," she tells the son. "It's really not looking good. At this point, we've given her all the medications we can." She pauses. "I don't know if you want us to continue to do this. You can come up to see her."

The son is a 45-minute drive away. The nurse offers to Face-Time, but he has an Android phone.

"She's failing, actively dying," the nurse tells the son. "I'm sorry to say that to you. We've given her 110 percent. But she's just spiraling back down . . . I think at this point, it's time to give her peace." Silence.

"Do you want me to put a phone to her ear, so she can hear your voice?"

In the hall, through the glass, everyone hears her son weep.

Jen walks away. At the nurses' station, she drops her head into her hands.

She tries not to think about all the patients she's lost, the children they won't see grow up, the grandkids they'll never know.

In Room 83, the family of a woman who has been in the ICU for 25 days has decided to take her off life support. She's 56. A wife and mother.

Orderlies roll a new patient onto Jen's ward. This woman is 54. She's been in the hospital for three days. She's wrapped in thick plastic, so she doesn't expose others to the virus. She looks like she's been swaddled in Saran Wrap. She needs to be sedated and put on a ventilator. Now.

As Jen hurries to meet her in Room 96, another nurse draws her into the coffee room. "Here, you need to eat," she says, shoving a fork toward Jen's mask.

For the first time all day, Jen laughs. "There's nothing like eating a tamale, then putting on an N95," she says. "Yummy!"

MASKS MUFFLE. Social distancing and masks make it almost impossible to overhear what people are saying. I had to ask Jen and the other nurses to repeat nearly everything they said. Usually just listening is enough, but those pandemic impediments make everything harder. Write what you think you hear, then confirm. And if you're still not sure of the exact quote, paraphrase.

3:20 p.m.

The woman in Room 84 codes again. Lights. Sirens. A dozen people rush to the room.

"We gotta stop. We're not doing anything for her," says a nurse.

"Her son says he's on the way," says another. "He wants us to keep her alive until he can say goodbye."

In Room 89, the man they had rolled over had his chest tube pop out. Jen sends someone to reinsert it. In Room 95, a woman's daughters have decided to let her go.

Then the woman in Room 84 codes again.

Every 20 minutes, the staff brings her back.

She has now coded seven times.

"This is something we don't do," Jen says.

Jen's not religious or spiritual. She doesn't ask why things happen, what they mean. Or what comes after death. She's cemented in the here and now, multi-tasking through every moment. Making life and death decisions.

Finally, the woman's son runs in. Two nurses help him put on a gown, gloves, mask and goggles. "Would you like the chaplain to be here with you?" asks a nurse.

The son looks stunned. He swallows, blinks back tears, nods.

He shuffles into the room, freezes and stares. Then he collapses on top of his mother.

Through the door, Jen motions for a nurse to unstrap the machine that's keeping her alive.

So her son can truly hug her.

5:50 p.m.

Near the end of her shift, Jen's back is sore. Her knees ache. She's thirsty. No time to fill her water bottle. She keeps yawning.

She can't stop thinking about the man who just lost his mom, and her own mom, who she lost in June to cancer.

A nurse from another COVID-19 ward comes to see Jen. She lost two people today and had heard ICU did, too. The nurses embrace, feeling each other's pain.

For the next half-hour, Jen works on scheduling, checks on her nurses, walks the ward one more time.

When the night nursing supervisor comes, she briefs her on each patient.

Room 83: She's CMO. Comfort Measures Only.

Room 84: The woman finally passed. But her son is still with her.

Room 86: This man brought pictures of his family. He told the ER nurse: Don't let me die.

Room 89: He's still prone, still struggling. He's got kids. He's not going to make it.

"But 93 is better, right?" asks the night nurse, referring to the young mom.

Jen drops her eyes and says softly, "Nooooo."

Saving sick people used to motivate her to keep doing this hard work. Now, she says, there's no joy to buoy her through the sorrow. "You wonder: How long can I do this for?" she says. "I've definitely thought about what I want to do next. I want to work with dogs."

She's grateful for her own health, her friends' and families'

MAKE BARGAINS. The hardest part of this story was watching nurses desperately struggle to keep people alive, and seeing two people die. We also had so many restrictions about what we couldn't include that we were bargaining with hospital officials throughout the process: Can we at least include ages? Genders? Room numbers? We didn't let anyone see the story ahead of time, but fact-checked with Jen and read sections to the public relations people— and kept negotiating even after the project published. Always ask for more access, and keep asking. But sometimes, to get anything, you have to acquiesce and make compromises.

health. And that she finally convinced her 18-year-old son to get the shot. "I had to bribe him with $100," she says.

She's incredulous at co-workers who won't get vaccinated. BayCare doesn't require its employees to, but it asks each patient.

For a while, the community was cheering for health care workers, bringing so many meals they donated some to the food bank. This summer, the love seemed to evaporate. On the "Heroes Work Here" sign, someone added the word "Still."

"I don't feel like a hero," Jen says. "I feel helpless."

6:10 p.m.

Like most of the nurses, Jen will drive home in silence.

Some try to process their day, so they don't take it to their families. Others try to block it out, so they don't have to relive it.

Jen tries to not think about anything during her commute to Palm Harbor, which, of course, is impossible. When she gets home, she works out or walks her two dogs.

Her kids don't ask about her day much. Her husband pours her a Chardonnay and lets her talk—if she wants.

He doesn't understand why she's putting herself through this.

But this job is what she does. And who she is.

She can't walk away. Not now.

AFTER THE STORY

Hundreds of readers from across the country wrote thanking Jen, and us, for sharing her story. Many were health care workers and retired nurses, grateful that we gave people a glimpse of their dark, hopeless days.

A bakery delivered breakfast to the hospital for Jen and her team. A deli sent lunch. A ninth-grade girl wrote thank-you notes to all the nurses.

Doctors and health care executives emailed praising the story's accuracy and intimacy, saying that their perspective needed to be shown, giving me hope that maybe they would welcome more journalists into their cloistered corridors.

Thousands more people shared the story on social media, tagging unvaccinated relatives and friends.

And the best payoff: Two readers wrote saying that they showed the article to their spouses, which convinced them to get the vaccine. Sometimes journalism works!

PART

—

03

NARRATIVES

Beginning. Middle. End. To me, that's the core of what narrative is. You can let a story unfold chronologically, start at the climax and work backward, or play around with structure — as long as there's a clear opening and ending.

I like to envision my stories as movies playing through my mind. What do I want readers to see, feel, wonder about? When do I draw them in? Where do I become a drone and rise above? Where do I weave in background or explanatory information, or provide historical context or bring in current events?

Narratives should take readers on a journey, give them reasons to question and care and — most importantly — keep reading.

The first story in this section was, at the time, the longest I had written, the one I had spent the most months reporting. It's about a feral child who was rescued and adopted by a hopeful family. It won the 2009 Pulitzer Prize for feature writing. The last story in this collection is about my son, who was four when I wrote it. That was the first time I ever tried writing a first-person story.

When the Lierows adopted Dani,
they had no idea what she had
suffered, or how to help her.
Photographer: Melissa Lyttle

17

MAKE A DIFFERENCE

Why do you want to write this story? Why should the subject let you in?

The Girl in the Window: Can Love and a New Family Save a Feral Child?

Reported over six months while producing 24 other stories; first draft written in one week. Published August 3, 2008

BEFORE THE STORY

Every year, a foster care agency sent a press release announcing hundreds of kids who needed to be adopted. Every year, I told the public relations director to pick just one child, or someone searching for a child, so I could zoom in on a single story. It's much easier to get readers to care about one family than to hit them with 200 needy kids.

Finally, the director called me. "I have your story," she said. She had been working with foster kids for 30 years, but she said she had never seen one like this. "We have a feral child."

I didn't know what that was. I imagined Mowgli from *The Jungle Book*, swinging through the trees with apes.

She told me about a girl, found curled in her own filth, in a horrible home in the middle of Florida. She was skeletal and couldn't talk, walk or feed herself. But a family had fallen in love with her haunted face and adopted her.

The girl's rescue had not been in the news. Her parents had told the girl's caseworker they didn't want any publicity. But the public relations director knew it was an amazing story. So she and the caseworker agreed to introduce me and a photographer to the parents.

I had never had anyone come with me to negotiate access, so that felt strange. But the parents trusted the caseworker, and she promised them we wouldn't bring any notepads or cameras—we'd just come to talk.

So they met us on their porch, didn't invite us inside. I told them what an amazing thing they had done, giving this girl a chance. Then I asked what they were worried about . . .

They were private people, they said. And they didn't want their new daughter to look "animalistic." I assured them I would respect her dignity and their wishes. If things happened that they didn't want me to write about, they could just tell me.

Then I made my pitch. What was in it for them? It helps so much to think about that ahead of time, to know not only why you want to tell a story, but why the subjects should let you.

I said, "If you can take in this girl, with all her needs, think of how many people might be inspired to adopt other children. Think of all the kids you could help."

They whispered together. Then opened the door.

THE STORY

Part 1: The Feral Child

The family had lived in the rundown rental house for almost three years when someone first saw a child's face in the window.

A little girl, pale, with dark eyes, lifted a dirty blanket above the broken glass and peered out, one neighbor remembered.

Everyone knew a woman lived in the house with her boyfriend and two adult sons. But they had never seen a child there, had never noticed anyone playing in the overgrown yard.

The girl looked young, 5 or 6, and thin. Too thin. Her cheeks seemed sunken; her eyes were lost.

The child stared into the square of sunlight, then slipped away.

Months went by. The face never reappeared.

Just before noon on July 13, 2005, a Plant City police car pulled up outside that shattered window. Two officers went into the house—and one stumbled back out.

Clutching his stomach, the rookie retched in the weeds.

Plant City Detective Mark Holste had been on the force for 18 years when he and his young partner were sent to the house on Old Sydney Road to stand by during a child abuse investigation. Someone had finally called the police.

They found a car parked outside. The driver's door was open and a woman was slumped over in her seat, sobbing. She was an investigator for the Florida Department of Children and Families.

"Unbelievable," she told Holste. "The worst I've ever seen."

The police officers walked through the front door, into a cramped living room.

"I've been in rooms with bodies rotting there for a week and it never stunk that bad," Holste said later. "There's just no way to describe it. Urine and feces—dog, cat and human excrement—smeared on the walls, mashed into the carpet. Everything dank and rotting."

Tattered curtains, yellow with cigarette smoke, dangling from bent metal rods. Cardboard and old comforters stuffed into broken, grimy windows. Trash blanketing the stained couch, the sticky counters.

The floor, walls, even the ceiling seemed to sway beneath legions of scuttling roaches.

"It sounded like you were walking on eggshells. You couldn't take a step without crunching German cockroaches," the detective said. "They were in the lights, in the furniture. Even inside the freezer. The freezer!"

While Holste looked around, a stout woman in a faded housecoat demanded to know what was going on. Yes, she lived there. Yes, those were her two sons in the living room. Her daughter? Well, yes, she had a daughter . . .

The detective strode past her, down a narrow hall. He turned the handle on a door, which opened into a space the size of a walk-in closet. He squinted in the dark.

At his feet, something stirred.

———

First he saw the girl's eyes: dark and wide, unfocused, unblinking. She wasn't looking at him so much as through him.

She lay on a torn, moldy mattress on the floor. She was curled on her side, long legs tucked into her emaciated chest. Her ribs and collarbone jutted out; one skinny arm was slung over her face; her black hair was matted, crawling with lice. Insect bites,

BUILD SUSPENSE. When he got to the run-down house, the detective had no idea what he might find inside. So don't let the readers in on that too quickly. Take them past the investigator sobbing outside, by the rookie retching in the weeds, into the cramped living room, down the narrow hall into the dark, through the door . . .

RECREATE SCENES. I started reporting this story two years after the officer carried Dani from her home. But I needed to know what that room looked like, what it smelled like, what it felt like to be stuck there. So I asked the officer if he still had evidence photos and if he'd look at them with me. He even remembered the sound of cockroaches crunching under his boots.

rashes and sores pocked her skin. Though she looked old enough to be in school, she was naked—except for a swollen diaper.

"The pile of dirty diapers in that room must have been 4 feet high," the detective said. "The glass in the window had been broken, and that child was just lying there, surrounded by her own excrement and bugs."

When he bent to lift her, she yelped like a lamb. "It felt like I was picking up a baby," Holste said. "I put her over my shoulder, and that diaper started leaking down my leg."

The girl didn't struggle. Holste asked, What's your name, honey? The girl didn't seem to hear.

He searched for clothes to dress her, but found only balled-up laundry, flecked with feces. He looked for a toy, a doll, a stuffed animal. "But the only ones I found were covered in maggots and roaches."

Choking back rage, he approached the mother. How could you let this happen?

"The mother's statement was: 'I'm doing the best I can,'" the detective said. "I told her, 'The best you can sucks!'"

He wanted to arrest the woman right then, but when he called his boss he was told to let DCF do its own investigation.

So the detective carried the girl down the dim hall, past her brothers, past her mother in the doorway, who was shrieking, "Don't take my baby!" He buckled the child into the state investigator's car. The investigator agreed: They had to get the girl out of there.

"Radio ahead to Tampa General," the detective remembers telling his partner. "If this child doesn't get to a hospital, she's not going to make it."

FIND AN INSIDE SOURCE. Doctors and nurses who took care of Dani at the hospital couldn't talk to me because of privacy laws. But her caseworker, who was there through those first few months, could—once Dani's adoptive parents agreed. Even they didn't know what their new daughter had been like when she was first taken into medical foster care, how she acted, what treatments experts tried.

Her name, her mother had said, was Danielle. She was almost 7 years old.

She weighed 46 pounds. She was malnourished and anemic. In the pediatric intensive care unit they tried to feed the girl, but she couldn't chew or swallow solid food. So they put her on an IV and let her drink from a bottle.

Aides bathed her, scrubbed the sores on her face, trimmed her torn fingernails. They had to cut her tangled hair before they could comb out the lice.

Her caseworker determined that she had never been to school, never seen a doctor. She didn't know how to hold a doll, didn't understand peek-a-boo. "Due to the severe neglect," a doctor would write, "the child will be disabled for the rest of her life."

MAKE A DIFFERENCE

Hunched in an oversized crib, Danielle curled in on herself like a potato bug, then writhed angrily, kicking and thrashing. To calm herself, she batted at her toes and sucked her fists. "Like an infant," one doctor wrote.

She wouldn't make eye contact. She didn't react to heat or cold—or pain. The insertion of an IV needle elicited no reaction. She never cried. With a nurse holding her hands, she could stand and walk sideways on her toes, like a crab. She couldn't talk, didn't know how to nod yes or no. Once in a while she grunted.

She couldn't tell anyone what had happened, what was wrong, what hurt.

Dr. Kathleen Armstrong, director of pediatric psychology at the University of South Florida medical school, was the first psychologist to examine Danielle. She said medical tests, brain scans, and vision, hearing and genetics checks found nothing wrong with the child. She wasn't deaf, wasn't autistic, had no physical ailments such as cerebral palsy or muscular dystrophy.

The doctors and social workers had no way of knowing all that had happened to Danielle. But the scene at the house, along with Danielle's almost comatose condition, led them to believe she had never been cared for beyond basic sustenance. Hard as it was to imagine, they doubted she had ever been taken out in the sun, sung to sleep, even hugged or held. She was fragile and beautiful, but whatever makes a person human seemed somehow missing.

Armstrong called the girl's condition "environmental autism." Danielle had been deprived of interaction for so long, the doctor believed, that she had withdrawn into herself.

The most extraordinary thing about Danielle, Armstrong said, was her lack of engagement with people, with anything. "There was no light in her eye, no response or recognition. . . . We saw a little girl who didn't even respond to hugs or affection. Even a child with the most severe autism responds to those."

Danielle's was "the most outrageous case of neglect I've ever seen."

———

The authorities had discovered the rarest and most pitiable of creatures: a feral child.

The term is not a diagnosis. It comes from historic accounts—some fictional, some true—of children raised by animals and therefore not exposed to human nurturing. Wolf boys and bird girls, Tarzan, Mowgli from *The Jungle Book*.

It's said that during the Holy Roman Empire, Frederick II gave

OVERREPORT. You can never know too much, and sometimes the rabbit holes you fall into help shape further reporting. I spent about three days reading about feral children, from the wolf boy who became the first emperor of Rome to the California girl who had been tied to a toilet. And I spent a lot of time trying to understand the science of what being discarded did to a young brain. That gave so much context to Dani's story.

a group of infants to some nuns. He told them to take care of the children but never to speak to them. He believed the babies would eventually reveal the true language of God. Instead, they died from the lack of interaction.

Then there was the Wild Boy of Aveyron, who wandered out of the woods near Paris in 1800, naked and grunting. He was about 12. A teacher took him in and named him Victor. He tried to socialize the child, teach him to talk. But after several years, he gave up on the teen and asked the housekeeper to care for him.

"In the first five years of life, 85 percent of the brain is developed," said Armstrong, the psychologist who examined Danielle. "Those early relationships, more than anything else, help wire the brain and provide children with the experience to trust, to develop language, to communicate. They need that system to relate to the world."

The importance of nurturing has been shown again and again. In the 1960s, psychologist Harry Harlow put groups of infant rhesus monkeys in a room with two artificial mothers. One, made of wire, dispensed food. The other, of terrycloth, extended cradled arms. Though they were starving, the baby monkeys all climbed into the warm cloth arms.

"Primates need comfort even more than they need food," Armstrong said.

The most recent case of a feral child was in 1970, in California. A girl whom therapists came to call Genie had been strapped to a potty chair until she was 13. Like the Wild Boy, Genie was studied in hospitals and laboratories. She was in her 20s when doctors realized she'd never talk, never be able to take care of herself. She ended up in foster care, closed off from the world, utterly dependent.

Danielle's case—which unfolded out of the public spotlight, without a word in the media—raised disturbing questions for everyone trying to help her. How could this have happened? What kind of mother would sit by year after year while her daughter languished in her own filth, starving and crawling with bugs?

And why hadn't someone intervened? The neighbors, the authorities—where had they been?

"It's mind-boggling that in the 21st century we can still have a child who's just left in a room like a gerbil," said Tracy Sheehan, Danielle's guardian in the legal system and now a circuit court judge. "No food. No one talking to her or reading her a story. She can't even use her hands. How could this child be so invisible?"

But the most pressing questions were about her future.

When Danielle was discovered, she was younger by six years than the Wild Boy or Genie, giving hope that she might yet be teachable. Many of her caregivers had high hopes they could make her whole.

Danielle had probably missed the chance to learn speech, but maybe she could come to understand language, to communicate in other ways.

Still, doctors had only the most modest ambitions for her.

"My hope was that she would be able to sleep through the night, to be out of diapers and to feed herself," Armstrong said. If things went really well, she said, Danielle would end up "in a nice nursing home."

———

Danielle spent six weeks at Tampa General before she was well enough to leave. But where could she go? Not home; Judge Martha Cook, who oversaw her dependency hearing, ordered that Danielle be placed in foster care and that her mother not be allowed to call or visit her. The mother was being investigated on criminal child abuse charges.

"That child, she broke my heart," Cook said later. "We were so distraught over her condition, we agonized over what to do."

Eventually, Danielle was placed in a group home in Land O'Lakes. She had a bed with sheets and a pillow, clothes and food, and someone at least to change her diapers.

In October 2005, a couple of weeks after she turned 7, Danielle started school for the first time. She was placed in a special ed class at Sanders Elementary.

"Her behavior was different than any child I'd ever seen," said Kevin O'Keefe, Danielle's first teacher. "If you put food anywhere near her, she'd grab it" and mouth it like a baby, he said. "She had a lot of episodes of great agitation, yelling, flailing her arms, rolling into a fetal position. She'd curl up in a closet, just to be away from everyone. She didn't know how to climb a slide or swing on a swing. She didn't want to be touched."

It took her a year just to become consolable, he said.

By Thanksgiving 2006—a year and a half after Danielle had gone into foster care—her caseworker was thinking about finding her a permanent home.

A nursing home, group home or medical foster care facility could take care of Danielle. But she needed more.

"In my entire career with the child welfare system, I don't ever remember a child like Danielle," said Luanne Panacek, ex-

TALK TO EVERYONE. Make a diagram of everyone who touched your main subject. I typed a timeline of Dani's life and tried to find each person who might have come in contact with her: her brothers, her birth father, other relatives, neighbors, the police officer, judge, social worker, psychiatrist, preschool teacher, speech therapist, horseback riding instructor. Each person illuminated different problems and had varying hopes for her.

ecutive director of the Children's Board of Hillsborough County. "It makes you think about what does quality of life mean? What's the best we can hope for her? After all she's been through, is it just being safe?"

That fall, Panacek decided to include Danielle in the Heart Gallery—a set of portraits depicting children available for adoption. The Children's Board displays the pictures in malls and on the Internet in hopes that people will fall in love with the children and take them home.

In Hillsborough alone, 600 kids are available for adoption. Who, Panacek wondered, would choose an 8-year-old who was still in diapers, who didn't know her own name and might not ever speak or let you hug her?

———

The day Danielle was supposed to have her picture taken for the Heart Gallery, she showed up with red Kool-Aid dribbled down her new blouse. She hadn't yet mastered a sippy cup.

Garet White, Danielle's care manager, scrubbed the girl's shirt and washed her face. She brushed Danielle's bangs from her forehead and begged the photographer to please be patient.

White stepped behind the photographer and waved at Danielle. She put her thumbs in her ears and wiggled her hands, stuck out her tongue and rolled her eyes. Danielle didn't even blink.

White was about to give up when she heard a sound she'd never heard from Danielle. The child's eyes were still dull, apparently unseeing. But her mouth was open. She looked like she was trying to laugh.

Click.

Part 2: Becoming Dani

RELUCTANCE, RESERVATIONS. What goes into people's decisions? When they're considering something life-changing, like starting a new job or adopting a child, what questions do they ask? What factors do they weigh? It's also good to explore regret, looking back. But what about the before? What was going through their heads? Giving them pause? Consider best- and worst-case scenarios.

Teenagers tore through the arcade, firing fake rifles. Sweaty boys hunched over air hockey tables. Girls squealed as they stomped on blinking squares.

Bernie and Diane Lierow remember standing silently inside GameWorks in Tampa, overwhelmed. They had driven three hours from their home in Fort Myers Beach, hoping to meet a child at this foster care event.

But all these kids seemed too wild, too big and, well, too worldly.

Bernie, 48, remodels houses. Diane, 45, cleans homes. They

At age 9, Dani Lierow couldn't talk or feed herself. Adoption workers called her a feral child. Photographer: Melissa Lyttle

have four grown sons from previous marriages and one together. Diane couldn't have any more children, and Bernie had always wanted a daughter. So last year, when William was 9, they decided to adopt.

Their new daughter would have to be younger than William, they told foster workers. But she would have to be potty-trained and able to feed herself. They didn't want a child who might hurt their son, or who was profoundly disabled and unable to take care of herself.

On the Internet they had found a girl in Texas, another in Georgia. Each time they were told, "That one is dangerous. She can't be with other children."

That's why they were at this Heart Gallery gathering, scanning the crowd.

Bernie's head ached from all the jangling games; Diane's stomach hurt, seeing all the abandoned kids; and William was tired of shooting aliens.

Diane stepped out of the chaos, into an alcove beneath the stairs. That was when she saw it. A little girl's face on a flyer, pale with sunken cheeks and dark hair chopped too short. Her brown eyes seemed to be searching for something.

Diane called Bernie over. He saw the same thing she did. "She just looked like she needed us."

———

Bernie and Diane are humble, unpretentious people who would rather picnic on their deck than eat out. They go to work, go to church, visit with their neighbors, walk their dogs. They don't travel or pursue exotic interests; a vacation for them is hanging out at home with the family. Shy and soft-spoken, they're both slow to anger and, they say, seldom argue.

They had everything they ever wanted, they said. Except for a daughter.

But the more they asked about Danielle, the more they didn't want to know.

She was 8, but functioned as a 2-year-old. She had been left alone in a dank room, ignored for most of her life.

No, she wasn't there at the video arcade; she was in a group home. She wore diapers, couldn't feed herself, couldn't talk. After more than a year in school, she still wouldn't make eye contact or play with other kids.

No one knew, really, what was wrong with her, or what she might be capable of.

"She was everything we didn't want," Bernie said.

But they couldn't forget those aching eyes.

———

FRAME BY FRAME. Getting subjects to recreate scenes requires slowing them down, having them walk through memories in stop-motion, pausing them to ask follow-up questions or jotting those down to save until after the interview. Mostly, it requires patience. Reporting for this section sounded like: What was Danielle doing when you first met her? What did she look like? How did she react? People don't know the level of specifics you need, so guide them carefully, draw them out and drill down for details.

When they met Danielle at her school, she was drooling. Her tongue hung from her mouth. Her head, which seemed too big for her thin neck, lolled side to side.

She looked at them for an instant, then loped away across the special ed classroom. She rolled onto her back, rocked for a while, then batted at her toes.

Diane walked over and spoke to her softly. Danielle didn't seem to notice. But when Bernie bent down, Danielle turned toward him and her eyes seemed to focus.

He held out his hand. She let him pull her to her feet. Danielle's teacher, Kevin O'Keefe, was amazed; he hadn't seen her warm up to anyone so quickly.

Bernie led Danielle to the playground, she pulling sideways and prancing on her tiptoes. She squinted in the sunlight but let him push her gently on the swing. When it was time for them to part, Bernie swore he saw Danielle wave.

That night, he had a dream. Two giant hands slid through his bedroom ceiling, the fingers laced together. Danielle was swinging on those hands, her dark eyes wide, thin arms reaching for him.

—

Everyone told them not to do it, neighbors, co-workers, friends. Everyone said they didn't know what they were getting into.

So what if Danielle is not everything we hoped for? Bernie and Diane answered. You can't pre-order your own kids. You take what God gives you.

They brought her home on Easter weekend 2007. It was supposed to be a rebirth, of sorts—a baptism into their family.

"It was a disaster," Bernie said.

They gave her a doll; she bit off its hands. They took her to the beach; she screamed and wouldn't put her feet in the sand. Back at her new home, she tore from room to room, her swim diaper spewing streams across the carpet.

She couldn't peel the wrapper from a chocolate egg, so she ate the shiny paper, too. She couldn't sit still to watch TV or look at a book. She couldn't hold a crayon. When they tried to brush her teeth or comb her hair, she kicked and thrashed. She wouldn't lie in a bed, wouldn't go to sleep, just rolled on her back, side to side, for hours.

All night she kept popping up, creeping sideways on her toes into the kitchen. She would pull out the frozen food drawer and stand on the bags of vegetables so she could see into the refrigerator.

"She wouldn't take anything," Bernie said. "I guess she wanted to make sure the food was still there."

When Bernie tried to guide her back to bed, Danielle railed against him and bit her own hands.

In time, Danielle's new family learned what worked and what didn't. Her foster family had been giving her antipsychotic drugs to mitigate her temper tantrums and help her sleep. When Bernie and Diane weaned her off the medication, she stopped drooling and started holding up her head. She let Bernie brush her teeth.

—

Bernie and Diane already thought of Danielle as their daughter, but legally she wasn't. Danielle's birth mother did not want to

DREAM BIG. People often are ashamed, or embarrassed, to share their dreams. But the ones they remember usually mean something and illuminate unconscious thoughts or motivations. When I asked Bernie if he had prayed about adopting Dani, he said God had handed Dani to him in a dream. He clung to that sign and never questioned his decision.

ZOOM IN. It's one thing to say Dani threw epic tantrums. But showing specific scenes and problems takes the story to another level: Writhing away from the toothbrush, screaming in the sand, tearing around while her swim diaper leaks all over the house. Readers cheer with Dani's parents as she learns to let Bernie brush her teeth, walk on the beach, use the toilet on her own.

give her up even though she had been charged with child abuse and faced 20 years in prison. So prosecutors offered a deal: If she waived her parental rights, they wouldn't send her to jail.

She took the plea. She was given two years of house arrest, plus probation. And 100 hours of community service.

In October 2007, Bernie and Diane officially adopted Danielle. They call her Dani.

———

"Okay, let's put your shoes on. Do you need to go potty again?" Diane asks.

It's an overcast Monday morning in spring 2008 and Dani is late for school. Again. She keeps flitting around the living room, ducking behind chairs and sofas, pulling at her shorts.

After a year with her new family, Dani scarcely resembles the girl in the Heart Gallery photo. She has grown a foot and her weight has doubled.

All those years she was kept inside, her hair was as dark as the dirty room she lived in. But since she started going to the beach and swimming in their backyard pool, Dani's shoulder-length hair has turned a golden blond. She still shrieks when anyone tries to brush it.

The changes in her behavior are subtle, but Bernie and Diane see progress. They give an example: When Dani feels overwhelmed she retreats to her room, rolls onto her back, pulls one sock toward the end of her toes and bats it. For hours. Bernie and Diane tell her to stop.

Now, when Dani hears them coming, she peels off her sock and throws it into the closet to hide it.

She's learning right from wrong, they say. And she seems upset when she knows she has disappointed them. As if she cares how they feel.

Bernie and Diane were told to put Dani in school with profoundly disabled children, but they insisted on different classes because they believe she can do more. They take her to occupational and physical therapy, to church and the mall and the grocery store. They have her in speech classes and horseback riding lessons.

Once, when Dani was trying to climb onto her horse, the mother of a boy in the therapeutic class turned to Diane.

"You're so lucky," Diane remembers the woman saying.

"Lucky?" Diane asked.

The woman nodded. "I know my son will never stand on his

WATCH AND LEARN. The subject of my story couldn't talk. I couldn't even try to get inside her head or ask how she felt. She didn't even seem to notice me or the photographer. So we spent long hours just watching her learn to navigate the world, which turned out to be a gift as much as a hindrance.

own, will never be able to climb onto a horse. You have no idea what your daughter might be able to do."

Diane finds hope in that idea. She counts small steps to convince herself things are slowly improving. So what if Dani steals food off other people's trays at McDonald's? At least she can feed herself chicken nuggets now. So what if she already has been to the bathroom four times this morning? She's finally out of diapers.

It took months, but they taught her to hold a stuffed teddy on the toilet so she wouldn't be scared to be alone in the bathroom. They bribed her with M&Ms.

"Dani, sit down and try to use the potty," Diane coaxes. "Pull down your shorts. That's a good girl."

Every weekday, for half an hour, speech therapist Leslie Goldenberg tries to teach Dani to talk. She sits her in front of a mirror at a Bonita Springs elementary school and shows her how to purse her lips to make puffing sounds.

"Puh-puh-puh," says the teacher. "Here, feel my mouth." She brings Dani's fingers to her lips, so she can feel the air.

Dani nods. She knows how to nod now. Goldenberg puffs again.

Leaning close to the mirror, Dani purses her lips, opens and closes them. No sound comes out. She can imitate the movement, but doesn't know she has to blow out air to make the noise.

She bends closer, scowls at her reflection. Her lips open and close again, then she leaps up and runs across the room. She grabs a Koosh ball and bounces it rapidly.

She's lost inside herself. Again.

But in many ways, Dani already has surpassed the teacher's expectations, and not just in terms of speech. She seems to be learning to listen, and she understands simple commands. She pulls at her pants to show she needs to go to the bathroom, taps a juice box when she wants more. She can sit at a table for five-minute stretches, and she's starting to scoop applesauce with a spoon. She's down to just a few temper tantrums a month. She is learning to push buttons on a speaking board, to use symbols to show when she wants a book or when she's angry. She's learning it's okay to be angry: You can deal with those feelings without biting your own hands.

"I'd like her to at least be able to master a sound board, so she can communicate her choices even if she never finds her voice,"

Goldenberg says. "I think she understands most of what we say. It's just that she doesn't always know how to—or want to—react."

Dani's teacher and family have heard her say only a few words, and all of them seemed accidental. Once she blurted "baaa," startling Goldenberg to tears. It was the first letter sound she had ever made.

She seems to talk most often when William is tickling her, as if something from her subconscious seeps out when she's too distracted to shut it off. Her brother has heard her say, "Stop!" and "No!" He thought he even heard her say his name.

Having a brother just one year older is invaluable for Dani's development, her teacher says. She has someone to practice language with, someone who will listen. "Even deaf infants will coo," Goldenberg said. "But if no one responds, they stop."

SEEK SIBLINGS. It would have been easy to overlook William. He was so quiet, often in the background, taking care of himself while his parents tended to Dani. But I sat on the floor with him while he was building Legos and learned how he was tickling her to try to get her to talk. And he was the only person who thought he had heard her say a word. Young kids can give great insight and provide details you never would have known.

William says Dani frightened him at first. "She did weird things." But he always wanted someone to play with. He doesn't care that she can't ride bikes with him or play Monopoly. "I drive her around in my Jeep and she honks the horn," he says. "She's learning to match up cards and stuff."

He couldn't believe she had never walked a dog or licked an ice cream cone. He taught her how to play peek-a-boo, helped her squish Play-Doh through her fingers. He showed her it was safe to walk on sand and fun to blow bubbles and okay to cry; when you hurt, someone comes. He taught her how to open a present. How to pick up tater tots and dunk them into a mountain of ketchup.

William was used to living like an only child, but since Dani has moved in, she gets most of their parents' attention. "She needs them more than me," he says simply.

He gave her his old toys, his "kid movies," his board books. He even moved out of his bedroom so she could sleep upstairs. His parents painted his old walls pink and filled the closet with cotton-candy dresses.

GET YOUR TOE IN THE DOOR, THEN DO FAN-KICKS. If you tell people you want to embed in their lives for six months, they'll run. So I never ask to spend a specific amount of time with someone or tell them how long the story will take. I just ask, "When can I see you again?" or "What's going on next week?" After four visits, Dani's dad invited us to spend the night. That's how we learned William was sleeping in the laundry room.

They moved a daybed into the laundry room for William, squeezed it between the washing machine and Dani's rocking horse. Each night, the 10-year-old boy cuddles up with a walkie-talkie because "it's scary down here, all alone."

After a few minutes, while his parents are trying to get Dani to bed, William always sneaks into the living room and folds himself into the love seat.

He trades his walkie-talkie for a small stuffed Dalmatian and calls down the hall, "Good night, Mom and Dad. Good night, Dani."

Someday, he's sure, she will answer.

Even now, Dani won't sleep in a bed. Bernie bought her a new trundle so she can slide out the bottom bunk and be at floor level. Diane found pink Hello Kitty sheets and a stuffed glow worm so Dani will never again be alone in the dark.

"You got your wormie? You ready to go to sleep?" Bernie asks, bending to pick up his daughter. She's turning slow circles beneath the window, holding her worm by his tail. Bernie lifts her to the glass and shows her the sun, slipping behind the neighbor's house.

He hopes, one day, she might be able to call him "Daddy," to get married or at least live on her own. But if that doesn't happen, he says, "That's okay, too. For me, it's all about getting the kisses and the hugs."

For now, Bernie and Diane are content to give Dani what she never had before: comfort and stability, attention and affection. A trundle, a glow worm.

Now Bernie tips Dani into bed, smooths her golden hair across the pillow. "Night-night," he says, kissing her forehead.

"Good night, honey," Diane calls from the doorway.

Bernie lowers the shade. As he walks past Dani, she reaches out and grabs his ankles.

Part 3: The Mother

She's out there somewhere, looming over Danielle's story like a ghost. To Bernie and Diane, Danielle's birth mother is a cipher, almost never spoken of. The less said, the better. As far as they are concerned Danielle was born the day they found her. And yet this unimaginable woman is out there somewhere, most likely still on probation, permanently unburdened of her daughter, and thinking—what? What can she possibly say? Nothing. Not a thing. But none of this makes any sense without her.

Michelle Crockett lives in a mobile home in Plant City with her two 20-something sons, three cats and a closet full of kittens. The trailer is just down the road from the little house where she lived with Danielle.

On a steamy afternoon a few weeks ago, Michelle opens the

BE THERE FOR BEDTIME. Whenever I'm writing about someone with kids, I always ask to be there when they're giving them a bath, reading a story or putting them down to sleep. I love the quiet intimacy of those moments—or the pushback when things get hard—and those routines are often so universal and relatable. Plus, once a parent gets their child to sleep, it's so much easier to interview them and gain introspection.

LOOK TO THE FUTURE. Dealing with Dani was constant and difficult. Even being there for a weekend was exhausting. Bernie tried to make light of the burden, joking and taking solace in bright spots when Dani shone through. Diane was a lot more reticent, reluctant to talk to me, much less share her fury and frustration. I didn't get either of them to admit second-guessing themselves, or even being disappointed, until I asked about their hopes for their daughter and what success would look like.

FIND BOO RADLEY. I didn't want to track down Dani's birth mom. I wanted to start with the girl's rescue and follow her rehabilitation. But my editor kept bugging me to find that scary creature everyone associated with evil. He named her after the neighbor in *To Kill a Mockingbird*. When I finally found Dani's birth mom, she provided so much insight into her daughter's beginning—and handed me all of Dani's medical records, which I never could have gotten on my own.

Dani often had temper tantrums when she got frustrated and couldn't communicate.
Photographer: Melissa Lyttle

door wearing a long T-shirt. When she sees two strangers, she ducks inside and pulls on a housecoat. She's tall and stout, with broad shoulders and the sallow skin of a smoker. She looks tired, older than her 51 years.

"My daughter?" she asks. "You want to talk about my daughter?" Her voice catches. Tears pool in her glasses.

The inside of the trailer is modest but clean: dishes drying on the counter, silk flowers on the table. Sitting in her kitchen, chain-smoking 305s, she starts at the end: the day the detective took Danielle.

"Part of me died that day," she says.

Michelle says she was a student at the University of Tampa when she met a man named Bernie at a bar. It was 1976. He was a Vietnam vet, 10 years her senior. They got married and moved to Las Vegas, where he drove a taxi.

Right away they had two sons, Bernard and Grant. The

younger boy wasn't potty-trained until he was 4, didn't talk until he was 5. "He was sort of slow," Michelle says. In school, they put him in special ed.

Her sons were teenagers when her husband got sick. Agent Orange, the doctors said. When he died in August 1997, Michelle filed for bankruptcy.

Six months later, she met a man in a casino. He was in Vegas on business. She went back to his hotel room with him.

"His name was Ron," she says. She shakes her head. "No, it was Bob. I think it was Bob."

———

For hours Michelle Crockett spins out her story, tapping ashes into a plastic ashtray. Everything she says sounds like a plea, but for what? Understanding? Sympathy? She doesn't apologize. Far from it. She feels wronged.

Danielle, she says, was born in a hospital in Las Vegas, a healthy baby who weighed 7 pounds, 6 ounces. Her Apgar score measuring her health was a 9, nearly perfect.

"She screamed a lot," Michelle says. "I just thought she was spoiled."

When Danielle was 18 months old, Michelle's mobile home burned down, so she loaded her two sons and baby daughter onto a Greyhound bus and headed to Florida, to bunk with a cousin.

They lost their suitcases along the way, she says. The cousin couldn't take the kids. After a week, Michelle moved into a Brandon apartment with no furniture, no clothes, no dishes. She got hired as a cashier at Publix.

She left Danielle at home while she worked. But it was okay: "The boys were with her," she says. She says she has the paperwork to prove it.

———

She goes to the boys' bathroom, returns with a box full of documents and hands it over.

The earliest documents are from Feb. 11, 2002. That was when someone called the child abuse hotline on her. The caller reported that a child, about 3, was "left unattended for days with a retarded older brother, never seen wearing anything but a diaper."

This is Michelle's proof that her sons were watching Danielle.

The caller continued:

"The home is filthy. There are clothes everywhere. There are feces on the child's seat and the counter is covered with trash."

MINE DOCUMENTS. The papers that Dani's mom gave me were invaluable for filling in her backstory. I spent hours reading psychological reports, doctors' examinations and investigations from the Department of Children and Families. I learned that Dani had been on the authorities' radar and, after two visits, was still left with her mother. Most of those records wouldn't have been available to me as a journalist. But since the mother handed them to me, I could include them in my story. Plenty of documents are available through public records, though: many court and police records, legal filings and lawsuits, real estate transactions and property values. Other documents can be obtained by filing Freedom of Information requests.

It's not clear what investigators found at the house, but they left Danielle with her mother that day.

Nine months later, another call to authorities. A person who knew Michelle from the Moose Lodge said she was always there playing bingo with her new boyfriend, leaving her children alone overnight.

"Not fit to be a mother," the caller said.

The hotline operator took these notes: The 4-year-old girl "is still wearing a diaper and drinking from a baby bottle. Ongoing situation, worse since last August. Mom leaves Grant and Danielle at home for several days in a row while she goes to work and spends the night with a new paramour. Danielle . . . is never seen outside the home."

Again the child abuse investigators went out. They offered Michelle free daycare for Danielle. She refused. And they left Danielle there.

Why? Didn't they worry about two separate calls to the hotline, months apart, citing the same concerns?

"It's not automatic that because the home is dirty we'd remove the child," said Nick Cox, regional director of the Florida Department of Children and Families. "And what they found in 2002 was not like the scene they walked into in 2005."

The aim, he said, is to keep the child with the parent, and try to help the parent get whatever services he or she might need. But Michelle refused help. And investigators might have felt they didn't have enough evidence to take Danielle, Cox said.

"I'm concerned, though, that no effort was made to interview the child," he said. "If you have a 4-year-old who is unable to speak, that would raise a red flag to me.

"I'm not going to tell you this was okay. I don't know how it could have happened."

REPORT THROUGH LIES. I seldom call people out for lying. But by grilling them for details, you can trap them in their own fabrications. Dani's mom claimed she took Dani to the library and park but couldn't remember which ones. She said they went for pizza, but Dani couldn't even chew back then. I didn't have to label her a liar. By repeating her replies, I let readers draw their own conclusions.

Michelle insists Danielle was fine. "I tried to potty-train her, she wouldn't train. I tried to get her into schools, no one would take her," she says in the kitchen of her trailer. The only thing she ever noticed was wrong, she says, "was that she didn't speak much. She talked in a soft tone. She'd say, 'Let's go eat.' But no one could hear her except me."

She says she took Danielle to the library and the park. "I took her out for pizza. Once." But she can't remember which library, which park or where they went for pizza.

MAKE A DIFFERENCE

"She liked this song I'd sing her," Michelle says. "Miss Polly had a dolly, she was sick, sick, sick . . ."

Michelle's older son, Bernard, told a judge that he once asked his mom why she never took Danielle to the doctor. Something's wrong with her, he remembered telling her. He said she answered, "If they see her, they might take her away."

———

A few months after the second abuse call, Michelle and her kids moved in with her boyfriend in the rundown rental house in Plant City. The day the cops came, Michelle says, she didn't know what was wrong.

The detective found Danielle in the back, sleeping. The only window in the small space was broken. Michelle had tacked a blanket across the shattered glass, but flies and beetles and roaches had crept in anyway.

"My house was a mess," she says. "I'd been sick and it got away from me. But I never knew a dirty house was against the law."

The cop walked past her, carrying Danielle.

"He said she was starving. I told him me and my sisters were all skinny till we were 13.

"I begged him, 'Please, don't take my baby! Please!'"

She says she put socks on her daughter before he took her to the car, but couldn't find any shoes.

———

A judge ordered Michelle to have a psychological evaluation. That's among the documents, too.

Danielle's IQ, the report says, is below 50, indicating "severe mental retardation." Michelle's is 77, "borderline range of intellectual ability."

"She tended to blame her difficulties on circumstances while rationalizing her own actions," wrote psychologist Richard Enrico Spana. She "is more concerned with herself than most other adults, and this could lead her to neglect paying adequate attention to people around her."

She wanted to fight for her daughter, she says, but didn't want to go to jail and didn't have enough money for a lawyer.

"I tried to get people to help me," Michelle says. "They say I made her autistic. But how do you make a kid autistic? They say I didn't put clothes on her—but she just tore them off."

After Danielle was taken away, Michelle says, she tripped over a box at Walmart and got in a car accident and couldn't work anymore. In February, she went back to court and a judge waived her community service hours.

She's on probation until 2012.

She spends her days with her sons, doing crossword puzzles and watching movies. Sometimes they talk about Danielle.

———

When Danielle was in the hospital, Michelle says, she and her sons sneaked in to see her. Michelle took a picture from the file: Danielle, drowning in a hospital gown, slumped in a bed that folded into a wheelchair.

"That's the last picture I have of her," Michelle says. In her kitchen, she snubs out her cigarette. She crosses to the living room, where Danielle's image looks down from the wall.

She reaches up and, with her finger, traces her daughter's face. "When I moved here," she says, "that was the first thing I hung."

She says she misses Danielle.

"Have you seen her?" Michelle asks. "Is she okay?"

———

Is she okay? Danielle is better than anyone dared hope. She has learned to look at people and let herself be held. She can chew ham. She can swim. She's tall and blond and has a little belly. She knows her name is Dani.

In her new room, she has a window she can look out of. When she wants to see outside, all she has to do is raise her arms and her dad is right behind her, waiting to pick her up.

STICK THE LANDING. Endings are as important as beginnings. A colleague once told me that if a reader gets all the way through your story, they deserve a bow on the package, and some sort of takeaway. Start thinking about where you're going to end before you start writing, and consider any theme or symbolism you have introduced. Neighbors first saw Dani's face in the broken window. Readers last see her when her dad picks her up to look out the window.

AFTER THE STORY

More than 2 million people have read Dani's story, on the *Tampa Bay Times'* website and through news outlets around the world. It was translated into a dozen languages and won the 2009 Pulitzer Prize for feature writing. Oprah Winfrey, Anderson Cooper, and *The 700 Club* welcomed the family onto their shows.

Hundreds of strangers sent cards, prayers and donations, captivated by this abandoned child—and moved by the possibility that she could be saved. Calls to child abuse hotlines soared after the story. Contributions to foster care agencies increased. In the first week alone, inquiries about adoption quadrupled. "I know of at least a dozen other children who were adopted because of her story," Bernie said. "She will never know how many people she touched."

A decade after being adopted, Dani still couldn't talk. But she seemed more content. Photographer: Lara Cerri

A few months after the story ran, the Lierows moved to Tennessee, where Dani and William were surrounded by horses, goats and dogs. I caught up with them three years later and wrote a follow-up: "The Girl in the Real World."

I kept up with Bernie, on and off, over the years. A decade after he adopted Dani, he invited me to come celebrate her 19th birthday with them. He and Diane had divorced, and he was living on another farm. He had put Dani in a group home near Nashville where, he said, she finally has friends. He visits her every month. I went with him to take her a cupcake in November 2017 and wrote another follow-up: "The Girl 10 Years Later."

Dani never learned to talk. The tantrums subsided; she seems more content. She's mastered eating and gobbles everything in sight. But she still needs help going to the bathroom and showering. She shares a bedroom with a woman about her age who also doesn't speak. Workers at the group home taught her to toss her laundry into the hamper, to make her bed and wait to eat until grace is done. Mostly, she still ignores everything around her, lost in her own world.

And what does she love doing most, the girl who spent her first seven years confined to a dark, miserable space? Sitting on the front porch or rocking on the swing out back, said a worker at the group home. "Just being outside."

18

INHABIT
THEIR HEADS

What were they think-
ing? Worrying about?
Praying for? What is it
like to be them?

Every Day Is Payday:
His First Real Check

Reported in two days; written in one. Published August 28, 2005

BEFORE THE STORY

I was covering the opening of a clubhouse for people with mental
illnesses as a daily news assignment. Afterward, I hung around to
talk to the director and some of the clients. I told them that once
the clubhouse was up and running, I'd love to follow someone the
program was helping, to show how it was working out.

A few months later, the director called. He told me about a man
named Ed, who hadn't worked in years and, at 39, was still living
with his mom. After spending time at the new clubhouse, getting
counseling and job education, Ed had gotten hired at a nearby sub
shop.

I didn't want to frighten him by tailing him on his first few days
of work. So I waited until it was time for him to pick up his first paycheck and asked if I could ride the bus to the sub shop with him.

In the best-case scenario, I get to interview, then observe — or
the opposite. But I get so tempted to break in and ask questions
while things are unfolding, I had to train myself to not interrupt. Instead, I take notes about people's body language, gestures and fid-

Edwin Wohlford hadn't worked in years.
But with the help of a clubhouse for
people with mental illness, he got a
job—and earned his first paycheck.
Photographer: Bob Croslin

gets, and mark my notebook margins with arrows, so I know where to go back and follow up.

I never assume what someone is thinking or feeling. You can always ask: What were you wondering about while you were staring out the bus window? What were you worrying about when you were wringing your hands?

Asking people what they were thinking, how they were feeling, taps into something deeper and gives you internal dialogue. You can use that to shape your own voice as a writer.

This is the first story where I ever thought, "What if I WAS my main character?"

THE STORY

He worries all the way to the bus stop. What if I'm too slow? What if the guys at work are just pretending to like me? What if I forget and put the salami on top of the pepperoni?

He shuffles along the sidewalk, his hands shoved deep in the pockets of his gray cardigan, blue eyes scanning the ground through square glasses. His shoulders hunch up as if he were trying to disappear inside himself.

What if I miss the bus? What if I weigh out too much turkey? What if no one talks to me? What if everyone talks to me? What if I get fired?

He has been fired before, 15 years ago. Or was it 20? He's 39 and can't really remember the last time he held a job.

This time is going to be different, though. He promised. He promised everyone: his mom, his new boss at the sub shop, the guys at the clubhouse. He has been taking his meds. He's working hard to make this work.

He has been on the job now, well, this will be his ninth day. Today is the last Friday in July.

Edwin Wohlford's first payday.

To save time this morning, he showered last night. He set two alarm clocks, for 5 and 5:30 a.m., and got up before either went off. At 6:40 a.m., he left the Clearwater condo he shares with his mom.

Now he's slumped on a bench, waiting and worrying, tugging on his black ball cap. He puts on his headphones and turns his Walkman up loud. Sometimes, when the classic rock is cranking, it swallows the noise in his head.

REPORT ROUTINE. Mornings are hard. Especially for someone starting a new job. So I asked Ed what had happened from the moment he got out of bed. Instead, he started with the night before, when he had showered to save time. He peppered his tasks with time stamps. So I incorporated that into my writing to show his mindset. Including routines—whether regular or new—helps take readers into the minutiae of someone's life, and perhaps compare it to their own.

At 7:12 a.m., the bus ambles up. Wohlford slouches into a seat near the front. He lost his driver's license years ago. After a few minutes, he has to transfer to another route. He gets out to wait on the shoulder of U.S. 19. Construction here. What if that backhoe dumps a load of dirt on me?

For Wohlford, who has schizophrenia and paranoia, just about anything can seem scary.

He rides the bus an hour and a half. Gets off at Vincent House in Pinellas Park, a clubhouse for people with mental illnesses. He stumbles through the door, shouting.

"I lost my glasses. I lost my darn glasses!" Wohlford's voice is always loud. But when he's upset, he bellows. Elliott Steele, a co-founder of Vincent House, comes over and claps a hand on his shoulder.

"How do you see without them? Can you work?" Steele asks.

"I don't know," Wohlford moans, patting his jeans pocket. "I don't know!"

Then, as quickly as it began, the crisis ends. "Oh, here they are," Wohlford says, untangling the glasses from inside his cardigan. "I was worrying what if I couldn't see to make the subs."

Every morning, before going to work at the sub shop, Wohlford stops by Vincent House to do some cleaning. He vacuums the dining area, scrubs the bathrooms, washes the dishes piled in the kitchen sink.

At 9:35 he pulls on his new shirt from Firehouse Subs.

"I'm ready," he says. But he doesn't see the counselor who is supposed to drive him to work.

"What if I'm late?"

In high school, before he knew what was wrong, Wohlford was sure all the kids hated him. He'd get to worrying about it, and his heart would start fluttering, and he'd get so upset he'd have to walk away. Or stand still and close his eyes and try to breathe slowly. Or collapse. Sometimes, he collapsed.

When he was 20, living in California, he started shutting himself in his room. In the dark. For days. Finally, he dragged himself to a doctor and got diagnosed.

"He's never been able to live on his own," his mother, Patty, says. "He lived under a bridge for a while. But I don't count that."

When Wohlford was 22, his mom moved him to Florida. For more than a decade, he went to day treatment in Pinellas Park. He played cards and did puzzles and shared during group therapy. He earned Monopoly money for participating. Every Friday,

SAVE THE LABEL. This story is about a man trying to work through his mental illness. But I don't point this out, or give his diagnosis of schizophrenia and paranoia, until the middle of this second section. I wanted to introduce Ed, to show him struggling and hoping, getting ready and worrying, to get readers invested in him as a human being before labeling him—or inviting assumptions.

WORK WORRY. Before something is about to happen, if I have the chance without interrupting the moment or interfering in the scene, I ask: "Are you excited? Worried? About what? Why?" Knowing someone is anxious or upset helps build tension in the scene and raises the stakes of the action—even when the stakes are small. Ed's anxiety overwhelmed him and often erupted in an endless stream of questions. I wanted readers to feel how hard this was for him.

TRY FRAGMENTS. Most of us don't think in full sentences. Especially not well-written sentences with clauses and adverbs and asides. So when I'm trying to capture what's going on inside someone's head, what it's like to be that person, I ask questions to draw out internal dialogue, then try to emulate that syntax when I write. Ed's speech was extremely staccato. So throughout this story, I used short sentences and sprinkled in fragments: Or collapse. In the dark. For days.

INHABIT THEIR HEADS

he cashed it in at the snack bar. Save $100 and you got yourself a Coke.

"He kept saying he wanted to work and earn real money," Patty Wohlford says. "But no one knew how to help him."

Just after Christmas, she found a listing for a place she thought might be good for her son. Vincent House, a nonprofit clubhouse in a strip mall on 49th Street N, is named for the painter Van Gogh, who suffered from mental illness. It opened in January 2003 and has seven staff and 195 members. People go there to make connections, gain confidence and learn life skills: balancing a checkbook, working on a computer, cooking in a commercial kitchen. Members can come five days a week, from 8:30 a.m. until 4:30 p.m. On Saturday, they have picnics and go bowling. Wohlford went there every day.

Until the late 1960s, most people like him were simply locked away. With the discovery of drug treatments in the 1970s, people with mental illnesses started moving out of hospitals and into group homes. Then came day-treatment programs and group crafts.

The next step was to give people real jobs.

"By the '80s, folks were deciding that people with mental illnesses might be able to work," said Dr. Sally Rogers, a psychologist at Boston University's Center for Psychiatric Rehabilitation.

Treatment centers set up "supported employment," in which counselors help clients get a job interview, then keep tabs on their work.

St. Petersburg's Boley Centers offer this program. Last year, counselors placed 340 people in jobs at more than 300 businesses: Checkers, McDonald's, Red Lobster and the Hilton.

But some seriously ill people, such as Ed Wohlford, can't handle the demands of supported employment.

That's where Vincent House comes in.

This spring, about the time Wohlford joined Vincent House, it launched a program called "transitional employment." Members earn the right to hold a part-time job by working in the clubhouse. They have to prove they can cope with the responsibility.

Then a counselor finds an employer willing to give a member a chance. The counselor trains for the job, then picks a member and shows him how to do it. That way, the member doesn't have to go through the stress of interviewing or explaining why he hasn't worked in 20 years. The counselor works alongside the member for as long as he or she needs help.

"They're all entry-level positions," says Steele, the Vincent

NO NUT GRAF. Some editors demand that dreaded paragraph, summing up why we're writing the story and what it all means. But those don't usually work well in narratives. They stop the story, pull readers out of the scene and can feel heavy-handed. I want readers to come along for the ride because they care—not because I told them they need to know this. But I do think background and context are important, so the paragraph that starts "Just after Christmas..." is probably as close to a nut graf as this story has.

House founder. "They all pay at least minimum wage. We have to explain to a lot of members that they can work part-time without losing their disability benefits."

Eight members of Vincent House have gotten jobs. Some file medical records. One ships plumbing supplies. Another works at a catering company.

Wohlford's name is the latest addition to the bulletin board. But his photo isn't up yet.

They'll snap that when he gets his first paycheck.

—————

"Where's Victor? I can't be late. Where's Victor?" Wohlford asks, pacing around the clubhouse.

Victor Taylor is the counselor who drives Wohlford to work. He also got Wohlford the job and trained him. For two weeks, Taylor went alone to Firehouse Subs in Pinellas Park to learn how to weigh lunch meat and wrap ham rolls. All last week, and for a couple of days this week, he stood beside Wohlford at the sub shop, showing him what to do, encouraging him and calming him and slapping high fives.

At 9:40 a.m., Taylor walks up, grinning. "You ready, brother? You're on your own today," he says, wrapping his arm around Wohlford. "Big day. Payday! That's what I'm talking about."

"I'm nervous," Wohlford says, rubbing his mustache.

"You're home now, brother. This is you!" Taylor says. Wohlford climbs into Taylor's Land Rover and hangs his head.

"I wish you could stay with me," he says. "I don't think they like me."

—————

EMBRACE ECHOES. You know how when a song is playing, and it comes back to the chorus, you sometimes feel this sort of connection: It's familiar. You know this part. You can sing along. Sometimes that works in writing, too. When I have parallel scenes—like worrying all the way to the bus stop, then the sub shop—I often play with repeating and slightly altering those opening lines. It doesn't always work. But when it does, it becomes a touchstone.

He worries all the way to the sub shop. What if someone crowds me? Or fusses at me? Or makes fun of me? What if I forget what I'm supposed to do?

Taylor helps Wohlford punch in, tie on his black apron, find his name tag and pin it on. "I'm Eddie," Wohlford says, showing off his name tag. "There was already an Ed here. So I'm Eddie."

Robin Blosser, the shift leader, shakes his hand. "We've got a busy day," she tells him. "Six platters got to go out in an hour. And I need three pans of Italians."

Wohlford's eyes widen. His shoulders start shaking.

Taylor puts his arm around him and hugs him hard. "Just keep focused, brother. You're gonna be great."

"You can do it Eddie," Blosser says. "You got it, man."

Wohlford tugs on plastic gloves. He glances at the TV in the corner; ESPN is blaring. Then he smashes his eyes shut, shakes his head, shuffles to the refrigerator and gets out one package of salami, one of pepperoni. He scans the sub shop until he finds Taylor, then walks over and waits. He stands there, blinking, until Taylor notices him.

"Hey, Robin, where do you want Ed to set up the Italians?" Taylor calls.

"Let's slide these cookies over and he can do it right here," she says, coming to his side. "You can do this, Eddie."

Taylor helps him slice open the packages of pre-cut meat. Wolford spreads a pile of deli sheets on the counter, then checks the scale.

Salami on the bottom. Pepperoni on top. Salami. Salami. Salami. Salami. Salami. Okay. That should do it. Check the scale. Two ounces. Pepperoni on top. Pepperoni. Pepperoni. Pepperoni. Stoop to see the scale. Two more ounces. Two and two. Four ounces all together. Perfect. The circles of meat are evenly spaced on the paper.

"Am I slacking off?" Wohlford asks, arranging another salami slice on the scale.

"No, brother. You're doing great," Taylor says. "You're doing awesome."

He watches Wohlford portion out six more Italian subs. Then he squeezes Wohlford's shoulder and smiles. "You don't need me," Taylor says. "I'm going back to the clubhouse."

"Do you have to?" Wohlford asks. His lower lip is quivering.

———

Just before noon, the manager comes over. He stands behind Wohlford, watching him straighten deli paper, squint at the scale. "Way to go, Eddie!" he says.

Wohlford jumps. He knocks the salami off the scale. He looks up, sheepishly, at the manager. "I'll try harder," he says.

"You're doing great, Eddie," the manager says. "Keep it up."

Kevin Ferlita didn't know much about mental illness, but he knew Victor Taylor. They'd been friends for years. So when Taylor stopped in, asking about work for some of his people, Ferlita created a job: sandwich portioner.

"It seemed like a good chance to give someone a second start," Ferlita says. Ed "kept wanting to quit last week. I said, 'Listen, we'll make sure you feel secure here.' We're all hoping we can help build his character."

Wohlford is loud, Ferlita says. He announces everything he's

PICK APART THE PROCESS. Watching Ed stack sandwich meat was incredibly boring. Especially after the first hour. But I knew how important the minutiae of his task was, and I saw how keenly he was concentrating. So I tracked his every move, wrote down the process and decided to make each step its own sentence as Ed counted off the salami slices. Later I asked him what else he had been thinking. He added "that should do it" and "perfect."

about to do. "And he's very serious," the manager says. "When he's finished doing what he's supposed to, he asks if he can do the dishes."

Just after 1 p.m., in the middle of the lunch crunch, black spots start spiraling in front of Wohlford's eyes. He puts down the pepperoni, yanks off his rubber gloves and glasses. He struggles to block out the chaos. He knows he needs to focus. "Dizzy," he says loudly. "I'm okay. Just dizzy." He bends and crushes his head between his elbows. "I can do this."

—————

He fills the three pans of Italians, rolls two trays of ham. He's earned a break. But he doesn't want one.

"I'm done with the meat," he tells the shift leader. "Can I do dishes now?"

The sinks are piled high: red plastic trays, pans slathered in meatball sauce, cartons caked with chicken salad. Wohlford sees the stacks and beams.

Soap. Rinse. Sanitize. Soap. Rinse. Sanitize. "I'm not that quick," he tells the guy slicing cheese behind him. "But I'm trying hard."

Just before 2 p.m., the manager starts making his rounds. Wohlford watches him talking to the cashier, the sandwich girls, the guy slicing cheese. When Ferlita comes toward the sink, Wohlford looks into the water. "Am I doing okay, boss?" he asks, softer than usual.

"Better than okay," Ferlita booms, stretching out his hand. "This is going to be a day to celebrate, sir." He shakes Wohlford's soapy hand with his right, offers him an envelope with his left. "Now you're back on track. You're part of the workforce."

Wohlford doesn't reach for the check. Ferlita thrusts it into his hand. Wohlford doesn't unfold it, doesn't see the bottom line: $114.70.

He stuffs it into his pocket and turns back to the sink of dirty dishes.

Later, back at the clubhouse, all the other members want to see the check. Wohlford holds it up while someone takes his photo for the bulletin board. Then he shoves it back into his pocket and picks up the vacuum.

"The money and all, it's great," he tells his fellow members. "But now every day is payday.

"I finally have a reason to get up and brush my teeth."

WHAT DOESN'T HAPPEN. It took me years to realize that sometimes the things that don't happen, the questions that get ignored, are as important as action that's unfolding. I learned to jot down when someone hangs their head or grits their teeth or suddenly falls silent. And when I expect a reaction, and it doesn't come, I remind myself that maybe that means something, too. Ed didn't reach for the check. Didn't unfold it or look to see how much he had made. What he didn't do said a lot: he wanted to work more than he wanted to get paid.

LAST WORDS. Young reporters often feel they have to give their subject the final say. Most of my early stories ended with a quote, usually one that summed up the story. While I try to write my own endings now, and often obsess over them, I can't ignore it when a perfect quote drops in my lap. Ed didn't just want to work. He needed "a reason to get up and brush my teeth." I couldn't come up with anything more powerful or profound.

BRAID
NARRATIVES

Find connections, make
timelines, current events,
historical background

The Last House in Rosewood:
No One Asked the Owner about
Her Story

Reported in three days; written over two. Published June 6, 2018

BEFORE THE STORY

The Realtor called me. Had I ever heard of Rosewood? Did I know
the story? The town's last house—the home of a hero—was for
sale.

I had seen the movie, read the book. But I had never been to that
remote part of Florida, a ghost town where, decades ago, a race
riot had resulted in almost every house being burned down.

I did some research, met the Realtor at the roadside property, where he introduced me to the owner. She was elderly and
afraid, didn't know much of the history. So I asked about her own
story, what brought her here. I didn't expect that to be more than a
couple of sentences in the feature about the house but wanted her
to know I cared.

As her story spilled out, and I learned all she had been through, I
started to see how it was similar to what the residents of Rosewood
went through. I made detailed timelines of the various aspects of

Fuji Scoggins didn't know the history of the home when she moved in. After 42 years, she was ready to sell it. And share her own story. Photographer: Martha Asencio Rhine

the story—of the owner's life, what was going on in the world, the history of the house (see the "Spotlight: Writing and Editing" feature on p. 202).

Later, while I was turning over the possibilities for story structure in my head, I realized I should braid those three narratives to point out the eerie parallels of prejudice and violence.

THE STORY

The house went on the market at the end of May—a three-story Victorian with stained-glass windows, surrounded by 35 acres. But there's no sign in the yard.

A state plaque is out on the road to Cedar Key, where tourists stop to take pictures. And others drive by, shooting holes into the metal marker.

"We aren't advertising it much locally," says the owner, Fuji Scoggins. "We don't want any trouble from the neighbors."

When she and her husband moved there 40 years ago, they didn't know about the history of the home, what the former owner did—or the town of 300 African Americans that a white mob torched into oblivion.

They had no idea that their house was the only remnant of Rosewood, Fla.

"Not until that reporter came around," says Fuji. "Then, all of a sudden, we had TV crews and people from all over jumping the fence."

On a hot, humid afternoon, she sinks into a red rocker on her screened porch, tired from sweeping cobwebs, trying to get the place ready to show. "I'm 84," she says. "I just can't take care of it anymore."

Her daughter and son-in-law are the Realtors. They wrote two separate listings: one for those who might want a big, old home with lots of land; the other for the National Trust for Historic Preservation.

The first listing describes a place "surrounded by majestic oaks, pecan trees, fruit trees."

The second says, "This is a property that should be preserved and the historical significance should never be forgotten."

For years, Fuji hated the house. It was too far out in the middle of nowhere, surrounded by dense woods of palms and palmettos and cypress swamp. The only neighbors were the hogs, deer and turkeys her husband loved to hunt. Plus, the home was too big for just the two of them.

"Please," Fuji kept begging her husband, "let this place be for vacations. Let's keep our house in Ozona." But he refused.

They had moved in during the winter of 1978; left her grown children a two-hour drive away.

On weekends, he sold honey to travelers heading into Cedar Key. And she waited tables at seafood restaurants in the tiny downtown, nine miles away.

"I know everyone here," says Fuji, who was born in Japan. "Everyone is always nice." Except that one time, her son-in-law reminds her. Her smile fades; her shoulders stoop. She doesn't like to talk about that.

She doesn't really like to talk about Rosewood, either. "So much sadness."

But if you beg her, she will tell you what she knows. No, what she heard. No one really knows the whole story. For 60 years, no one talked about it.

———

In early 1982, *St. Petersburg Times* reporter Gary Moore drove up to Cedar Key, searching for a story.

He didn't know to ask about Rosewood. But soon people started wondering, whispering: Had he heard about what happened here?

Moore spent months tracking down survivors, finding newspaper clippings, dredging up deeds. He hiked miles through tangled marshes and found tracks from the abandoned railroad.

And, of course, he knocked on the door of the only house around, which sat off the south edge of State Road 24.

Fuji's husband, Doyal Scoggins, knew nothing of his home's heritage, or previous owners. But he invited Moore to come in and look around. Moore stayed for hours, Fuji said, and told them what he had learned.

"It was a special town," Moore later wrote of Rosewood. "Almost all its inhabitants were black. A world unto itself, it was a village deep in the Suwannee River swamps and wilderness of Levy County . . ."

When a post office and train depot opened in 1870, officials named the unincorporated stop Rosewood, for its abundant pink cedars. Residents worked in lumber yards, turpentine mills, and later, at a factory that turned the trees into pencils. Families built

DROP GOLD COINS. When you're writing a news story, it's important to get all of the information in early—the who, what, where and when at least. But in a narrative, you need to draw your readers in, make them want more. A wise man once called it "dropping gold coins." If you leave little gems, questions and promises along the way, they'll want to keep reading. Why had no one talked about Rosewood? What had happened there? What happened to Fuji?

LET READERS UNRAVEL IT. Share the story behind the story. When you're researching something, take your readers with you. Who first reported it? How did they track down the truth? Make readers feel like they're helping sort out the mystery. I never knew Gary Moore and came to the *St. Petersburg Times* long after he left. But his 1982 story was the perfect jumping-off point for my reporting.

houses, churches, a school, a baseball diamond and a Masonic lodge.

They shopped at a store near the tracks that was run by one of the few white men in Rosewood. John Wright and his wife, Mary, bought that big, white house with stained-glass windows in 1900. They had three children, who all died before age 5. They were kind to the black kids who hung out at the shop, giving them candy.

For years, the little town thrived, mostly isolated and undisturbed.

"Then came New Year's week," Moore wrote, "1923."

———

Fannie Taylor was white, 22, with two small children. She and her lumberman husband lived in Sumner, a few miles west of Rosewood. On Jan. 1, 1923, she woke her neighbors, screaming that a black man had broken into her house and attacked her. Her husband gathered a group of men, who followed a tracking dog to the railroad.

Which led to Rosewood.

"The story of what happened next," Moore wrote, "is a maze of conflicting tales ..."

Some said the intruder had escaped from a chain gang. A black woman who washed Fannie's laundry said Fannie had a white lover, who had hit her that morning. There was no black man. Just a story to explain a black eye.

But no one stopped to ask questions. Or wait for the sheriff.

The hound raced into an open house and sniffed some shoes, Moore wrote, then ran back out and stopped at a row of wagon tracks. Had the homeowner harbored that fugitive? "Who was in your house?" the white men demanded. When the black man said, "Nobody," the mob tied him to a Model T and dragged him down the dirt road.

Then they hunted down the wagon owner, cut off his ears and hand, hanged him in a tree and shot off his face.

All week, killings continued. The mob grew to more than 300, drawn by newspaper headlines of a "negro assaulter." Black families huddled in their homes and barricaded the doors. Some shot back.

So the white men poured kerosene on all the houses and set them ablaze, forcing black women and children to flee into the swamp. Some shivered for days in the dark, wet and cold, waiting for the shooting to stop.

KEEP IT ALIVE. It's unsettling to dig up grim, violent details from the past, to transport yourself to something so horrific. But it's also important to remind people what communities of color endured, to recount how falsehoods spread, prejudices fueled flames—and innocent people were murdered. Hopefully, by knowing, we can prevent it from happening again.

Others escaped to the only house still standing, the one owned by the white storekeeper. Wright hid some people in his attic, some in a secret closet in the master bedroom. He lowered others into his deep well out back.

"If it hadn't been for this house, we wouldn't be here," a survivor named Lee Ruth Davis told *60 Minutes* in 1983. "We wouldn't have had anywhere to hide."

Survivors said the storekeeper also helped persuade two white conductors to stop their freight train in Rosewood, in the early morning of Jan. 6.

After it was all over, officials reported that eight people had been killed—two white, six black.

Survivors counted up to 27 dead, said a dozen were piled in a mass grave in the woods. No one was ever arrested. No black families ever returned to Rosewood.

"We didn't talk about it," survivor Minnie Lee Langley told *60 Minutes*. "Because I didn't want my grandkids to know what the whites done to us."

Wright, Moore wrote, "lived in the ruins of Rosewood till he died, served as undercover emissary to his dispossessed black neighbors who lived in secrecy in distant places, and for a while, kept a pistol on every table."

Ostracized by white townsfolk, Wright started drinking. One night, he passed out. They found him on his porch, frozen to death.

"For the longest time," Fuji said, "he didn't even have a tombstone in town."

COLLECT ALL COVERAGE. With sites like newspapers.com, it's easy to go back in time and find original coverage of events that happened even a century ago. I read accounts from six cities across the state, coverage from Black publications and city council meetings. I watched a CBS special and a Hollywood movie, read a nonfiction book by a former journalist. By gathering every account I could, I hoped to be able to get closer to the truth.

When CBS reporter Ed Bradley filmed from Fuji's front porch, the story made international news. Survivors staged a reunion.

A decade later, the Florida legislature commissioned a report about what really happened in Rosewood. Researchers determined that officials had failed to protect residents. The state issued checks of up to $150,000 each to 10 people who could prove they lived in Rosewood in 1923 and set up a scholarship for survivors' relatives. It was the first time a state had paid compensation to African Americans for racial injustice.

A book about Rosewood, *Like Judgment Day*, came out in 1996. Director John Singleton turned the story into a movie, starring Jon Voight as John Wright.

"That's when the tourists really started coming by," Fuji said. "We had busloads from as far away as California."

In 2004, she watched Gov. Jeb Bush erect a historical highway marker at the end of her driveway. Within days, she saw truck-loads of teenagers taking aim at the names of the victims. "They knocked down that sign many, many times," Fuji said. "Some-times, I got scared."

She never read the book. Or saw the movie. "I was working double shifts," she said. "I never had time."

And in all those years, with all those reporters, historians and tourists, no one ever asked about the woman who lived in that house—who had survived a different massacre.

————

The blasts were blinding, she remembers. For days, bombs rained down. "I saw a lot of dead people," Fuji said.

She was 10 when planes attacked her island of Saipan, where Americans wanted to build a World War II air base. Her house was destroyed. Her parents and their eight children had to sleep on the beach. "I don't know for how long—until we were cap-tured, and they put us in barbed-wire fences."

She was so hungry, she ate maggots. So thirsty, she couldn't spit. But when a U.S. soldier offered his canteen, she refused. "I was afraid of Americans. I thought it was poison," she said. "So the soldier drank it himself, to show me it was safe. Then I drank and drank and drank."

When her family was freed, they headed to Okinawa to find relatives. "There, things got even worse," Fuji said. Bombs oblit-erated that island the next year. "We stayed forever in a shed," she said. "The roof leaked, with all that rain."

As a teenager, she lied and said she could read and write En-glish, then dropped out of school to serve food on the Air Force base. She married an American, had a son with him. In 1957, for the first time, she saw the United States.

They landed in California, had a daughter. But Fuji's husband suffered from his time in the war and had to be committed to a mental institution. A friend from church introduced her to an-other serviceman, Doyle Scoggins, who had grown up in Palm Harbor, Fla.—and wanted to move back.

"I did what I had to do," Fuji said. "I survived."

In 2002—five years after the Rosewood movie, two years be-fore Jeb Bush dedicated the road sign—Fuji's husband told her he was leaving. He had reconnected with an old flame and would sell Fuji the house and property for $100. "I didn't expect a di-vorce," she said. "I thought we got along real good."

For 16 years, she kept cutting the 5-acre lawn with a push mower, scraping paint from the porch, chopping wood for the

BE INTERESTED. When you let people know you care, they'll usually let you in. All those journalists who had come to tell the story of Rosewood, all those photographers who had taken portraits of the house, no one had ever asked Fuji about her own story. When I did, she shied away, saying, "This is not about me." But it was. Like that house, and the chil-dren who escaped the massacre, she was a survivor.

ADMIT: I CAN'T IMAGINE. You can approach an interview trying to find common ground: I'm a mother, too. I live in an old house. I don't like being alone. Or you can admit, you have no way to relate to what that per-son has gone through, what it was like to lose everything and have to sleep on the beach, to be contained by barbed wire. When Fuji told me about her hunger, I asked, "What did that feel like?" When she told me she ate maggots, I had no reply.

NOTICE JEWELRY. What people wear reflects their priorities and personality. Are they wearing dangly earrings? What kind of necklace? Always check for wedding bands. Once, I noticed a man had a tan around where his wedding ring had been. He smiled and said, "I'm on vacation." Fuji had been separated for years but still wore her gold band, hoping her husband would come home.

stove. She left her husband's framed photo on her nightstand and refused to take off her thin, gold wedding band. She never moved, she said, because "I never thought he was going to stay away."

Her children have been trying for years to get her to sell the house and move near them. They worry about her all the way out there. And they are scared she will be subjected to more prejudice.

A while back, when Fuji was still waiting tables in the still mostly white town of Cedar Key, an older customer wearing a WWII ball cap kept glaring at her, snapping each time she approached. Finally, he hissed, "I hate your people."

Fuji stepped back, dropped her head, then looked up—and looked him in the eye. "I understand," she remembers saying. "I'm very sorry that you feel that way. But war is war. It's not the people."

She said she didn't cry. But he did.

KNOW THE NOW. If you're going to explore the past, you have to poke around in the present. In 2018, when I researched and wrote this story, I was surprised to learn how much white supremacy still existed. I spent a day researching hate crimes and racial injustices around where Rosewood once was and learned that just five years earlier, a KKK leaflet had been thrown into the yard of a Black city councilwoman, and a white mother wouldn't let her daughter ride in the homecoming parade with a Black boy. Now, as this type of history is coming to light regularly, I realize how naive I was— and how important it is to provide that past and current context.

Word got out five years ago: Fuji was thinking of selling her house. Neighbors heard that a group of African Americans wanted to buy it and turn it into a shrine. Soon, one dropped by with a warning: You don't want another riot around here.

That same year, 2013, a black council member in nearby Bronson reported that someone had thrown a Ziploc bag into her yard, with a rock and leaflet from the Traditionalist American Knights of the Ku Klux Klan. Four other African Americans found the same threats on their doorsteps.

And at Cedar Key School, for the first time anyone could remember, a black student was elected to the homecoming court. But the mother of the white girl who was chosen as his partner refused to let her daughter ride in the car with him.

"People are trying to keep things quiet," says Greg Dichtas, Fuji's son-in-law. "There's still a lot of discrimination around here."

"I thought it was over," says Fuji's daughter, Connie Dichtas. "Shouldn't that all be in the past? But around here, it's still an open wound."

The last house in Rosewood still has its original floor-to-ceiling windows, which Wright climbed out of to stand on the porch and fire at the mob. The horse-and-buggy wallpaper still blankets the foyer. In the covered well, where the children hid, clear water still bubbles from the ground.

All four bedrooms, and two baths, are still decorated with the furniture Fuji inherited when she moved there. If the next buyer wants it, she says, it's theirs.

Fuji's son, John R. Smith, hopes a university turns the house into an educational campus.

Her son-in-law fears someone might want to build a campground on the property or, worse, a Stuckey's.

Last month, just before listing it, he met with historian Sherry DuPree, who runs the Rosewood Heritage Foundation. She is writing grants, talking to the state's humanities council, trying to raise money to buy the house. "Every culture has its own Rosewood," she says. "We need to keep the word alive, to protect this place and prove this town existed."

Her group can't afford the $500,000 asking price. But they can't afford to forget.

"We paid an architect to study that land. We could have a nice garden, buildings for classrooms and research," she says. "Maybe even a small hotel."

She knows not everyone would welcome the idea.

"But if those walls could talk, they would tell the story of cultures working together, a white man opening his doors to save his black neighbors."

Edward Gonzalez-Tennant, an archaeology professor at the University of Central Florida, wants the home to be put in a public trust, repaired and turned into a museum. "It would be important to have it cover the history of Rosewood," he says, "not just the riot."

As neighbors were knocking on Fuji's door, and historians were weighing in, the last survivor of Rosewood died in Jacksonville last month. Mary Hall Daniels was 3 years old when the mob killed her relatives and burned down her town. When she died at age 98, more than 350 people came to her funeral.

"Events like Rosewood live on in the minds and hearts of survivors and their descendants even after almost 100 years," DuPree says. "We're just trying to get the word out, to keep the story alive."

Fuji sits quietly rocking, nodding as her son and son-in-law discuss the possibilities. She says she doesn't really know what the best future for her house would be. But she hopes someone steps in to save it soon.

"Whatever happens," she says softly. "I just want it to go peaceful."

ASK WHO ELSE CARES? The Realtor wanted to sell the house. Fuji wanted to feel safe. I asked, "Is anyone else interested in the property?" They told me about a historical preservation group, mostly Black volunteers who wanted to protect the house and share its story. Finding other people who care about a place helps elevate its importance.

INTERVIEW ACADEMICS. Sometimes, it helps to have an outsider, with nothing at stake, to put things in perspective. Professors are great sources to show how things fit into history, what matters and why. They provide expertise and context. Whenever possible, reach out to an academic. The University of Central Florida professor I talked to confirmed how important Rosewood was. And is.

WRITING AND EDITING

Beyond the specific Tips & Takeaways embedded in the individual stories, here is some more in-depth advice about writing and editing stories.

WRITING

Get ready: Before I start to write, I read through all my notes and take notes on the notes. So for long stories, each legal pad of reporting would be reduced to a single page of notes—the most important parts. I make a detailed timeline, starting back as far as I can, with whatever details I happen to know. For the one I made for "The Last House in Rosewood" (chapter 19), I included the history of the house, of Rosewood, of the original and current owners (see p. 204). I also make a list of characters and scenes.

Plant notepads: Never sit down to a blank computer screen. You can't start there. You have to tumble images, ideas, sentences around in your head long before you start to write. I compose most of my openings while showering, folding laundry, walking my dog, doing dishes, driving, thinking while I'm engaged in some menial task. I keep notebooks on the back of my toilet, in my car's glove box, by the kitchen sink to record my thoughts. That way, when I start to type, I already have a beginning and often more.

Stash your notes: A wise editor once told me: "The story isn't in your notes. It's in your head. And heart." Then he took away my notepads and told me to go write. Now, I often stash my notes in my car or kitchen while I write. I leave things I don't know in brackets. *The [yellow?] blanket.* Then, when I'm done writing, I go back through my notes and fill in the blanks. You'll be surprised how freeing—and often how much faster—it is to write without flipping through your notes.

Work to a reward: Try seeing your story in sections, instead of one long narrative. I often alternate parts of my piece into Scene / Information / Scene, trying to end each with a question or cliffhanger. I make myself write an entire section before getting up. I can draft an average section in the time it takes me to drink a can of Diet Coke. So when I finish a section, I can go get a refill.

Outline or no outline? Do what works best for you, but definitely it's good to know where you plan to start and end the story and what big question you want it to answer. I enjoy talking through my reporting with an editor or a colleague, and that helps me find my focus and see the path. I can work both ways. Sometimes I'm following a detailed outline. Sometimes I'm going with the flow in my head.

Don't try too hard: You don't have to use fancy words or lots of phrases or think of yourself as "writerly." If the metaphors and similes don't come easily, don't force them. Lots of long, eloquent sentences also can distract readers from the scene or information you're trying to convey. Write like you talk. That's the best way to find your voice.

EDITING

Search and slice: After I edit myself on the computer, I print my story out and edit on paper. You can see things differently when you edit with a pen. Cut *And*, *But*, and *Yet* from the beginning of sentences. Get rid of clichés and boring quotes. Watch hedging: Do you need every *some*, *might*, *may*, *could*? Eliminate jargon. Split long sentences and lose needless attribution. Check for active voice and strong verbs. Look for repetition and too many modifiers. Did you tell when you could have shown?

Read out loud: Once you're done writing, have someone read your story to you. Listen for rhythm, tangled clauses, clarity. Where does the reader trip up? Where does she get confused or bored? You'll be surprised how many things you can find to fix when you listen to your story. If you don't have anyone to read it to you, record yourself reading it on your phone's voice memo app.

Cut the last lines: Endings are as important as openings. If someone took the time to read all the way to the end, they deserve a reward. Not a pithy quote to sum things up. A walk-off home run of a thought, image, idea. People always joke about storytellers "burying the lead." But writers often bury the ending. To make your last words sing, try cutting off the last sentence. Or two.

ROSEWOOD: A TIMELINE

1845	Rosewood established with turpentine mill, red cedar trees
1870	Post office and train depot opened, house and store built near tracks around this time
Jan. 1871	John M. Wright born
May 1, 1889	Wright marries widow Mary Jacobs
May 9, 1900	Wright buys property from estate of Charles B. Dibble, store and boardinghouse
1900–1904	Wrights have two sons and a daughter, all die before age 4
1915	Rosewood peak population 355, mostly black
1919	Wright sells two acres to Lexie Gordon for $10, sells 10 acres to the Methodist Church
1920	At least 30 homes in Rosewood, mostly black owners
Jan. 1, 1923	Massacre begins after Fannie Taylor, 22, of Sumner says a black man attacked her
Jan. 4, 1923	Mob of 400 armed white men surround Sarah Carrier's home, black residents fight back
Jan. 6, 1923	Wright helps get conductors John and William Bryce to evacuate women, children
Jan. 7, 1923	Mob burns rest of structures in Rosewood, except for Wright house
1931	Mary Jo Wright dies, John starts drinking
Jan. 3, 1938	Wright gets drunk in Cedar Key, guys bring him home, dump on porch, he dies
1942	A. H. Wilson, administrator of Wright's estate, sells to Sherman and Rosa Cannon of Sumner
1957	Fuji comes to U.S., California, on big ship, married to U.S. military man
1958	Rosa Cannon, widow, sells to Lester and Lorena Johnson
1971	Johnsons sell to Lillian Piombo
1972	Fuji, Doyal, Connie and Joe move from California to Florida
1976	Piombo sells to J. K. and Olive Thigpen of Cedar Key

Dec. 14, 1977	Thigpens sell to Doyal and Fuji Scoggins, house and 35 acres for $90,000
1982	*St. Pete Times* reporter Gary Moore publishes first account of massacre
1983	Ed Bradley does *60 Minutes* report from Rosewood
1985	First Rosewood reunion, about 50 people come
1993	FL legislature commissions 100-page report on events; Klansmen protest in front of home
1994	Checks to survivors, 400 claims, 70 up to $5,000, first racial reparations; bus tours start
1995	FDLE searches for mass graves
1996	Book *Rosewood, Like Judgement Day* published by Michael D'Orso
1997	Movie directed by John Singleton
2002	Doyal and Fuji divorce after 33 years, he sells house and land to Fuji for $100
2004	State designates Rosewood as Florida Heritage Landmark, Jeb Bush commemorates sign
2013	Cedar Key School, 300 kids, ninth-grade homecoming: white girl's mom won't let her in car with black boy; KKK recruiting, throws rocks in yards of two black Bronson council members; Fuji sick, quits waitressing, daughter wants her to sell house, neighbor threatens: not to black buyers
May 2, 2018	Mary Hall Daniels, last of the 10 survivors, dies at age 98
May 16, 2018	Sherry DuPree visits to talk about tours, university buyers, historic site
May 18, 2018	House listed for sale for $500,000

Eleana Frangedis, 18, lived in an eight-bedroom house in a gated community on the water. She wanted to go camping with troubled girls who had been sent to a program deep in the woods.
Photographer: Melissa Lyttle

20

FOLLOW
THE STORY

Watch and wonder,
be open, expand
the frame

A Walk in the Woods: Miss Teen America Finds Freedom, for a Day

Reported in five days; written in two. Published July 17, 2013

BEFORE THE STORY

While covering stories about foster care, I heard about this camp
for troubled girls tucked far into the woods. The girls were isolated for weeks or months as they dealt with anger issues, suicidal
thoughts, addiction, grief and loss.

I called the public relations director for the agency that ran the
camp, asking if I could spend a night there and profile the program,
talk to some of the girls. She told me I couldn't name or identify any
of the campers. They were wards of the state or privately funded
by parents. Instead, she said, Miss Teen America was scheduled to
stay there the next week. Could I come while she was there?

Of course! An added layer to the story, someone I could name
and quote and focus on. An interesting contrast and quest: Beauty
queen goes camping. I planned to frame it around her day and night
in the woods. I thought I knew how the story would unspool.

But within an hour, I started seeing signs, feeling the story shift,
struggling with so many questions. I had to take the turns as they

came, pay attention to everything I heard, without saying anything, saving my queries for later.

By bedtime that night, I knew I had to meet Miss Teen's parents.

THE STORY

Before she finished her reign, before she moved out of her mom's house to start college, the beauty queen wanted to go camping.

Eleana Frangedis, 18, lives in an eight-bedroom house in a gated community on the water in Tarpon Springs. She had never hiked or chopped wood or gone more than a day without washing her hair.

But in March, in her role as Miss Teen America, she had spent an afternoon at a wilderness camp for troubled girls. She had planned to tell the girls at Camp E-Nini-Hassee they could be anything they wanted to be. Instead, they had inspired her with their stories of survival.

In their thank-you letters, they invited her back for a week. She wanted to prove she was strong, that she could make it in the woods, like them.

Eleana's mother said she wouldn't be able to handle it. Besides, her mom said, why would you want to do that?

Finally, Eleana's mom relented. She could go for one night.

So on a drizzly Tuesday in April, Eleana packed a backpack with shampoo and conditioner, jeans and bug spray, and new shorts from T.J. Maxx. Usually, it takes her three hours to get ready, but that morning, she was out the door in less than an hour. No jewelry, no makeup, no curling iron. This time, she left her satin sash at home.

The drive to rural Citrus County took almost two hours.

It was morning, but the forest was dark. Only small squares of sunlight seeped through the live oaks. The camp director led Eleana up sand hills, around a grove of palmettos. The forecast called for rain.

"If it gets really bad, do the girls still sleep outside?" Eleana asked.

"Oh, yes," said director Jo Lynn Smith. "Come on, we still have a ways to go. The girls here walk more than 3 miles a day."

E-Nini-Hassee means "her sunny road." The 840-acre camp opened in 1969, the first therapeutic outdoor program for girls in

COMPARE AND CONTRAST. Ask people what they have and haven't done. Be specific. Not just "Have you ever been camping?" But "How long have you ever gone without washing your hair?" Ask what they'd usually pack, how long it typically takes them to get ready versus this time. What are they leaving behind?

SANDWICH INFORMATION IN SCENES. This section starts and ends as a narrative, putting you in the car with the beauty queen, overhearing dialogue. In the middle, while you're still driving to the camp, you get the information you'd find on a brochure: The basics readers need to know. By tucking those facts into the scene, you don't have to stop the narrative. And yes, I was in the back seat on that drive.

the Southeast. More than 10,000 at-risk teenagers have stayed there, for six months to two years. It is run by a nonprofit called Eckerd that is dedicated to helping kids and families.

The girls' quarters are deep in the woods.

They arrive with a host of issues: addiction, defiance, anger management problems. Some are runaways, some suicidal. About half come from foster care. Others are sent by parents, who pay up to $225 a day.

The girls eat in an air-conditioned dining hall, but they're mostly outside—building lean-tos and working rope courses, chopping trees and reading Maya Angelou, setting goals, talking through their problems.

They don't have TV or Internet. Cellphones are forbidden. Eleana had already surrendered hers.

"How often can the girls call their parents?" she asked the director.

"Once a month."

Eleana had never gone more than a day without talking to her mom.

———

In a clearing rimmed with tall pines, a dozen girls were sitting cross-legged in a circle.

"Okay, Cliff Dwellers. This is Eleana. She's going to stay with you," Smith said. "This time, she's going to be a camper too."

The girls opened their circle, making room for one more.

As they went around introducing themselves—age, hometown, how long they had been there—Eleana wondered what had brought them here.

Many of the girls had scars running up their wrists. One had a constellation of cigarette burns on her right arm. Another kept picking her acne. The oldest, 16, had been beaten by her cocaine dealer; she had been there six months. The youngest, 11, kept back-talking to her mom, and had been there six days.

They came from all over Florida, and from as far as New Orleans. Black, white, Hispanic, mixed. Some got food stamps. Some had housekeepers.

Out here, in the woods, they were all Cliff Dwellers.

"Okay, I'm Eleana, I'm 18, and I'm Miss Teen America," she said when it was her turn. "I was a little intimidated when I came last time, but I got your notes, and they made me cry, and now I'm really excited to be here."

Counselor Bethany Richards, 28, went over the schedule:

SEE SCARS. I once was at a writers' conference where everyone had to share stories about their scars—an interesting and emotional way to introduce ourselves. Always look for, and ask about, scars. If you don't see any, still ask—about the physical and emotional ones. Like tattoos, every scar tells a story. It may reveal something about the person's suffering or obstacles they've overcome.

Clean camp, clear trails, get lunch. Haul supplies, birthday fun, guitar practice. Shower, dinner, powwow. Lights out by 9.

"That's not so bad," Eleana told the girl next to her. "My step-dad has to get up early—he's a doctor. So at my house we're not allowed to talk above a whisper after 8 p.m."

———

During cleaning time, the girls showed Eleana around. The washup was a shed with 12 tubes of toothpaste strung around a spigot. The open-air bunks were covered by tarps, the beds swathed in cones of white netting, gauzy clouds that seemed to breathe in the breeze.

"Did they tell you about the skeeters? And the coyotes?" asked the 11-year-old. "You can hear 'em howling all night."

Eleana swallowed, tried to smile. "As long as I don't wake up with a spider on my face."

The little girl showed Eleana how to use a broom handle to knock bugs off the tarp. "This is where the watchman sits all night," she said, pointing at a stool. "They take our shoes, so we can't run away."

One other thing, the girl said. "If you have to go to the bath-room in the middle of the night, you have to go in a bucket."

"A real bucket?"

They were scrubbing bird poo off a railing when the girl noticed Eleana's sparkly silver manicure. She squealed, "Oooh, I love your nails! Are they real?" She wanted to know how Eleana got to be Miss Teen America. "I mean, are you, like, famous?"

Eleana was 14 when she saw the Miss Universe pageant and decided she wanted to be a beauty queen. When she was 17, her mom found the website for Miss Teen America, a for-profit pageant. Florida didn't have a competition, so Eleana mailed a head shot and statement to the national director, touting youth empowerment and antibullying as her platforms, and the director interviewed her by Skype.

That was it. Her sash and crown came in the mail. Last spring, Eleana and her family flew to Tennessee, where she represented the Sunshine State—and won the national competition. Plus a scholarship of up to $10,000. The pageant wasn't televised, but someone put clips on YouTube.

"What did you do for talent?" asked the little girl.

"There wasn't any talent."

"You mean you just had to look pretty?"

———

CLICK AROUND. If you've never heard of something, research every-where you can. The camp promo-tor said "Miss Teen America," like it was a household name. Some quick searches on Google, Facebook, Twit-ter and, especially, YouTube showed how much of a scam that title was. I had that information before I went to camp. When the girl asked about it, she gave me a place to weave it into the scene.

Just then, counselor Bethany called a huddle. Two girls were fighting over a branch cutter.

"I don't like it when you argue," sobbed the girl who kept picking at her face. "It reminds me of home."

They all stood in a circle, kicking the sand, while the counselor tried to help them patch their problems. It took a half-hour because one girl was sulking and refused to say what was wrong.

"Sometimes these things go on for hours," the oldest girl whispered to Eleana. "The longest huddle ever lasted until 3 a.m."

Eleana gasped.

"It helps, though, to really talk things through," said the oldest girl.

"Yeah," agreed Eleana. "We don't ever have time to do that at home."

Lunch was served family-style around big, square tables in the mess hall: salad, a sweet potato and hard-boiled egg. For dessert, each girl got 15 grapes.

Eleana asked them about school. They do math and science in the morning, or sometimes reading groups. In the afternoons, they have music and crafts. There is little downtime, no chance to be alone.

In the afternoon, after hauling supplies, everyone gathered for a celebration. It was the sulky girl's 16th birthday, and the counselors had agreed to let the campers sing karaoke.

In the high-ceilinged room, papered with posters of Queen Victoria and Wilma Rudolph, the campers sang songs by Taylor Swift. When someone put on the anthem from *The Little Mermaid*, Eleana joined in. "Out of the sea, wish I could be, part of their world . . ."

"You know, it's really nice to be with girls my age who are just doing regular stuff," Eleana told the oldest girl while they ate cake. "I mean, I don't really have any friends; they all kind of chiseled away, or I had to pull away because they were leading me down the wrong path. I feel like I missed all that teenage stuff, just hanging out and sharing."

Girls had bullied her in elementary school, she said. She had gone to two middle schools and three high schools. This year, she had been doing her senior classes alone via virtual school while she made appearances.

"I wish I had a senior prom. I keep seeing all the girls from

LYRICS MATTER. Pay attention to music and words, even if they're only playing in the background. Especially when someone is singing. Sometimes you can find connections in the song and subject or scene. I jotted down most of the karaoke songs the girls sang at that celebration, but they didn't seem to mean anything. Until the beauty queen joined in, wishing she could be "part of their world . . ."

MARK YOUR NOTES. When I'm trying to write down quotes or dialogue, I nearly always want to stop people and ask follow-up questions. As this scene was unfolding, I realized there was so much more to the story than I'd thought. I sat on the floor watching, wondering, writing down everything I could. And at each place on my notepad where I needed to come back and ask more, I drew a giant arrow in the margin. Instead of interrupting the scene, you can go back later and fill in those blanks.

other schools on Facebook in their new dresses," Eleana said. "I won't have a graduation. I guess they'll mail me my diploma."

The oldest girl asked about Eleana's parents. Eleana's relationship with her father was so strained that they hadn't spoken in a year. Just the day before, she had gone to court, dropped his last name and taken her mother's maiden name, Loulourgas.

Eleana told her campmate, "They split up when I was 2, but I've always been caught in their divorce. They have been to court 160 times."

The girl who had been beaten by a drug dealer shook her head and said, "That must be so hard."

———

That night they gathered near their bunks for the powwow. It was drizzling. A few pale stars pinpricked the black sky.

"You know, it's actually kind of nice not having my phone," Eleana told the oldest girl as they sat cross-legged on the platform.

"I'm proud of you for coming to camp with us," said the girl.

"Thanks for letting me," said Eleana. "I've never really had a slumber party."

Soon a counselor collected all the girls' shoes, hugged each camper and turned off the lanterns. The oldest girl helped Eleana string the mosquito netting above her bed.

Long after everyone else fell asleep, Eleana lay staring at the dark, listening to insects and an owl, wind ruffling the branches. Deep in the woods, under constant guard with no chance of getting away, she felt free.

———

During powwow the next morning, each girl planted a stick in the fire and announced her goal for the day: Build each other up, listen and don't judge, take responsibility for your actions.

"My goal," said Eleana, "is to make this the best day possible."

The girls gave her work gloves, taught her how to chop wood, shave the bark for kindling, clean the fire pit. In the afternoon, to release some tension, the counselors led the girls in a round of silly sounds and dance moves.

Eleana squawked and flapped her arms like a crow. "It's so awesome to get to be goofy," she said, laughing. "I mean, how often do you get to just let go and not care what people think?"

She looked younger now, with no makeup to cover her freckles, her green eyes aglow without liner.

MAKE THE CALL. Some writers hesitate to include their own thoughts. As I've gained confidence, I've learned to trust myself more and note my own feelings and observations on the margins or inside large parentheses. I try to avoid inserting my opinion. But I like being able to help readers see something, like how much younger the beauty queen looked without makeup.

"Can you braid my hair like yours?" a girl asked when they took a break.

"Of course!" said Eleana, pulling the rubber band from her own French braid. "Here, sit down in front of me. You're going to look so cute."

They had to get permission to touch each other. Soon, half of the Cliff Dwellers had beauty queen braids.

The youngest girl asked if she could hug Eleana goodbye, then everyone piled around her. "I had a blast spending time with you all. I grew here," said Eleana. "Thank you. I never really had a group of girlfriends. Or even really just one."

On the way back up the hill, counselor Bethany dropped back to walk beside Eleana. "What about before you were Miss Teen? Did you have friends then, when you were just you?"

Eleana shook her head. She had people she hung out with, but she and her mother agreed they weren't good for her. "I had to learn to distance myself."

In the parking lot, someone offered to give Eleana her phone back.

Eleana's smile faded. "I don't really want it back. Not just yet," she said. "I don't really want to go home. Can't I just stay here?"

ALTERNATE ENDINGS. The story was supposed to end here. It's a great ending for the narrative: Rich beauty queen doesn't want to leave the woods. But she had raised so many questions at camp, seemed so sad about her home life, so happy to be in the wilderness with girls who'd had such hard times. Sometimes you have to extend the storyline and do more reporting.

Some of the stories Eleana told at camp left me wondering. Was she really as lonely as she seemed? Why had she gone to so many different schools? And what had her parents been fighting about in court for 16 years?

I drove to the courthouse and asked for the divorce file. It turned out to be 13 folders thick. It describes a divorce that was finalized in 1997 but never really finalized at all.

Eleana's parents fought about who would pay for her horse-back riding lessons and where she would go to school. The court had established "divorce rules" to display in both houses, times Dad could call, places he had to drop off Eleana. Each side accused the other of contempt of court.

I went to see Michael Frangedis, 49, at his home in Safety Harbor. He hasn't seen Eleana since he moved in a year ago. The bookshelf in the living room is crowded with silver-framed pictures of her. In a bedroom Eleana has never seen, he displays the construction paper cards she designed for him, the scrapbooks they made together, her first tiara from when she was Miss Greek Independence 2011.

INSERT YOURSELF. Up to this point in the story, I haven't been part of it. But when I set out to learn more about the beauty queen's past, to see if her camp stories were true, I took readers with me as I researched public records and met both parents. It was hard talking her mom into meeting me, even harder to carry on that contentious conversation. But that scene made the story so much stronger. The dad surprised me even more.

Frangedis hopes to write a book. He says he'll call it *Total Control*, with a subtitle about the damage done to kids in divorces.

"I just try every way I can to reach out to my kid," he said. "All I want is to have her back in my life again."

Emilia Giannakopoulos, Eleana's mom, agreed to meet me at a restaurant in Clearwater, near her office.

She runs her father's plastics company and her new husband's neurosurgery practice and has two school-aged kids, plus Eleana.

"I'm very busy," she said when we met. "I have 45 minutes. You're lucky I got away at all."

I started by asking her to spell her name. Then I asked her age.

"How dare you!" she said. "And you, a woman!"

While I stammered to explain, Eleana arrived. Her mother hadn't said she was coming. Eleana looked confused about the tension in the air.

"So what did you think of Eleana staying out in the woods?" I asked, trying to move on.

"I wasn't thrilled with her going there," said Eleana's mother—who is 41, according to the divorce file. "She wanted to stay for five days, but no way would I allow that."

And what about sleeping outside? With only a bucket for a bathroom?

"What bucket?" asked her mother. She looked at Eleana, then back at me. "I was traveling," she said. "I didn't have time to talk to her."

She told some of her story: After the divorce, she went back to school even though she was raising a 2-year-old. "And I graduated from USF with honors."

What was Eleana like as a child? I asked. What did she want to be when she grew up?

Her mother looked annoyed. "I was too busy to remember what she wanted to be."

The bullying began in elementary school, said Eleana's mother. "All those mean girls, she came home crying a lot." She enrolled Eleana in private school, paid for it all, "since her father wouldn't." (He says he couldn't afford to.)

Eleana's mom said she did all she could to shelter her daughter during the divorce. But Eleana must have been affected, I said, what with rules about where she had to stay and for how long . . .

"This is not about my divorce," Eleana's mother said. "If I

had known you were going to ask me all this, I never would have agreed to talk to you."

I said I just wanted to know how the divorce affected Eleana.

Her mother didn't think it was relevant. Turning to Eleana, she said something angrily in Greek. Eleana stared at her lap, trying not to cry.

Finally, Eleana looked at her mother and said softly, "The divorce was hard on me."

"No it wasn't," said her mother. "It was not."

———

All spring, Eleana had been counting down the days. When I called her after lunch, she already knew the numbers.

Forty days until she hands her crown to the new Miss Teen America.

Thirty-one days until she moves out of her mother's house.

Thirty-two days until she starts college.

Eleana wanted to live in a dorm at Florida Atlantic University, to have girlfriends and slumber parties. Instead, her mother got her an apartment in Boca Raton.

So that when she comes to visit, she can stay with Eleana.

SHINE LIGHT ON PEOPLE IN THE SHADOWS. There's an old adage that the best thing journalism can do is let people be heard. Some of my favorite parts of sharing stories are illuminating alternative worlds and viewpoints, imparting knowledge, helping people see each other—and themselves. When the beauty queen finally told her mother, "The divorce was hard on me," her mother shut her down. Of course. But at least, for the first time, she heard her daughter say those words.

AFTER THE STORY

Eleana moved across the state, studied international business at Florida Atlantic University. Her maternal grandparents and mom paid her way. "But we kept butting heads," she said. "It was their way or the highway."

For three years, Eleana didn't talk to her mom or her mom's parents, except for on holidays.

Then on Father's Day 2016, when she was a junior in college, she started thinking about who she was, who she wanted to be. She wants to help people. "And I can't do that until I take care of my own business at home," she said. So she called her dad and saw him for the first time in five years.

She gave him a box she'd made, filled with 250 memories—one for every week they'd lost being apart. She wrote each on a slip of paper, like a fortune cookie message: the first time he took her fishing, that day he made a mudslide in their backyard, her birthday party when he helped her build a sandcastle. "And you were the only dad there."

"I never wanted him to forget all the things he did for me growing up," she said.

She spent that night in her room at his new house. "It was like a time capsule from when I was 13," she said. "He'd taken everything from his old house and recreated my room exactly as it was. The pencils and colored erasers were even still in the desk, everything just as I left it."

Eleana and her dad went to Greece, to see his dad. They judged a beauty contest together.

In 2020, she met Pedro. He convinced her that despite differences, your family is still your family, and no one can replace them. He wanted to meet her grandparents and her mom.

Eleana started with her grandparents. Then she ran into her mom at a restaurant. The next day, she introduced them all to her partner. "I had to learn to accept who they are, and love them regardless," she said. "You grow up and learn grace, to say it's okay."

She talks about her time at the camp for troubled girls "all the time," she said. "I'd love to go back." But she hasn't been camping since.

21

FIND THE BRUISE ON THE APPLE

Ask uncomfortable questions, celebrate conflict, mine regrets

The Old Daredevil: Evel Knievel Comes Back to Earth

Reported over four days; written in two. Published August 5, 2007

BEFORE THE STORY

A former editor has this theory: If an apple looks too shiny, too perfect, it probably isn't real. If it has a bruise, you know it is. So if a subject seems too good to be true, search for the bad spot. Ask about mistakes they made, things they wish they'd done differently, regrets.

This isn't the story I set out to tell. And my editor made me put myself in it—because I discovered the dark spot when Evel Knievel made me cry.

Someone had seen the old daredevil at a bank and called the newsroom: He's still alive! In the 1970s, my dad and I had watched him fly a rocket-powered motorcycle over the Snake River Canyon.

When I called Evel, he said I could come over. When I got there, he started yelling: "Your questions are so stupid! Why are you wasting my time? Just get me a beer, then go!"

I phoned my editor from the car, still shaking. My editor asked, "Did you write everything down?"

For his last trick, daredevil Evel
Knievel returned to Butte, Montana,
where he had grown up—and gone
to jail. Photographer: Melissa Lyttle

THE STORY

The old daredevil tips back in his recliner, nursing a blue lollipop. His small white dog, Rocket, slumbers in his lap. On the Food Network, a chef is shouting. Evel Knievel grabs the remote, fumbles with the buttons. "Blasted thing," he growls. "I can't turn it down." He slams the clicker on the table beside him. Buries his face in his hands. "I spend my days right here, mostly," he says, without lifting his head.

It's been three weeks since his second stroke. He is always tired, sometimes addled. Knievel is 68 but has the body of—well, of a man held together with pins and plates. "I used to go all over the world," he grumbles. "I used to travel eight months a year. Now I can't even drive."

He takes 11 pills in the morning, a dozen at night. They keep his blood flowing and his transplanted liver working. They ease the arthritis that burns his back, arms and legs. It hurts like hell, being mortal.

It's a hot morning in July. In two weeks he is supposed to fly to his hometown of Butte, Mont., for the annual festival in his honor: Evel Knievel Days. He'll wave from the passenger seat of a pickup, sign some autographs, try to impersonate the man he used to be.

"This is my last performance," he says. "If I make it."

If I make it. How many times do you think Evel Knievel has said those words?

———

Usually he did make it, piloting his motorcycle over cars, snakes, sharks, buses. But we remember him just as well for the times his cycle came up just a teensy bit short. Knievel scattered pieces of himself at Caesars Palace, in Wembley Stadium, in San Francisco's Cow Palace.

He was the first Jackass.

His aim was uncertain, but his timing was exquisite. In the mid-1970s, America was booing its returning soldiers and booting its president. In vroomed Knievel, wearing a red, white and blue leather jumpsuit, a hero's cape and a showoff's thick gold chains.

"Evel was the king of bling," his friend Bill Rundle says. "And they didn't even know what bling was back then."

He gave Americans someone to cheer for, or at least provided

RANTS ROCK. I used to shy away from people railing at city council meetings, car crashes, Little League games. Now I relish those outbursts. How someone handles frustration and anger illuminates a lot about them. Pay attention to body movements, gestures, facial expressions, tone of voice. Evel was grumbling long before I asked the first question. And I wrote it all down.

WRITE TO KICKERS. Of course the ending of a story is important. But the ending of each section is, too. If you want readers to stay with you, you have to give them something to wonder about, care about or need to know. It could be a cliff-hanger. A telling quote. Or a question: Will he make it?

CELEBRITY STATUS. When you're writing about a celebrity, it's important to recap their career—maybe even more important to put it in context. How did he gain such a following? Why was he famous at this time in history? What did he mean to America? I tried to sum up his accomplishments and failures, and make him relevant for a younger generation who hadn't heard of him: He was the first *Jackass*. He rose to such stardom in the 1970s because our country needed a hero.

a welcome distraction. Twelve days after Richard Nixon resigned, Knievel jumped 13 Mack trucks. On Oct. 25, 1975, more than half the country watched him leap over 14 Greyhound buses in Ohio—more than watched the "Thrilla in Manila" fight between Joe Frazier and Muhammad Ali. Knievel had money, fame and—he doesn't mind telling you—"oh God, more than 1,000 women."

And now here he is, struggling just to breathe. White wisps are all that's left of the thick hair that once spilled from his helmet. After weeks in the hospital, his golf course tan has paled. Gone are the gold chains, the diamond pinky ring, that swagger.

If life delivered neat endings, Evel Knievel would have gone out in a flash of glory, at the far end of a row of buses, or maybe in the bottom of the Snake River Canyon, which he famously failed to clear in 1974. Instead, after two marriages, four kids, a liver transplant, lung disease and a couple of strokes, the old daredevil sees this year's annual Evel Knievel Days as his ending. It will have to do.

"He was such an icon," Rundle says. "You don't believe icons can get old."

His wife, Krystal, 38, calls him by his given name, Bob.

They live with two spoiled Maltese in a modest Clearwater condo. You have to punch in a code to get through the lobby. The name above their code is an alias. When it said Knievel, drunks kept coming by late at night, buzzing their number.

An oil painting of Evel dominates his front hallway. A bronze statue of him stands on a bookshelf, surrounded by photos of his 11 grandkids.

The dog is snoring in Knievel's lap. Another chef is yelling on TV. Evel turns to a visitor and says, "Why don't you get up and get yourself a beer?"

It's 11 a.m. The visitor declines, thanks him. Knievel barks, "Then why don't you go get me one?"

"Christ almighty," he grouses when he finally gets his Michelob Ultra. He takes a swig.

"Forgive me," he says, "for using the Lord's name in vain."

"Okay, ask your questions. Hurry up. I don't have all day."

He doesn't want to waste whatever time he has left repeating things everyone already knows. For God's sake, people have written books about him. George Hamilton played him in a movie.

FIND THE BRUISE ON THE APPLE

The Bionic Woman wrapped her arms around his waist on an episode of her show.

He is tired of people pestering him, asking stupid questions. What kind of questions? "That's a dumb question."

What was your favorite jump? "Jesus. Any jump I landed was my favorite."

What does it feel like to crash? "What the hell do you think it feels like? Christ almighty. It hurts."

Why did you do what you did? "Because I could. I could do the impossible. And it sure beat selling insurance."

Was it worth it? "What kind of stupid question is that? I'm still here, aren't I? Now hurry up. I'm running out of air."

———

From the time he could pedal a bike, Robert Craig Knievel wanted to fly.

He was born in 1938, in the desolate mining town of Butte. His parents divorced before he was 2 and left him and his younger brother to be raised by grandparents. "Bobby" was 8 when he got his first wheels. He taught himself to ride, then jump. By 12, he'd totaled four bikes and moved on to motorcycles. Everyone around Butte knew Bobby. He'd race through flower beds, leap curbs, pop wheelies through parking lots.

He wanted to be as flashy as Liberace, as brave as Roy Rogers, as beloved as Elvis. The legend goes that when he got tossed in jail for—what else?—reckless driving, a judge nicknamed him Evil Knievel. Later, Evel changed the spelling so he wouldn't seem so bad.

He worked as a hunting guide, then sold insurance and Hondas. If you beat him at arm wrestling, you won a free motorcycle. Some say he scammed people with a security guard business.

"A lot of Butte people really resent him to this day," says Mike Byrnes, who went to school with Knievel and now runs Butte Tours. "He's the most famous guy to come out of Butte. But we don't have any Evel sites on our tours. We've got a T-shirt, though. 'Butte, Montana: Birthplace of Evel Knievel. We apologize.'"

Knievel was 27, married and a father, when he set out to become a professional daredevil. He did everything: built the ramps, booked the venues, promoted the show. Pay him $500 and he'd jump two cars.

Then sponsors began upping the ante. Think you can jump six cars? We'll give you $1,500. Try seven—we'll make it $2,000.

EMBRACE THE EVIL. If someone yells at you, don't take it personally. Try not to react. Write down everything—even your reaction. Those moments might elevate your story. Evel made me feel like the worst, most annoying reporter ever. I didn't know what to do to salvage the interview. So I just kept taking it, and taking notes, as tears dripped onto my legal pad—trying to buy time. I never envisioned that scene as the opener.

NOW AND THEN. An easy and effective way to structure a narrative is to bounce between present and past. Many of my stories are structured around scene/background/scene/background, with the narrative unfolding every other section. If you get readers sucked in, they'll follow you through what you need them to know: the history, context or science. When you entice them with chocolate, they're more likely to eat the broccoli.

TAKE IN THE TOWN. Where someone comes from often shapes their personality or view of the world. Go there, if you can, or take readers there if you're from there. Walk the streets, smell the trees, talk to the locals. Wonder what it would have been like to grow up there, 70-some years ago. Almost everyone in Butte knew Evel. No one had anything nice to say.

Soon Knievel was coming up with his own stunts. How much would you pay me to jump buses? Sharks? The Grand Canyon?

"He always figured he'd at least try," says Rundle, who traveled with Knievel's entourage.

"This one time at the Cow Palace, he knew his bike wasn't getting up enough speed to make the jump. But Evel would never back down. He jumped anyway. That one broke him up pretty good."

Rundle was with Knievel in 1974 when the federal government said he couldn't jump the Grand Canyon. So Knievel had to settle for the Snake River Canyon. Promoters promised him $6 million.

For a week before the jump, ABC showed specials on how the stunt could go wrong, why the "Skycycle"—more rocket ship than motorcycle—wouldn't make it.

"They kept going over all the ways he could die," Rundle says. "And I don't think Evel thought he'd make it, either. But you know he'd just sit there watching all the reports and he never said anything to anyone. He never seemed to react. It was eerie."

———

Knievel needs oxygen. He lifts the dog from his lap, heaves himself out of the recliner.

He shuffles across his living room in white socks, past the Evel Knievel light-switch plate in his bedroom hall, past the photo of his second wedding, at Caesars Palace, where he once crashed so badly he spent a month in a coma.

Knievel opens his closet and pulls out the tubes that tether him to a tank. He flips on the machine, drinks in the air.

On the way back to the living room, he passes a table piled high with fan mail. A guy from St. Paul, Minn., sent an old photo of Evel leaping in front of a Ferris wheel. "I'm just wondering how you're doing," the man wrote. "You're extremely brave. I respect you." Knievel answers every inquiry—as long as he gets a self-addressed envelope, with postage.

"I never thought the empire would last this long," he says, easing back into his chair. He closes his eyes. The shadow of a smile seems to tug at his mouth.

Then he looks up, confused. "What year is it again?"

———

In the winter of 1976, Knievel wiped out after jumping a tank of live sharks, crushing both arms and his collarbone and suffering a severe concussion. He also smashed into a cameraman, who eventually lost an eye.

He did a few exhibitions after that—some with his son Robbie, now a grownup daredevil—then quit. He spent his time on golf courses and in casinos, gambling on everything, sometimes $100,000 on a football game.

Years later, after the IRS took some of his homes, Knievel cruised the highways in his custom RV, visiting car dealerships and Harley shops, towing a trailer filled with his past: the rocket he'd ridden into the canyon, five motorcycles, a skeleton illustrating the 35 bones he'd shattered. His appearances helped sell cars, put money in his pocket.

Then came liver disease and the strokes. Knievel can't go on the road anymore. He still does a few endorsements: Mini Coopers, a slot machine, a line of custom motorcycles. Last year, Evel toys were re-released. Even so, money is tight now; Knievel is trying to sell his custom RV.

These days, he says, he doesn't need an adrenaline rush. "The most joy I get now is waking up and wrapping my arms around my wife," he says. "But sometimes she sleeps way over on the other side of the bed and it's hard to get to her. Especially with the dogs between us."

More and more, he thinks about the life after this one. He says he knows God has a place for him. "My grandmother who raised me, she lived to 103, she'll be there waiting for me. And I hope she'll forgive me for all I put her through," Knievel says.

"She'll point her finger at me and say, 'I told you so, Bobby. I told you everything you wanted to do in life, you could. You can fall many times, but as long as you keep getting up, you'll never be a failure.'"

———

Evel Knievel needs a nap.

It's a couple of hours into the interview and he's talking about a stunt he never got to do. He wanted to jump out of a plane without a parachute and land in a haystack. "They never let me do it," he says. "That's the only . . ."

He nods off. Ten seconds go by, then 20. The dog licks his hand.

When Knievel wakes and sees the visitor still sitting there, he gets angry. He's embarrassed, frustrated, in pain. "You have to go," he says, narrowing his eyes. "I have been known to have quite a temper. And I'm taking medication to stop it. But now I've got to get some sleep."

He's yelling now, pointing a crooked finger. "You gotta go. NOW!"

FIND JOY. Many people are quick to share their complaints. It's also important to ask them what makes them happy. Something as big as watching their kids grow up. Or as small as their tomatoes sprouting. Asking about joy also is a good way to turn around a bad conversation and find something to like in even the most angry people. Evel just wanted to hug his wife in bed.

FACE DEATH. It's not always easy to ask people about dying. But when they're living in its shadow, you have to know. How often do you think about death? What do you think it will be like? What happens next? Are you afraid? Why? Or why not? Exploring the end is powerful. Most people have thought about it, picturing angels or an abyss. Evel was sure his grandmother would greet him.

As the visitor exits, Knievel waves. "Thanks for coming," he calls. "Maybe I'll see you in Butte."

———

A couple of weeks later Knievel makes it to Montana, but barely. Instead of staying with his daughter or in a hotel, he checks into an assisted living facility because he's weak and having trouble breathing.

"He's not doing very well," says his old friend, Bill Rundle. "But he says he'll hold on, at least long enough to lead the parade."

Rundle created Evel Knievel Days in 2002 as a way of honoring his buddy. The event brought bikers from across the West. Rundle hired stunt cyclists and built a dirt ramp in the middle of town and even got Robbie Knievel to be there for his dad.

Last year, about 30,000 people packed Butte for Evel days. More than 100 paid $100 each to dine with "Himself," as the program calls him. Organizers had sold tickets to this year's event long before Knievel had the stroke.

The day before the festival, Rundle is concerned. "We had a tearful two-hour conversation last night," he says. "Evel says he's not going back to Florida. He's going to get through this last show. Then he wants to die right here in Butte."

Late Friday afternoon, more than 1,000 cycles—Hondas and Harleys, trikes and choppers—fill the street in front of the Finlen Hotel. A white pickup is parked at the head of the pack. It's striped with red and blue, sprinkled with stars. Even the leather seats are custom Evel. This is his ride.

Soon Rundle slides into the truck. He looks tired and worried. Are those tears in his eyes?

The bikers follow, revving their engines. The ground seems to tremble.

"Where's Evel?" people in the crowd keep asking.

Four teenagers climb into the painted pickup. Turns out they're Evel's grandchildren. The truck pulls forward, without Knievel.

Evel misses his own parade.

———

That night in the hotel banquet room, Evel images are everywhere. Plastic place mats show a blurry Knievel in his Skycycle. A mannequin in his jumpsuit is propped by the bar.

The head table is empty.

"Ladies and gentlemen," Rundle says. "Welcome to the Evel

Knievel social." He pauses. A few people clap. "Evel wasn't feeling too well tonight. They had to take him to the hospital to find out what's wrong.

"But you know him. He just called. He's already checked out. He's on his way back here to join you," Rundle says.

"He doesn't want anyone saying they want their money back."

The salads have just been served when Knievel limps in, leaning on two friends. He sits down gingerly, then waves. The hospital band is still around his wrist.

"Everyone, please, let's enjoy our dinner," he says. "I just had a little spell with blood pressure. I think it was too much heat and overexertion on my part. But I'm okay now. Let's eat."

Breathing heavily, pausing between bites, Knievel shovels salad into his mouth while people walk up to shake his shaking hand.

After the entree is served, Knievel summons one of his helpers. He pushes back his chair, leans on the handle of his oxygen tank. "Thank you all very much. I had a tough day," he says.

He unfolds a small square of paper, thanks his doctors and his sponsors, says he has a new custom motorcycle company and there's a rock opera being written about him. It's like that time at Wembley Stadium, where he crashed and broke everything and got up and talked to the crowd anyway.

"I hate to duck out right now," he says. "But I just have to. Thank you so much for coming to see me. God bless all of you."

When he stands up the audience does too, clapping and chanting "Evel, Evel, Evel!" Forty-two minutes after he arrived, Knievel makes his way to the door, propped up by a friend, but still standing.

END ON HOPE. When I interviewed Evel at his home, I saw how frail he was. But I never doubted he'd make it to Butte. I expected to watch him emcee the festivities, sign autographs, regain some semblance of his celebrity self. When he barely made it to the banquet, I thought about ending with how people had to prop him up. But I watched him struggle to get there, to still be the man they had admired. That was his last public appearance. He died a few days later.

Counselor Kedine Johns thought girls at
the drop-out prevention school should
learn more than reading and math. So she
started an etiquette class, with plastic
forks. Photographer: Kathleen Flynn

22

USE THEIR VOICES

Listen to their language,
write like they talk,
let them characterize
themselves

The Swan Project: For Troubled Girls, Etiquette Classes Open Another World

Reported in two months; written in a week. Published March 30, 2010

BEFORE THE STORY

At first, I wasn't sure this was a story. When the school director called me, saying they were about to start an etiquette class for troubled teenage girls, I thought, "Don't they have a lot more to worry about than which fork to use?" But I agreed to meet the young teacher who was putting the program together.

She told me her students made her sad. They had suffered such hardships and loss, were struggling with self-esteem. She wanted to teach them so much more than manners. She hoped to help them learn to accept themselves—and each other—and give them skills to navigate the world.

Every Tuesday for two months, a photographer and I went to the school and sat silently in the class, watching and listening. Each of the girls had their own vernacular, but they used a lot of the same slang. The banter between them was funny and often revealing. I used a lot more dialogue in this story than I usually do, because I was privy to all their conversations and I wanted to capture their individual voices and viewpoints without just paraphrasing. Instead of describing them, I let them characterize themselves.

After each class, we'd interview the girls and their teacher and talk about what we'd witnessed, how they felt, what it meant.

I could have done a story on the class of 10 young women or told it from the teacher's perspective. But I quickly zeroed in on three girls I wanted to be my main characters. These three were totally different, in looks, background and personality. I wanted to capture that diversity and see if the program would change them. Fortunately, they were willing to let me in — and let me come home with them.

THE STORY

BUILD THE SET. Giving readers a sense of place, dropping them into a scene, puts them there with the characters and gets them more invested in the story. Think of it like designing a stage set: What do you want the audience to see? How do you want them to feel? Which details matter?

They had just finished lunch, were just crumpling paper napkins into trash bins, when the call came through the school speakers:

"Will the following girls please report to the conference room . . ."

The teenagers looked at each other. What was going on?

"Lindsey," said the voice coming through the speaker. A girl with green bangs hung her head.

"Spring," the voice continued. In the corner of the lunchroom, a 15-year-old huddled behind her black curtain of hair. Dark liner smudged her eyes. She looked as if she had been crying.

The voice called several other names. Finally it said: "Chayna." A girl with a short ponytail cringed. The look on her face said: What did I do now?

They trudged into the conference room, 10 girls wearing a kind of slacker uniform—jeans and flip-flops and baggy school T-shirts. They dropped into swivel chairs around a long table.

A whiteboard listed some of the things that could get you in trouble here at PACE Center for Girls: "Racist slurs. Smuggling drugs or weapons. Bad behavior."

On another wall, a framed print showed a dirt road winding beneath cherry trees. The picture carried a quote from Norman Vincent Peale. "People become really remarkable when they start thinking that they can do things."

The girls didn't read the walls. They spun in their chairs, played with their hair.

Guidance counselor Kedine Johns waited for them to get settled. She was 25, slender and graceful, with long dark hair, almond eyes and perfect posture. On weekends, she modeled for charity events. At school she always wore pencil skirts, stiletto heels and just enough makeup. To the girls at PACE, such a woman seemed completely alien.

"Today, I'm starting a new class for you all," the counselor said. "It's a semester-long group session on etiquette."

The girls groaned. One yawned. Another propped her feet on the table.

"Do any of you know what etiquette is?"

None of them did.

The PACE Center for Girls—a free school operated by a state-wide nonprofit agency—is in a long, low office building in downtown Lakeland. It has 45 students. They are 12 to 17, almost all living in poverty, each struggling with something.

Their parents are in jail or they have been locked up themselves. They have drug problems. They have babies. A few have hurt people. Several have tried to kill themselves. Many have dropped out or been kicked out of other schools.

PACE is their last resort.

The acronym stands for Practical Academic Cultural Education. Students learn English and math and history, but also how to look for a job and get along with their parents. They work in small groups, and they know it's okay to leave class to cry or scream or just talk to someone.

Kedine Johns—the students call her Miss Kedine—became a PACE guidance counselor in January 2009, after receiving her master's degree in counseling. At first, she cried every night. The girls were all so hurt, so damaged. She worked with one girl who got adopted after her mother died—only to have her adoptive mother die, too. Another teen got pregnant and miscarried three times in a year.

"So much sadness," Miss Kedine recalled telling her own mother.

What struck her even more was how the girls behaved. Miss Kedine grew up in a big family in rural Jamaica, sheltered and loved. She was raised to be a lady and to appreciate manners. She never fidgeted, never seemed flustered. In the hard plastic chairs at school, she sat like a queen.

She never imagined girls could be like this.

The PACE girls swore. They mumbled and slouched. They ate with their fingers and let boys call them, "Hey, Baby." Many had never had their hair done or used makeup. They wore un-

SET OFF A SENTENCE. Letting a single sentence have its own paragraph gives it power, alerting readers that this idea or detail is important. Don't do it too often, though. It only works if it stays unusual. And the sentence, of course, has to be meaningful and intriguing—something that you might Tweet out to entice people to read the story.

dershirts because they couldn't afford bras or didn't know how to buy them. They didn't say thank you.

Other instructors could teach the students to master algebra and read a map. But what good would that do if the girls went for a job interview wearing flip-flops, chewing their hair, not knowing to cross their ankles or look the interviewer in the eye?

Last fall, Miss Kedine approached her principal with a plan. She wanted to create a new class in etiquette. She would write her own curriculum, using information from books, the Internet and the skills she had learned in childhood. Over eight weeks, with a small group of girls, she would cover everything from deodorant to dating to dinner parties.

Principal Michele DeLoach was intrigued. Certainly the girls needed polishing, and she wanted to get to them before life hardened them even more.

She just wasn't sure they would listen, or care.

Would a girl who had been sexually abused want to hear about proper behavior on a date? Would a teenager who was always hungry have the patience to learn about dinner parties?

It was *My Fair Lady*, with a young Jamaican teacher as Henry Higgins and a bunch of coarse small-town kids as Eliza Doolittle.

"We don't have funds to start a new program," the principal told Miss Kedine. "But if you want to try it, I'm behind you. You can handpick your girls."

The counselor called her class *Introduction to Etiquette*.

The principal called it *The Swan Project*.

———

In the conference room, on that warm Tuesday in October, Miss Kedine smoothed her skirt and looked over her girls.

Lindsey seemed angry: arms folded, one foot tapping under the table. Spring was still hiding behind her dark hair. Chayna looked bored.

Miss Kedine took a breath.

"Sooo, etiquette," she started. None of the girls looked up. "You know, manners, class, being a lady."

"Who wants to be a lady?" someone muttered. Someone else laughed.

"You are all ladies, whether you want to be or not. This is about how you carry yourself, how you present yourself to the world."

Lindsey leaned forward, cut her eyes. "Okay, I mean that's cool and all," she said. "But is there a reason we have to do this? I don't really want to be here."

The counselor forced a smile, soldiered on.

"We're going to learn a lot of interesting stuff this semester, like how to shake hands and address people. No, 'Whuzzups?' or 'Hey girl!' in here," she said.

The girls looked confused. "What's wrong with that?" Lindsey asked.

"We're going to learn about grooming, hygiene and makeup," Miss Kedine continued. "Posture, eye contact. The proper way to sit."

"There's a proper way to sit?" someone asked. At least now some were listening.

"We'll talk about buttering bread and cutting meat. Eating soup and setting a table. And at the end of the semester, there will be a treat."

A few girls looked up.

"A final exam."

They looked away again. Some treat.

Miss Kedine explained: The last class would be a field trip. She would take them to a fancy restaurant with china plates, linen napkins and a full setting of silverware. She would join them all at a proper luncheon.

"What's a luncheon?" asked Chayna.

Most of these girls had never left Polk County; one thought Tampa was a state. Of the 10 in class, only three had ever eaten at a restaurant other than a fast-food joint. Spring asked: Does Golden Corral count?

Miss Kedine had grown up with elegant restaurant dinners, big formal family meals at home. Until she moved to Florida when she was 15, she had never been to a Burger King, never seen people eat with their fingers. Now she would have to help these girls understand her world.

"It will be so much fun and we'll get all dressed up, and we'll get to see how beautiful you girls can be," she told them. Again, the girls groaned.

None of them—not one—owned a dress.

Lindsey

The second week, Miss Kedine moved her girls from the conference room to the cafeteria, where the air smelled like fried food, body odor and cheap perfume.

The students slid into plastic chairs and crossed their arms. Spring cupped her chin in her hands. Chayna balled her fists. Two girls already had been kicked out of the group for fighting.

CHANNEL THEIR THOUGHTS. The girls didn't utter, "Some treat." Those were my words, not in quotes. When the teacher mentioned the final exam, I watched them turn away. I knew that's when she lost them. So afterward, I asked them what they thought of having an exam, and they said if the class was supposed to be fun, why'd they have to take a test? That wasn't in the moment as the scene unfolded. I paraphrased their thoughts instead.

"Okay, sit up straight," Miss Kedine said. "Both feet on the floor. Today we're going to talk about respect."

"Oh I got a lot of respect," one girl said, rolling her eyes. "For me."

The counselor let it pass. She started to talk about how you should respect your parents when she noticed she was one girl short.

Lindsey was missing. Again.

"Does anyone know where she is?"

Lindsey Kennedy, proud to be "almost 18," was the oldest girl in etiquette class, and the most popular. She was a good listener, patient and always eager to help. Buy someone a soda, give someone a ride.

But the other girls didn't know much about her, didn't understand why she missed school so often. They didn't know that helping others was Lindsey's way of masking her own hurt.

Lindsey's parents split when she was little. She and her younger brother and sister bounced between their homes for years. Both parents later married other people and then divorced again. Her dad lost his job, and her mom got mixed up with meth.

Lindsey had been a good student, a cheerleader, even a coach for her little sister's squad. Now she was skipping classes, hanging out with the wrong kids, crashing on people's couches. She dropped out of school in 10th grade.

"I've been pretty much grown and on my own," she said, "since I was 14."

She had sex with a boy once, but it felt wrong. Soon she started dating girls. When she told her dad she was gay, he wouldn't speak to her at first. She told herself she didn't care; what did she need his approval for?

Lindsey's closest friend was a girl she had known most of her life. Candy was the kind of friend, she said, who made you believe in yourself. You're smart, Lindsey remembered her saying. You can do anything. Candy wanted Lindsey to go back to school and become a nurse, just as Lindsey had always said she would.

One night about a year ago, Candy came over to Lindsey's uncle's house, where she was staying. The girls watched TV and listened to music. They didn't drink or take drugs, Lindsey said (the police later confirmed this). The next morning Lindsey learned that Candy had been killed in a car accident on her way home.

CONFIRM IF YOU CAN. I didn't ask Lindsey if she and her friend had been drinking or doing drugs the night Candy died. But she offered that detail, as if it was important to her. I wanted to include that but had to prove it was true. So I pulled the police report from the accident. Whenever possible, get public records. They give authority to writing and often contain great details.

She got Candy's name tattooed on the back of her neck, to honor her. She started going to PACE, got a job slinging tacos at Tijuana Flats and saved enough money to buy an ancient Camaro. She put Candy's picture in the dashboard, by the instrument panel, for inspiration.

Lindsey's classmates didn't know about her loss, or what her life was like now. Most afternoons, after a full day of school, she picked up her nephew at daycare, took him home, changed his diaper and fed him peanut butter and jelly—or something. She sat next to him at the breakfast bar, eating cereal or a sub or whatever passed for her dinner that night.

Forks were not usually required.

When her uncle got home, Lindsey went to work, often pulling a full shift, 3 to 11 p.m. After that, she just wanted to go somewhere and collapse. Lately she was staying with her uncle, though sometimes she bunked with friends, or at her dad's, or in the Camaro.

After all that, she was often too tired or overwhelmed to go to school. Sometimes she stayed away for days, and Miss Kedine would go looking for her. She always found her asleep.

Lindsey still talked to Candy even though Candy was gone. Behind her cracked steering wheel, smoking a Marlboro Menthol, Lindsey would tell Candy about her job, her new girlfriend, even about etiquette.

When the class met for the third time, Lindsey strolled into the lunchroom and plopped into a chair beside Chayna. No one asked where she had been, and she didn't offer.

She picked at her fingernails while Miss Kedine talked about hygiene—brushing your teeth, showering and shaving. Stuff she already knew.

Lindsey didn't think she needed this class. Anyone could see she was more refined than some of the other girls. She wore lots of jewelry: three necklaces, jangly bracelets, rings on every finger. She underscored her eyes with navy liner and smiled when she spoke. And she highlighted her hair with a different color every week, often pulling it into a ponytail or fountain.

Today her hair was dark eggplant, streaked with gold.

Besides, she knew how to behave in a nice restaurant: She had been to Olive Garden.

But Miss Kedine had chosen her for a reason: Lindsey would graduate soon, and the counselor saw this as a chance to give the girl a shine.

She also knew that if Lindsey bought in, the other girls might do the same.

When Miss Kedine began talking about looking for work, Lindsey sat up.

"Do you know the right way to greet a stranger," the counselor asked, "someone who might meet you for an interview?"

She showed the girls how to introduce themselves and shake hands firmly. "You don't have to squeeze, but don't be flimsy," she said. She made each of them practice with her. "Okay," she told Lindsey. "But don't pull away so fast. You want to hold on for at least a couple of seconds." Lindsey nodded.

"And look me in the eye," said Miss Kedine. "You want to make eye contact, let people know you're listening." Lindsey stared at her counselor, still holding her hand. Miss Kedine laughed. "It's okay to blink."

Next, they worked on posture. Back straight, shoulders squared, no slouching—whether you're sitting or standing. "The way you carry yourself says a lot about you," said Miss Kedine. "Your bearing, the way you sit and walk."

She told the girls to get a book. Any hardback book. Lindsey grabbed a Stephen Hawking book, and Spring took one about co-dependency. "You're going to need to hold yourself very straight to balance your book," Miss Kedine said, planting a thesaurus on her head. "Don't shuffle. Lift your feet. Chin up, don't look down."

She glided across the lunchroom, the book barely wobbling. She stopped in front of Chayna, who hadn't bothered to get a book, and placed the thesaurus on her head. It slid off. "You're going to have to practice this," she said. "You've got to be able to do this in heels."

Chayna shook her head, dislodging the book. "No way, never. I can't walk in those."

"That's why you need to practice," Miss Kedine said. "Now let's see you all try."

Lindsey led the way, taking small steps, holding steady. The other girls tried to follow. But Spring kept staring at her feet. Chayna padded heavily in her flip-flops. Their books kept sliding off.

Soon Miss Kedine turned to a new subject: how to behave on a date.

"What do you do when someone holds the door for you, or pulls out your chair?"

TAKE IN TITLES. When you're introducing books to a scene, always check the titles. They might not matter, but they usually do. In this case, I'm not even sure the girls or teacher looked at the words on the spines. But I did. And the titles they chose seemed to sum up aspects of their personalities, even if it wasn't on purpose.

"Why they pulling out your chair?" asked one of the girls.

"Oh," the counselor smiled. "They're not trying to dis you. It's a common act of courtesy. And you don't plop into your chair, you slide. Smoothing your skirt beneath you."

The girls laughed. As if any of them would ever wear a skirt.

Soon the hour was over, and Miss Kedine told the girls she would see them next Tuesday.

That weekend, Lindsey had a job interview at the coffee shop in Lakeland Square Mall. She liked Tijuana Flats, but this job sounded better and it paid more. She was nervous as she drove to the interview, tumbling over everything Miss Kedine had told her.

When the manager of Barnie's Coffee & Tea Co. extended his hand, Lindsey shook it, smiled and met his eyes. When he pulled out a chair for her, she slid in gracefully, in her new, non-ripped jeans. She told him she had experience, worked hard, loved people and wanted all the hours he could give her.

She said, "I can handle a lot."

She started the next week.

Spring

For the fourth class, Miss Kedine brought in a big cardboard box. She set it on the long table in front of the lunchroom and greeted her girls.

Another student had been kicked out for fighting. Seven of the original 10 remained.

"Today you're going to get to do place settings," Miss Kedine said, bouncing a bit in her high heels. "I brought us all sorts of plates and cups and silverware."

She reached into the box and began unloading foam dishes and plastic utensils. The school couldn't afford china or flatware, so these items would have to do.

The utensils had colored dots on them, each one carefully applied by Miss Kedine herself. She handed out a printed guide to the colors. The fork with the red sticker was the dinner fork. The orange one was the seafood fork. Green was salad, yellow, cake.

The forks and plates and so forth were to be arranged according to a guide to holiday entertaining that Miss Kedine had printed from the Internet.

"Four forks?" Lindsey laughed. "Who needs four forks?" Her hair was ash blond now, with walnut streaks.

SET GUIDEPOSTS. Long stories need to be broken into sections, to make them less daunting, more digestible. Subheads can separate the segments. But I prefer signposts signaling a change in time, character or circumstance. To move through a school year, I've used months: August, September ... To move through police training, I used weeks: Week 2, Week 22. I separated this piece with people, each girl getting her own installment as we moved through the semester.

"You'll get four forks when we go out for our luncheon. And you'll need to know which one to use for what," Miss Kedine said. "Haven't any of you ever set a table?"

Chayna yawned. "I saw someone do that on TV one time. I didn't get it." Most of Chayna's diet—burgers, chicken nuggets and fries her mom brought home from her job at McDonald's—required no silverware.

Miss Kedine just shook her head. "Okay, girls, now come on up and get your place settings."

In the back of the room, Spring sat alone. As usual. When the other girls came forward, she didn't move. She just stared at the diagram, breathing hard, her hands shaking.

"Spring, you okay?" asked the counselor. All the girls turned to look. Spring covered her face with her sweaty hands. "Spring?"

Miss Kedine crossed the room, put her hand on Spring's shoulder, rubbed her back.

"It is a lot, isn't it? So many things to remember," the counselor said. Spring started sobbing. "It's okay. We'll all help you. You still have a month. You can practice at home."

The girl took her hands from her face, looked up at Miss Kedine. "You don't understand," she sighed.

"At my house we don't even have four forks."

———

Spring Waterloo could always feel the panic coming, small waves building to big. Whenever she was overwhelmed or scared, she had attacks. Her body would go numb. Her face melted into a blank mask.

It feels, she said, like someone is pressing a heavy board on your chest and you can't gulp enough air. It looks all wavy, like seeing everything in a funhouse mirror. It sounds as if you're underwater, everything all muffled and far away. It tastes like bile.

Miss Kedine had been working with Spring for months, even before this class started, trying to calm her. She felt she knew Spring's story, why she suffered.

Spring didn't think Miss Kedine could understand. The counselor was too pretty; everybody loved her.

What if you weren't like that? What if you hated your body, your face, even your stupid smile? What if your brother was smart and your sister was popular and your mom worked long hours and was always stressed and your daddy was the only one who really loved you—but then he died?

"How would you feel," Spring asked, "if that was you?"

She was 11 when her father had the heart attack. Spring remembers lying on the living room floor, watching Jerry Springer, calling her dad's cell phone to see why he hadn't come home. When her mother finally showed up with her brother and sister, everyone knew but her.

She wore a flowered dress to the funeral. She hadn't worn a dress since.

Over the next few years, she moved a dozen times. "We were always getting kicked out of places," she said. "Mostly we just couldn't make the rent."

By the time Spring got to Lakeland High, she was having panic attacks every day. She would be walking down the hall, daydreaming in math class, or standing in line in the cafeteria, and she'd just freak out. The second semester of ninth grade, she stopped going to school. Stopped going anywhere.

She got so scared of being alone, she wouldn't even take a shower. She was 14, and her mom had to bathe her.

She would sit in her room all day, using a razor blade to carve long, thin slices into her thighs. The feeling of warm blood trickling down her legs was like a drug, she said, "like I was blocking out all the other hurt and releasing happiness. Or something."

Did she want to kill herself? "I don't know," she said. "I didn't really care."

A private counselor suggested PACE and spent months convincing Spring that she could cope there. She finally enrolled in April 2009. And though the attacks came less frequently, they were just as strong.

She sat by herself at school, barely talked in class, never ate the free lunch. She wouldn't let anyone see her eat.

"Who wants to see a fat girl stuff her face?"

Spring's brother and sister were grown and gone. She lived with her mom, a paralegal, and her mom's boyfriend, "who sells cars or something."

When her mom had enough money to put gas in her van, she picked Spring up from school. Otherwise, Spring got a bus pass from one of the teachers and rode a couple of miles to her lonely duplex.

Laundry filled the living room—jeans and T-shirts wadded on the sofa, sweats and underwear spilling across the floor. Spring couldn't remember what was clean, what was dirty. The only table, in a corner that was meant to be a dining room, ached under weeks of newspapers, a CD player and a box of panty liners.

EXAMINE INDEFINITE ARTICLES. Using "the" instead of "a" adds emphasis, gives the event gravity. If I had written: "when her father had a heart attack," it wouldn't have seemed as important as "when her father had the heart attack." Changing the article made the sentence seem so final. And that's the way Spring saw it and said it.

LET HER SAY IT. When I described Spring, I talked about her hair and eyeliner. I didn't mention her size, though that was inexorably tied to her self-image. But when she said that quote about a fat girl stuffing her face, I knew I was going to include it, because that's how she sees herself. It's always a gift when people describe themselves, and you don't have to.

Spring and her mom never ate at the table. They almost never ate together.

Sometimes, when there was food, Spring would make herself a frozen pizza or waffle and eat sitting on her bed. Sometimes her mom would bring home a Publix sub. Sometimes Spring went hungry. She stashed packages of ramen noodles under her bed.

In her best moments she imagined a different future. She hoped to get a job at Publix, or maybe Winn-Dixie. She would start jogging and finish high school and maybe even go to college. Someday, she hoped, she would be a model, like Miss Kedine.

———

Each week in class, the counselor reiterated the finer points of table-setting.

She set the plastic foam cups before the girls, helped them position the plasticware. Start with the outside utensil, she told them, and work your way in.

She showed her students how to eat soup: "Scoop the spoon away from you; don't slurp." How to break off a bite of bread and butter that instead of spackling the whole slice. How to unfold their napkins, place them on their laps, and dab at their lips instead of wiping.

"And when you're cutting meat, you don't cut up the whole thing before you start eating," said Miss Kedine. "You cut a single bite, then eat that."

"Man, you should've brought us steak so we could practice!" Lindsey said.

"Well, I didn't bring steak," said Miss Kedine, reaching into the big box. "But I brought chicken."

Spring got scared. Was Miss Kedine going to make her eat in front of everyone?

The counselor pulled out squares of paper. The school couldn't afford real meat. So the girls had to practice on paper chicken.

———

The lessons continued: Hair care and color. Manicures and nail polish. Walking in high heels.

As the weeks passed, Miss Kedine showed the girls how to trim their cuticles, slide on a pair of stockings, use oatmeal to make a cleansing mask. She gave the girls facials. None of them had ever had a facial.

Miss Kedine saw the girls growing less resistant. They made

fewer snide comments, didn't slouch as much. Sometimes they stopped by her office to borrow deodorant.

Two days before Thanksgiving, she canceled class. PACE teachers went to Publix and bought turkey and stuffing, cornbread and cranberry sauce, and served a feast in the lunchroom.

Miss Kedine couldn't wait for her girls to show off their new manners. "Okay, everyone bring a plate up here and help yourselves," she called.

She smiled as her girls placed paper napkins in their laps. Nodded approvingly as they cut one bite of turkey at a time.

But when dessert arrived, etiquette excused itself and left the room.

A girl picked up the whipped cream and squirted it into her mouth. Another smeared some across Chayna's face. Someone flung banana pudding across the room and shouted, "Food fight!"

In the back of the room, Spring licked the frosting off an orange cupcake. It was the first time anyone had seen her eat.

On the eighth Tuesday, a tall girl strode into class, sporting long, scarlet nails, a hint of gloss shimmering on her lips.

"Oooh, look at Spring!" someone shouted. Her hair was mahogany now, with thick auburn highlights, tied with a white ribbon.

"Don't you look nice," said Miss Kedine. Blushing, Spring slid into her seat. But her hands didn't sweat, her stomach didn't clench. A month had gone by since she'd had a panic attack.

"I'm so glad you ladies are here. You know, this is our last class," said Miss Kedine. The girls groaned. The teenagers who had hated the idea of etiquette class now didn't want it to end.

"You all learned so much. You ladies surprised me," said Miss Kedine. "Now, let's go over what we have learned."

On the first day of class, the counselor had asked the girls about self-esteem. Lindsey liked herself, was proud of her independence. Chayna said she was "working on it." Back then, Spring wouldn't even look in the mirror.

"So where are you all today?" Miss Kedine asked. "Has anything changed?"

One girl said she felt fancy now, because she knew what rich people knew. Another said she was ready to meet the queen.

Spring crossed her ankles, combed back her hair with her fake nails.

PARSE PARLANCE. Most of this story is told from the girls' perspective and with their language. But when the food fight happened, I couldn't escape the irony: here they were trying to learn manners, and they start slinging banana pudding. So I switched the voice to sound proper, employing etiquette as a character, excusing itself and leaving the room.

FOOD MATTERS. What people eat, what's in their cabinets and refrigerators, whether they cook, get meals delivered, grab and go from a gas station or dine at a fancy restaurant says a lot about people and how they live their lives. Ask not only what they eat, but where. In their car? On their bed? In front of the TV? Food—or lack thereof—was a prevalent theme throughout this story.

"Okay, I'm about to be really honest with y'all here," she said. She glanced around the room at the faces of her new friends, then locked eyes with Miss Kedine.

"I've been working on this. You've helped me see it, some," she said, touching her forehead. "I guess, except for this pimple, maybe, like you been telling me, I am beautiful."

———

Chayna

As the girls left class, they talked about what they were going to wear to the luncheon three days from now.

Miss Kedine told them they had to wear skirts or dresses and heels. Or at least nice flats.

One girl had borrowed her sister's homecoming dress. Spring's mom had bought her a new dress, purple and white and black—the first one she had owned since her dad died.

Chayna shuffled past her classmates, not saying a word. Miss Kedine stopped her in the hall. "How about you? Do you have your outfit ready?"

Chayna kicked the floor with her flip-flop. Her mother kept telling her she would give her money to go shopping. But she never did.

Miss Kedine squeezed Chayna's shoulder.

"It's okay," she said. "We'll figure out something."

She started to ask Chayna what size she wore, whether she needed shoes too. But the girl was already running to catch her bus.

Chayna Castro lives in public housing in a small, dark apartment on the edge of Haines City. Chayna moved in with her mom only a few months earlier. She hardly knew her.

She had grown up mostly with her dad and sisters. Her brother was in jail, and her older sister had quit high school and had a baby at 15—Chayna's age now.

Years earlier, while Chayna's father was still working in the phosphate mines, they all shared a house and ate dinner together. Then her daddy got hurt at work.

They had to move into an apartment, then into a trailer, a motel, and the homes of relatives and friends. In 14 years, Chayna moved 15 times.

"My daddy just couldn't get it together," she said. He was frustrated, she said, and sometimes took it out on her.

"Mama was on drugs for a while. But she went to rehab. Daddy, I don't know. I wanted to stay with him."

USE THEIR VOICES

She was in sixth grade when she got kicked out of middle school for fighting. The other girl was asking for it, she said.

They sent Chayna to an alternative school, but she got expelled.

About that time, her daddy started leaving her alone with her little sister. First for a few hours, then a night, then two or three days at a time.

Chayna, who was 12, said she would make macaroni and cheese, heat a can of beans, tell her 10-year-old sister, "Don't worry. Daddy will be home soon."

After a few months, her daddy put her and her younger sister on a bus and sent them to live with their mom.

They found the rooming house address their dad had given them. But their mom was gone. An aunt took them in, then handed them off to another relative.

Chayna got so angry and frustrated. Nobody wanted her. Finally, she slashed her aunt's tires and wound up in foster care.

They stayed in strangers' homes for six months or a year, Chayna can't remember. She kept trying to kill herself: slashed her wrists, wrapped a radio cord around her neck, smothered herself with a pillow.

"I kept wanting to go home," she said. Only she didn't have one.

Finally, her dad came to get her. He sent her to PACE, where she learned she was three grade levels behind. When her mom got a subsidized apartment, she moved in with her.

She had been a student at PACE for more than a year, longer than she had ever lived in one place.

Now, she got up at 6 a.m. every weekday, walked a mile in the dark and rode three buses to get there—a 2½-hour trip each way.

———

Two days before the luncheon, Miss Kedine called Chayna into her office. The girl immediately wondered again what she had done wrong.

"So, you ready?" asked the counselor, stepping from behind her desk. She grabbed the keys to the school van and walked toward the front door.

Confused, Chayna followed. "Where we going?"

"We're going shopping."

Chayna hid her smile with her hands. She didn't want Miss Kedine to see how excited she was.

"Okay," she said. "But I'm not wearing no dress or no high heels."

They pulled up outside a strip mall. Miss Kedine led the way to Marshalls. As they walked through the double doors, toward the first few racks of clothes, Chayna's eyes got wide.

She couldn't remember the last time she had gone shopping. She didn't know what size she was or even what department she should be in. Girls? Juniors? Women's?

Miss Kedine looked her over, trying to guess. Chayna's T-shirts were so baggy you couldn't tell if she was square or hourglass-shaped. "Let's try a size 5," Miss Kedine said. "Looks like you might already be in women's."

Chayna followed Miss Kedine through the aisles, looking all around, never stopping to pull out a dress.

Miss Kedine held out several—a flowered skirt, a sundress, one with short sleeves.

Each time, Chayna scrunched her nose and shook her head.

"You're not even trying," the counselor said. "Here."

She started piling dresses into Chayna's arms, short ones and long ones, prints and solids. On the top, she draped a black dress with a golden sash.

"Hey, that one's cute," Chayna said. "Look at the skirt . . . it's all bubbly."

She dropped the other options on the seat in the fitting room and pulled on the black dress. Miss Kedine tied the sash behind her.

"Beautiful. Just beautiful," she said, turning Chayna in front of the mirror. "Who knew you had such a cute figure?"

"I feel naked," Chayna said into her fingers. But when she looked up and saw herself, she just stared. She had never seen herself in a dress, never dreamed she could look like such a lady.

"Now, we just need to get you some shoes," said Miss Kedine, helping her unzip the dress. "You said they had to be flats, right?"

"Well, I never walked in heels before," Chayna said.

"Then now is the time."

The counselor picked out low heels first, but Chayna wanted something spikier—like Miss Kedine's—so they settled on a pair of strappy black stilettos.

"I feel fake," Chayna said, wobbling down the aisle. "Like it's not me."

"Oh, it's you," said Miss Kedine. "Just look at you!"

"Thank you, Miss Kedine!" Chayna cried, taking off the shoes and cradling her new clothes. She kept unfolding the dress to look at it. "Oh, thank you."

Miss Kedine gave the clerk her charge card. The total came to $69.52; she would pay for this out of her own pocket.

At the subsidized apartment Chayna shared with her mom, that much money would cover a month's rent.

———

Chayna's mom was already there when she got home that afternoon.

"How was work?" Chayna asked, heading for her bedroom, swinging the Marshalls bag on her arm.

"Actually not too bad today," said Chayna's mom, Kathy Young, 47. "What you got there?"

Chayna had told her mom about etiquette class, about how they were learning to do facials and sit straight. But she didn't want to spoil the surprise about the dress.

"You'll see," she said.

Chayna spent a couple of minutes behind her closed door, then re-emerged.

"Do you like?" she asked, twirling down the narrow hall. The gold bow was crooked behind her back. She teetered in her heels.

Chayna's mom was sitting on the couch with her back to her daughter. When she turned and saw her, she gasped. Then she collapsed, sobbing.

"Oh my God, giiirl! Oh my God, I got chill bumps!"

You're so pretty, Chayna's mother told her. So grown.

"I wish I could be there to see you at the luncheon," she said, wiping tears.

She had never been to one of Chayna's school events. And she had never been to a luncheon.

———

Final Exam

Some girls celebrate their emergence into the adult world with a cotillion or a coming out party. For others it's a quinceanera, bat mitzvah or sweet 16. For the students in Miss Kedine's etiquette class, their proving party was lunch at a cafe overlooking the lake.

They had been working toward this for eight weeks, dreading it at times. But not now. They saw it as a chance to make Miss Kedine proud, to debut their new, grownup selves.

"Okay, ladies, let's get going. You only have an hour here to get ready," Miss Kedine called, leading them into the PACE

TRANSITION BETWEEN SECTIONS. Sometimes you have to jump from one scene to another or weave information into the narrative. Try to find ways to hand off the end of one section to start the next, like a baton in a relay race. At the end of the last section, I introduce Chayna's apartment and her mom. To start the next—another day entirely—I open with Chayna's mom in that apartment.

BE INCLUSIVE. I wanted to signify what this meal meant to the girls, what was at stake, how defining the moment might be. So I tried to give readers from different cultures context by comparing the luncheon to various coming-out parties and rituals. Just using Sweet 16 or Quinceañera would have been too narrow of a lens.

conference room that Friday. "Anyone need help with hair or makeup?"

The girls weren't listening. They were too busy ogling each other's dresses and shoes.

"Oooh, Chayna, that's so fine," one girl said as Chayna pulled the black dress from her backpack. Chayna looked angry: hands clenched, jaw set, like she might haul off and hit the girl. "Hey, what's wrong?"

Chayna kicked off her flip-flops, stomped into her high heels. "Broke up with my boyfriend on the bus this morning," she said. "He weren't treating me right, and I know better now." She pranced around, practicing her posture. "Hey, I got this," she said, suddenly sounding proud. "Only, heels hurt."

"I didn't bring no high heels," said Spring, shuffling by in dirty flip-flops.

Miss Kedine planted her hands on her hips. "I said no flip-flops."

"I don't have no other shoes."

"Why didn't you tell me?" snapped Miss Kedine. She marched into the hall, smoothed her skirt, then her hair, took two deep breaths and got out her key ring. The teachers kept rewards for the girls in a glass case in the front hall. Perfume and hair clips and rhinestone sandals.

"What size?" asked Miss Kedine, opening the case.

"I don't know."

So Miss Kedine took one of Spring's flip-flops and held it up to the new shoes until she found the right size. Spring's Cinderella moment.

Heading back into the conference room, Miss Kedine looked over her girls. Someone was helping Chayna with her hair. Someone else was spritzing on body spray. Another had left the class. But where was Lindsey?

No one had seen her. A couple of girls had called her cell phone, but it was dead. Lindsey had promised she would be there for the luncheon. It was the last thing she had to do to graduate. How could she miss this?

Miss Kedine asked another teacher to look after the class. She drove a few blocks to Lindsey's uncle's house, the last place she had heard Lindsey was staying.

The front window on the little green house was broken. Someone had taped cardboard over the hole. Lindsey's old red Camaro was parked out front.

Miss Kedine knocked on the door. "Come in," someone called. So she walked down the hall, calling, "Hello, I'm Lindsey's counselor . . ."

In the first bedroom on the left, she found Lindsey, fast asleep, her face blanketed by her hair, which was now brown.

"You've got five minutes," said Miss Kedine.

Sitting up slowly, Lindsey rubbed her eyes. "I don't have a dress."

———

They pulled out of the PACE parking lot 20 minutes later, six would-be ladies, their counselor and principal.

"I'm sorry," Lindsey told everyone. She had worked late, come back and cleaned her uncle's house, then got into a fight with her mom and slept through the alarm. After Miss Kedine woke her, she stopped by a friend's house to borrow a turquoise dress.

Soon they pulled into the parking lot of Zorah's restaurant. "Okay, ladies," Miss Kedine called into the rearview mirror. "Remember your manners."

"You girls all look so gorgeous," said Ms. DeLoach, the principal.

As Spring walked up the path, she started breathing hard. Lindsey watched a scarlet rash creep up Spring's neck, spread across her face. She saw Spring's lower lip begin to tremble.

"You okay?"

"Scared."

"It'll be okay," Lindsey said, squeezing Spring's elbow. "I got your back."

All the girls froze when they walked inside. The restaurant had been a waterfront residence, and was still homey and elegant, like a scene from one of Miss Kedine's magazines. Lace curtains kissed the wide windows. A fire licked at the hearth. And on every table, a scarlet poinsettia.

The hostess led them to a private dining room in the back, where a wall of windows overlooked the sun-striped lake.

"Okay, ladies, let's take our seats," said Miss Kedine. They pulled out their own chairs, slid into their seats, crossed their ankles. Chayna planted her elbows on the table, then remembered.

She touched the edge of the chocolate-colored tablecloth, then lifted the corner of the snowy one laid diagonally across it. "This two tablecloths here?" she asked. "This a tablecloth too, right?" Miss Kedine nodded. "Wow," Chayna breathed. "I never even been anywhere with one."

What's a butter dish? What's tomato bisque? What's hummus?

They regarded the nine utensils and three plates with the caution of bomb defusers. They didn't dare touch the black fabric blooming from their crystal water glasses. "Ladies," Miss Kedine said gently, "remember, napkins in our laps."

Spring fingered the carefully folded cloth, seeming confused. "This is our napkin?"

They didn't know what vinaigrette was. Of six dressing choices, they all ordered ranch. "Like the sauce for McNuggets?" asked Chayna.

LOWS AND HIGHS. When Lindsey didn't know what a red pepper was, I felt her embarrassment. But I jumped right from that moment to the funniest part of the luncheon, fast-forwarding through 45 minutes to pair the despair with laughter. And told in Spring's voice, the joke about ramen noodles almost seemed like her way of comforting Lindsey after the earlier moment.

Lindsey poked a piece of red pepper, held it up and asked Miss Kedine, "What's this? Some sort of fancy tomato?" She thought all peppers were green.

About 45 minutes after they arrived, while the girls were still picking at their salads, Spring leaned into Lindsey and said, "This meal's taking forever. Ramen noodles be ready in, like, three minutes."

Then, the disaster Spring had dreaded.

She stabbed at a crouton. It sailed off her plate and plopped onto the tablecloth. Her face went blank as she confronted the evidence: Who did she think she was, pretending she could fit in somewhere like this?

Stomach tightening, she sank into her chair and buried her face in her clammy hands.

"It's okay," Lindsey laughed quietly. "I told you, I got your back." She jabbed her own fork into a piece of lettuce and flicked it onto the table.

––––––

The girls were quiet during most of the meal. You could hear ice clinking in lemonade glasses, knives scraping plates. "You can talk, you know," Miss Kedine encouraged them.

No, they really couldn't. To do this right, they needed the focus of a surgeon.

Cutting real chicken was the hardest part. The plastic knives and paper poultry hadn't prepared them. "You should have at least gotten us Play-Doh chicken to practice," someone told Miss Kedine.

The counselor corrected the girls, gently, when one held her fork in her fist, when another buttered a whole slice of bread at once, when Chayna left her spoon in her soup bowl instead of setting it on the saucer. Miss Kedine nodded when they sat up straight and dabbed at their mouths.

When the chocolate pie and strawberries were served, Miss Kedine clinked her spoon on her glass and said, "Ladies! I'm so thrilled with you all." She beamed at her students, at their transformation. "Now I don't expect you all to remember everything. But if you take even one thing with you from this, as you enter the world, I know it will make a difference."

They had just finished lunch, were folding linen napkins in their laps, when Miss Kedine stood and addressed them again.

"Will the following girls please step forward to receive their certificates of completion . . ."

One by one, the students rose to accept their awards.

The girl who had been on her own since she was 14, who worked 30 hours a week and kept her dead friend's picture in her car. The girl who lost her daddy, who used to cut herself, who couldn't look in a mirror. The girl who had moved 15 times, who had been so sullen and angry, whose own mother hadn't seen her in a dress, hadn't known she was beautiful.

"Lindsey," the counselor called. "Spring." She named the other three girls, who all stood up beside the table. "And Chayna."

They held their paper diplomas in front of them. "I'm hanging this in my room," Chayna whispered.

When the girls started the etiquette class, they thought they would simply learn how to use a napkin and where to place a salad fork. If they knew how to walk in heels and shake hands properly, their teacher had told them, the world would see them differently.

But it turned out that Miss Kedine's class had accomplished much more: It had changed the way the girls saw themselves. Understanding how to behave, they gained confidence, began to think they were worthy, started aspiring to lives they never thought possible.

This wasn't about salad forks or crossing your ankles or saying "Please." It was about knowing you belong. Believing you can make it out there.

With their principal and Miss Kedine between them, the girls posed for a picture. Then, suddenly, it was over. Everyone piled into the PACE van, and the counselor hurried them back to school.

_____

Lindsey had to get to her new job. Spring's mom had promised to drive her home, so she could see her dressed up. And Chayna had to catch her bus. She still had that 2½-hour trip ahead of her.

"Thank you, Miss Kedine," Chayna shouted, waving as she crossed the school parking lot. She wore her purple backpack over the golden bow on her dress, a girl and a woman at the same time. In her hand, she carried a plastic bag with her old jeans and her new certificate, the only award she had ever received.

"Hey!" called Miss Kedine, seeing her in her nice clothes, "aren't you going to change?"

Shaking her head, Chayna climbed onto the bus in her new high heels.

She already had.

23

WALK A MILE IN THEIR SHOES

Ride the bus,
live their life,
invite yourself over

Mr. Newton: A 99-Year-Old Man Still Sweeps a Seafood Factory

Reported over five days; written in one. Published December 15, 2015

BEFORE THE STORY

A reader called one day: "There's this man who works at our shrimp factory, sweeping up the place. He's been here for as long as I can remember. I knew he was old, but I just found out he's 99. He never misses a day at work."

The next day, I drove to meet Mr. Newton, who was kind, warm and accommodating, but could barely hear me. He also couldn't speak much English. I asked if I could watch him work. Then, after three days at the factory: "Can I follow you home?"

He didn't have a car. Though he lived just a couple of miles from work, the complicated, unreliable bus trip took two hours. As I sat behind him, I watched riders ask about his health, wish him well.

At his house, I learned of his life and how he now lived: a solitary centenarian who fell asleep with talk radio, who still had the curtains his wife put up long ago, who still read the sign she had written on the door for their boys.

I framed this story around a single day in Mr. Newton's life. But

At 99, Newton Murray still swept up a
shrimp factory and its sprawling parking
lot—and inspired his coworkers with
his work ethic and cheerful greetings.
Photographer: Melissa Lyttle

I spent an entire work week with him, watching and wondering, gaining access and intimacy. It wasn't just what I witnessed in one day. Because I had learned his routine and gotten to shadow him at work, then follow him home, I could write with authority. I had started to know and understand him.

This story was a welcome reminder that there are people all around us living quiet but remarkable lives, often unnoticed, sometimes inspiring strangers in ways they may not even realize. Their stories are worth seeking out and sharing.

THE STORY

His alarm beeps at 3:30 a.m., drowning out the talk radio that keeps him company all night. He rolls over slowly and prays: "Please, Lord, give me the strength to get up."

It takes a half-hour, sometimes longer, but eventually he hobbles to the kitchen to make tea.

And three days a week, no matter how the old man feels, he steps into the cotton pants with the torn right knee and pulls on the white shirt with "Bama Sea Products" stitched above his pacemaker. Then he wraps a paper towel around a piece of fried chicken, packs it into his Coleman cooler, and leaves his house.

By now it is 5:45 a.m. The two-block walk to the bus takes him 20 minutes, his tiny steps scraping the sidewalk.

Four hours after he wakes, he arrives at work.

"Morning, Mr. Newton!" a moustached man calls.

"Hello, Cap'n!" he says, raising his hand. "Beautiful day."

To him, every day is.

Newton Murray—everyone calls him Mr. Newton—is 99 years old, making him the oldest employee of Bama seafood and probably among the oldest anywhere. But he has no thoughts of retirement. After he puts away his cooler, he will set to work tidying up Bama's vast parking lots.

If you saw him there, you might think he was just holding up a broom. But it's really the other way around.

Bama Sea Products used to be in downtown St. Petersburg. But in 2000, owner John Stephens sold the waterfront property and bought the former Harry H. Bell & Sons cold storage on 28th Street between I-275 and the tracks.

Stephens acquired two warehouses with a walk-in freezer, offices and a retail shop—90,000 square feet of enclosed space—

SPEND ALL DAY. If you're going to shadow someone, be there as they wake up—even if it's 3:30 a.m. Or have them recreate that part of their routine in detail. Be there when they make breakfast. Walk to the bus stop. Sit behind them on the bus. Go to work with them. Follow them home. Go inside.

LEARN TO LISTEN. Sometimes even background noise matters. Ask why someone sleeps with the TV on. Or listens to rap while they do homework. Or turns on the oldies station in the car. When I approached Mr. Newton's house that morning, I heard loud voices but didn't see anyone. When he opened the door, the noise got louder. "Talk radio," he said, hobbling to turn it down. I asked if he kept that on all night. "Keeps me company," he replied. That's when I first felt his loneliness.

plus parking lots and loading docks. Total area to sweep: two city blocks.

The Bama seafood people were moving in when an old man showed up. He had a dark, wrinkled face, milky eyes, spindly arms.

"I am here for work," he told general manager John Jackson.

"They sold the building," Jackson remembers telling him. "This is no longer Harry Bell's."

"No matter, Cap'n," Jackson remembers him saying. "I come with the property."

Jackson let him stay. "What was I going to do?"

The next day, the old man brought his own broom.

Mr. Newton, then 86, had been working as a janitor at the complex for more than 20 years, ever since he moved here from Trinidad. His salary then and now: minimum wage.

"Bama became my new family," he says. "I am blessed."

"He's just an amazing, quiet, old man with an unbelievable attitude," says Bob Joseph, who does Bama's purchasing.

"He cares about everyone around him but doesn't really share much of himself," says Brian Jackson, his supervisor.

What does maintenance man Karl Holycross see when he looks at Mr. Newton? Job security. "If they don't let him go, I have nothing to worry about."

"He's here more for morale than productivity," says Michael Stephens, Bama's lawyer and son of the owner. "In some ways, he's a liability. Everyone worries he's going to tumble down the stairs.

"But he just makes you smile, makes you realize you have nothing to complain about. I know he must be hurting, but he's always in a good mood."

Besides, the lawyer says, no one has the heart to fire a 99-year-old man who never arrives late or leaves early, who never says no or asks for a raise.

"A couple of years ago, his supervisor came to my dad and said he was really worried about Mr. Newton. My dad agreed: We have to let him go so he doesn't get hurt. 'Okay,' said the supervisor. 'When are you going to tell him?' But my dad couldn't tell him. So it stopped there."

It takes Mr. Newton eight hours to clear both parking lots and the warehouse, if you include bathroom breaks and naps.

"We could probably get a young guy with a leaf blower to do

his job in an hour," says the lawyer. "But this place just wouldn't be the same without Mr. Newton."

His home base at Bama is next to the rear loading dock. On his way there, he stops to rest every 25 steps or so. He has outlived one pacemaker and has had the second for six years.

He says he keeps going because the people at Bama depend on him. "I cannot let them down. They need me."

Just before 8 a.m., he reaches the stairs: seven of them, narrow and steep. Mr. Newton shifts his cooler to his back, grabs the railing with both hands and heaves himself up, pulling and panting, pausing after each step.

A forklift operator calls, "Morning, Mr. Newton!"

"Morning, Cap'n!"

He approaches the boiler room, steps inside. "High Voltage," says a sign on the door. He limps past walls filled with fan belts, bins of screws, broken motors. Behind the throbbing boiler, the door to the storage closet says, "Keep Out." Inside: a small refrigerator, two swivel chairs and a filing cabinet.

Mr. Newton's "office."

He takes the chicken out of his cooler, wraps it in another paper towel, eases it into the fridge. He pulls his bifocals from his shirt pocket, folds them into two paper towels. His gold Walmart watch gets three towels. His slim wallet merits four—each treasure wrapped according to its worth, each with its own space in the filing cabinet's bottom drawer.

He unbuttons his shirt, smooths it across a metal hanger, hangs it on the back wall; replaces his pants with coveralls, the same he has worn for 13 years. He's the only employee at Bama who still wears a uniform. In all that time, Stephens says, Mr. Newton has asked for only one thing: a new ball cap.

But he won't wear it to work. "Only when I get dressed up."

At 8:30, he straps a too-big weight belt around his fragile waist, steps into white rubber boots and shoulders his worn broom. His supervisor bought him a new one months ago, but he won't use it until he wears out the old one.

He was the third of 11 children, the oldest boy, born on the island of Tobago in April 1914, a couple of months before World War I erupted. His father suffered a hernia and couldn't work; his mother sold coconuts and melons from their garden. In their

COUNT THE STEPS. If you don't struggle to move, it might not matter how far you have to walk to work. But when every step is a strain, and you have to keep resting, that's a telling detail. I wanted readers to know how long it took Mr. Newton to walk two blocks to the bus stop, how many steps he could go before resting, how many stairs he had to climb, so they could feel his effort—and pain.

ACTIONS SPEAK. The way a person makes their lunch, or gets ready for work, or unpacks their pockets says something about them: Are they careful? Careless? Those details aren't always worth including. But when you see someone painstakingly going through the motions of the most mundane tasks, they matter. Mr. Newton had a process for everything. And was ploddingly slow. But that kept him from forgetting anything.

CHART HISTORY THROUGH HIS STORY.
When you're writing about someone, try to see them in the context
of the world's progress: he was born
before airplanes or interstates. Mr.
Newton had lived a whole century,
so I wanted to encompass that experience by telling it through what
he saw with his grandmother on the
remote island of Tobago.

cramped house at the edge of town, Newton and his siblings slept on the dirt floor.

When he was 8, he went "down the hill" to visit his grand-mother and never returned home. She raised him, taught him to cook and clean. Together, they watched the first car cross the is-land, the first electric lights pierce the darkness. He lived through World War II and English rule, island independence and the first election.

"Queen Elizabeth is still my boss lady," he says.

Newton was in seventh grade when he dropped out of school to work as a yard boy. Since 1926, he has seldom taken a day off.

"Papa has always been a workaholic," says his stepdaughter, Daphne Brown.

He moved to Trinidad as a young man, to work for Texaco. After a day in the oil fields, he would "come home and take care of cows, goats, pigs, this huge garden. And he was a minister. On Sundays, he would lead 60 people at the Baptist church and get everyone on fire.

"The day he stops working," she says, "will be the day he dies."

Mr. Newton married Daphne's mother, Mimie, in 1956, when Daphne and her sister, Verina, were teenagers. Verina moved to Miami in 1971, and five years later persuaded her mom and stepdad to come. When Mr. Newton relocated to Florida, he was 63—just retired from Texaco after 40 years. He and his wife brought twin boys, age 12, whose mother asked them to give her sons a chance in America.

"He's always been such a loving, generous man," says Daphne, 74, who lives in Washington, D.C.

"Stubborn, bull-headed, has to have his own way," says Ver-ina, 75, who lives down the street from her stepdad. "He just won't slow down."

Mr. Newton could have lived on his Texaco retirement, but as soon as he landed in St. Petersburg, he started looking for work. Someone introduced him to the folks at Harry Bell, where he worked until Bama bought the building and inherited its custo-dian.

In 1976 he bought a three-bedroom, $15,600 home, took out a $500 monthly mortgage, and paid off the loan in 28 years.

"I wish my wife could have seen that," he says. "She was a good cook, a good mother, a good seamstress. She died in

1985 and I never looked for another. Oh, she was a darling of a lady."

For years, he walked the 2.5 miles to work. It took almost two hours. He would leave before first light, get home in the dark. Later, he bought a bike, then a used Plymouth. One of the twins—he doesn't remember which—crashed the car into a wall in 1986. Since then, Mr. Newton has taken the bus.

The monthly senior pass costs $35—almost five hours' worth of sweeping. "I am lucky," he says. "God bless America!"

———

Just after 9 a.m., he starts clearing the back lot, a daunting expanse of asphalt about three football fields wide. Mr. Newton's broom is one foot across.

He takes small swipes, brushing straw wrappers and cigarette butts into neat piles the size of dinner plates. A Milky Way wrapper, a Sun Chips bag, a yellow lighter. Near the walkway, a mound of shrimp shells, a McDonald's cup.

Mr. Newton smiles and shakes his head. "It is okay. It keeps me working."

He bends to scoop soggy leaves from a drain. Lopes after a blue hair net, blowing like a tumbleweed. For a half-hour, in the morning sun, Mr. Newton listens to the scritch-scratch of his broom, his soundtrack for more than 30 years. Step, step, sweep. Step, step, sweep. Rest a minute, leaning on his broom like a cane. Step, step, sweep . . .

"I am slowing down," he says. He means in general, not just today. "My breath is short. I am getting tired." He has been forgetting things: whether he ate dinner or picked up his paycheck. In an hour, he clears only four parking spaces.

Then he heads inside, out of the heat, to take a break.

"How you feeling, Mr. Newton?" asks marketing director Dottie Guy.

"Never been better," he smiles. "And you?"

He builds his days on routine, every move an echo. Lunch is always at noon and the menu never changes: Wonder bread cradling a piece of fried chicken. A $15 bucket from Walmart lasts him 10 days.

Sometimes he eats in his "office," on the swivel stool by the fridge. Other times he holes up in a closet by the front loading dock. He always eats by himself. Often he falls asleep. "A few times we couldn't find him, and when we did, we worried he was dead," lawyer Stephens says.

MONEY MATTERS. Folks who live on fixed incomes have to count every penny, and most don't mind talking about it; it defines the way they live. Ask about income and expenses. It also helps to calculate the context: How many hours did Mr. Newton have to sweep to buy a senior bus pass? FIVE! After all these years in the same job, how much did he earn? MINIMUM WAGE! How much did his bucket of chicken cost? $15—but he made it last 10 days.

DO THE MATH. Measurements and dimensions are great details, but not everyone can envision a parking lot that's 500 feet wide. Help readers put numbers in perspective, so they can see the scene in terms they can understand. Find comparisons: What else is 500 feet wide? About three football fields. Mr. Newton had to sweep that expanse with a one-foot broom. I measured it.

KEEP GOING. If you only spend a few hours, or one day, with someone, you can't really learn their routine. Go back, watch and wait, dip into their world over the course of a couple of days. If you can't, ask them to recount the things they do every day, step by step. After shadowing Mr. Newton for one day, I learned how much of his life revolved around routine. And that I wanted to spend the whole week with him, to see how similar every day was, to try to understand him.

"They let me rest here. And I know they will always come looking for me," says Mr. Newton. "I know here I am never alone."

———

His youngest sister, who lives in Connecticut, mails him cartons of frozen soup. She wants him to come live with her. His stepdaughters have offered to take him in. He has 17 grandchildren, he lost track of how many greats, plenty of family who would care for him.

But Mr. Newton is determined never to lean on anyone. He treasures his work, his independence. "I don't know God's plan," he says. "I keep asking, and he keeps me going."

"He's just trying to do the best he can until God takes the breath out of his body," stepdaughter Verina says. "And when he falls on his face and calls me, I come prop him up and he keeps on going."

Tuesdays Mr. Newton does laundry and rakes his yard. Thursdays he cooks a week's worth of suppers, mostly rice and beans. Neighbors drive him to Walmart to pick up prescriptions on Saturdays. A woman from church drives him to Unity of St. Petersburg every Sunday. "He brings Mother's Day cards, Father's Day cards, he's always in the same seat in the middle section," says the Rev. Fred Clare. "He's just a loving, sweet soul who touches people—a great example of how to live."

And three days a week, shivering in the winter and sweating in the summer, Mr. Newton clocks in at work, earning around $10,000 a year. Every two years, he saves $600 toward a ticket back to Trinidad; Bama gives him a $200 bonus to cover the rest. He never eats seafood at home—"Never anything so fancy, just by myself"—but he spends a week's wages on shrimp and mahi to bring to his relatives.

FIND MEANING. Search for universal themes, connections, meaning. Stories that resonate the most with readers are about things nearly everyone experiences: love, loss, hope, fear. This could have been a day-in-the-life story about a 99-year-old man. But when I saw how his coworkers loved him, when they told me how inspiring he was and why they kept him around, as he talked about why he stayed, I realized this was a story about finding purpose—and knowing you matter. Something we can all relate to.

"It is nice there," says Mr. Newton. "For my 100th birthday, I will go back. But not for good. How could I? My job is here."

In all his years of working—more than 84—no one has ever asked him if he likes his job. "Life can't always be easy, but you do your best and be grateful," he says.

It's not much, earning minimum wage to move dirt around a parking lot. But for now, Mr. Newton has a purpose, something to do. He matters.

People tell him he inspires them. If he misses a day for a doctor's appointment, his co-workers worry. When he's gone, he will leave a hole.

The meaning of life? "Only God knows," says Mr. Newton.

But with his beaten broom, sweeping a sprawling seafood warehouse, he seems to have found the secret to not dying.

———

The parking lots are clean, the dustpan has been dumped. Mr. Newton inspects his work, then starts an exact reversal of the morning's routine: Unstrap the worn weight belt, climb out of coveralls, into the torn cotton pants. Button on the shirt with the company logo.

Slide out the bottom drawer of the file cabinet, unwrap wallet, glasses, and gold Walmart watch, pack them all in pockets.

Finally, he fishes out what's left of his lunch: half a drumstick. He rewraps it in another paper towel, shoulders the cooler, and turns out the closet light. "Night, Mr. Newton," calls the maintenance man.

"Night, Cap'n," he says. "See you Wednesday."

At 3:30, he hauls himself up a long flight of stairs to Bama's main office and fills out his timecard. Nobody requires him to do this, or cares if he doesn't. Then he eases himself back down the 30 steps and pads across the parking lot. At the bus stop, he stands beside a light pole, hiding from the sun in its 6-inch sliver of shade.

When his bus finally arrives, other riders greet him by name. "Hey, Mr. Newton!" calls a 40-something woman, a 20-something guy. "Hey, beautiful!" he calls. "Hey, Cap'n!"

An hour later, he is back in his yard, where the watermelon vines twine around his fence and the mango trees droop with fruit. Through his bedroom window, talk radio is still blaring.

"I could not stay here all day, alone in this house. What would I do? Watch Judge Joe Brown?" he asks, fingering his keys.

He unlocks the gate, then the door. Sinks into a chair draped with a bed sheet. He's too tired to make tea. Looking up, he can see framed portraits of Jesus, the twin boys he raised, his wife.

Across from him, on a faded poster in the hall, is a list she wrote almost 30 years ago. She made it for the boys, but Mr. Newton still follows it religiously.

Things to do today:
1. Read Bible and talk to God.
2. Be considerate of everyone.
3. Show my family I love them.
4. Do my best in all my work.

READ THE WALLS. Jot down sayings from posters, pillows, picture frames. The words people surround themselves with give a glimpse into what inspires them and how they see the world. Ask why they hung that photo or kept that quote or where they got that small statue. What does it mean? Why does it matter? When I saw the poster in Mr. Newton's house, I knew I'd found his mantra.

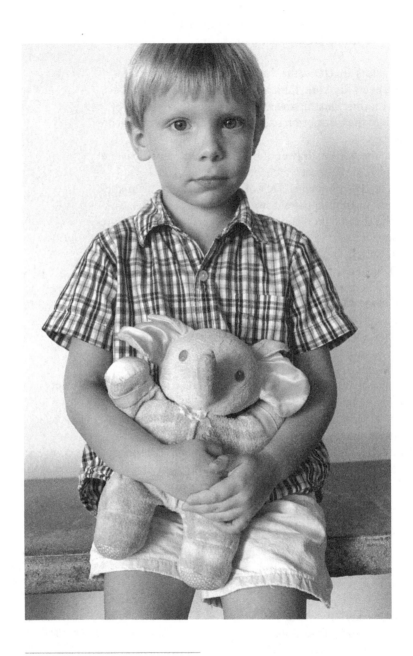

When Tucker DeGregory was four, he took his best friend, Bobo, everywhere.
Photographer: Patty Yablonski

24

GET PERSONAL

Share your life, open up, tell your own stories, take risks, see yourself as a character

I Brake for Bobo: A Boy Loses His Stuffed Elephant

Experienced in one evening; written the next day. Published September 3, 2005

BEFORE THE STORY

We were waiting for our staff meeting to start, talking about our weekends. My boys and I had driven to Atlanta, to my cousin's wedding. My youngest son, then four, was in the back seat when I heard him howl. His best friend, a stuffed elephant named Bobo, had flown out the window.

I didn't know what to do, whether to be a hero or teach him a lesson.

My colleagues shared their own stories of lost teddy bears and toys. Everyone, it seemed, had a Bobo story.

"Go home. Skip the meeting," said my editor. "Go write that."

First-person pieces can be dangerous. You have to open yourself up to share scars. You have to be ready to absorb the world's judgment. When first-person pieces are bad, they're very bad — sometimes embarrassing. So unless you really have something to say, or can bring a unique perspective, beware.

I had never wanted to write about myself, never thought my stories could compete with the people I profiled.

But my editor insisted: If no one has heard a story before, or everyone has had a similar experience, it's worth writing about. Besides, he said, it wasn't just about me. I would serve as an everywoman. I could represent all the other children who had lost their best friends, and parents who had to decide whether to find them.

So that day, at age 35, I poured out my angst as a mother and, for the first time, wrote about myself.

THE STORY

We'd been on the road for almost eight hours. Me and my two boys. We were driving home from my cousin's wedding in Atlanta. Well, I was driving.

Ry, who's 6, and Tucker, who's 4, were strapped into their car seats in the back seat.

It was past 10 p.m. It was raining.

I was riding the right lane of I-75, about 11 miles north of Brooksville, figuring we had about another hour to go.

Then Tucker starts screaming. "EEEIIIAAAK! EEEIIIAAAK!" Out of nowhere, he starts screeching like he's been shot or something. "EEEIIIAAAK! EEEIIIAAAK!"

"What's the matter? What's the matter?" I shout, gripping the wheel with both hands. I turn down the radio. Look up into the rearview mirror. Tucker is thrashing around in his car seat, straining against his seat belt, beating his fists against the car door. "EEEIIIAAAK! EEEIIIAAAK! EEEIIIAAAK!"

So Ry starts screaming, too. Both of them, in stereo, wailing and railing in the back seat.

There's nowhere to pull over. No exits in sight. In the darkness, a metal guardrail is rushing past on my right. Semis are speeding by on my left.

"What's the matter?" I cry, almost in tears myself. "Please, boys, what's wrong?"

"Mommy!" Ry whines. Then he chokes on his sobs. "Mommy," he tries again. "It's horrible! You won't believe it!

"Bobo just flew out the window."

Bobo is a stuffed elephant. He's about 10 inches tall, almost as wide. He wears plaid pajamas, which have faded from all the washings, and a white bow around his neck. His stubby front feet are lined with white satin. So are his big, floppy ears. His pale

SAVOR SOUNDS. Opening sections can transport the reader into a scene. Reporting for all five senses really helps. But sometimes, one sense overwhelms the others. The lead of this story is loud and hopefully captures what it's like to be driving on the highway late at night in the rain listening to the radio when suddenly you are bombarded by screams, screeches, thrashing, straining, beating, wailing, railing, guardrails rushing by, semis speeding past.

blue face is made of terry cloth, like a soft towel. His trunk is almost bald from too much loving.

Uncle Mark sent Bobo to Tucker as a baby present. When I brought Tucker home from the hospital, Bobo was waiting in his crib.

Whenever Tucker is upset, or tired, or scared, or even sometimes when he's really, really happy, he squeezes Bobo tight and rubs that terry cloth trunk against his nose. Bobo has been thrown up on, colored on and had almost every imaginable kind of juice spilled on him. Tucker wipes his nose on Bobo, wipes his hands on him. Uses Bobo to dry his tears. He talks to Bobo, sings him songs, tells him secrets. He slides Bobo down the slide at the playground, feeds him Teddy Grahams during snack time, takes him to Grandmom's house, to the grocery and McDonald's.

Every morning when Tucker goes to preschool, Bobo goes with him. Tucker kisses Bobo "bye" at the door and tucks him into his cubby, until nap time. Tucker can't fall asleep without Bobo.

And now that little blue elephant is lying somewhere on I-75, with the rain splattering down, the headlights streaming past and the semis whizzing by at 80 miles an hour.

And there's no place to pull over. Only darkness, now, on my right.

And I don't know what to do.

By now, Bobo is miles behind us. He has probably bounced down the embankment. Or been crushed under an 18-wheeler.

"He's probably scared," Ry says.

"Is he in heaven?" Tucker asks through his tears. "Do they have Teddy Grahams in heaven?"

Now I see the blue sign. There's a rest stop ahead. A mile later, I pull over and park between a silver Airstream and an old Winnebago. I try to think things through.

"Are we going back for Bobo now?" Ry asks.

"I don't want him to go to heaven!" Tuck screams. "Is he already in heaven?"

The way I see it, here in the dark, on the side of the highway, I have two choices: I can go back and look for Bobo, maybe become a hero to my kids. Or I can tell my boys I'm sorry. Bobo's gone.

Maybe that way Tucker would learn a lesson. After all, hadn't

MAKE IT MATTER. It's one thing to say your kid lost his stuffed elephant. But you have to help readers understand how monumental that loss is. I tried to show readers Bobo first—his physical description. Then I shared what the little animal did for my son, things I thought might be universal for other kids who carried around their best friends.

SHARE YOUR PAIN. So much of writing relies on confidence. It's hard to let yourself be vulnerable, especially to strangers. First-person stories about heroic deeds seem indulgent. The more relatable ones reveal weaknesses, show warts, admit regret. I didn't write this story to say I saved Bobo. I wrote it to show the angst of indecision, not knowing what to do.

I told him umpteen times to roll up that window? Not to dangle Bobo out in the wind?

And even if I find him, I probably won't be able to get to him. I couldn't find a place to pull over before. What if we see him again, then have to let him go?

And what if I do stop the car? And climb out, into the rain, into highway traffic, and try to fetch the would-be flying elephant? And what if, just then, a semi whizzes by and, God forbid, I get crushed?

"Maybe Mommy can buy you another Bobo," Ry offers, trying to console Tucker.

But Bobo is extinct.

———

Two years ago, Tucker's great-grandmother got worried about what would happen if Bobo ever got lost. So she called Playskool, the company that manufactured Bobo (not his given name), and asked to order three more. The Playskool official told her that particular stuffed elephant had been discontinued. There might be one more in stock, somewhere, the official said. But that was it.

So Tucker's great-grandmother bought the last blue elephant wearing plaid pajamas in America and sent it to Tucker, as an extra, just in case. That Bobo lived in the top of my closet for months. Then, just before we moved to Florida, while we were riding bikes around our old neighborhood, while Tucker was riding on the back of my bicycle, he dropped Bobo into a storm drain. We had to abandon the elephant. I raced home, got the other Bobo and stopped Tucker's sobs.

So now there's no backup Bobo.

Over the ages, across the cultures, how many Bobos (or teddy bears or dolls or blankets) have been dropped out of windows? Left in Wal-Marts? Lost along the way?

Teach a lesson . . . risk your life . . . be a rescue hero: What would you do if you had to make that call for your kid?

———

I can't sit here all night.

I drive back onto I-75, still heading south. A sign says the next exit is 10 miles ahead.

At Brooksville, I take the exit and turn around. Pull back onto the highway, heading north this time. Eleven miles and I pass another rest stop, on the opposite side of the road. Then another mile to the place I think Bobo might have fallen. Another mile past that and I finally find another exit where I can turn around again.

"Are you going to get Bobo now, Mommy?"

"I don't know," I tell Tucker. "I'm going to try."

I pull back onto I-75, heading south for the second time. I flick the headlights onto bright. I squint through the downpour, scanning the skinny shoulder. "Help me look," I call over the back seat. "See if you can see Bobo."

I'm going about 55 miles per hour, about as slow as seems safe on the interstate. I drive over a bridge, down a slight incline. SUVs, pickups and semis keep speeding by. We pass Burger King bags, shreds of blown-out tires, lots of skid marks.

But no Bobo.

"I bet he's having apple juice in heaven right now," Ry says.

Another 2 miles. Another two dozen trucks. Then we reach an overpass and a long metal guardrail starts rolling by on my right.

"There's Bobo!" Ry screams. "I see him!"

I see him, too. A small blue blob, wedged against the guardrail. But I can't pull over. The shoulder is too narrow.

Tucker starts shrieking again. "At least we know!" he's crying. "At least we know now, Mommy. He's not dead! He's still there! You can get him!"

I don't know how.

I drive on, heading toward Brooksville—again. I'm thinking about the last time we lost Bobo, when Tucker left him in Subway, and he got locked inside the sandwich shop, and I had to call the emergency, after-hours number on the door and get the manager to open it so we could get Bobo out.

And I'm thinking, as I'm driving, that I love that silly little blue elephant, too. That if we lose Bobo, my son will lose part of his childhood.

Without Bobo, he won't seem like such a little boy.

And I won't seem like I can help him with the one thing that matters most in his young life. And he might realize Mommy can't fix everything.

————

I exit at Brooksville again. Head north again, 12 more miles, past the rest stop and onto the next exit. Then I turn around. Again.

This time, I drive even slower. Maybe 45 mph, tops. When I think I'm nearing the overpass, I pull over onto the narrow shoul-

LISTEN TO THE CHILDREN. Capturing the way kids speak, showing how they see the world, is so revealing. I always try to include as much children's dialogue as I can. My sons' quotes are my favorite part of this story, worrying about whether there are Teddy Grahams in heaven, or if Bobo was drinking apple juice. It was the first time I'd heard my older son console his little brother—a powerful rite of passage.

WHY OF THE WHY. Every motivation has another motivation behind it. To get to the core of your story, a wonderful journalism teacher once said, "You have to find the why of the why." I had to find that elephant so my son would stop shrieking. So he would be able to sleep. So I wouldn't feel guilty. But it wasn't until the end of this section that I shared why I really had to do this: So Tucker wouldn't have to grow up. So I could still be his hero, if only for this one night.

der. Those wakeup strips, or whatever you call them, are criss-crossing the asphalt every few inches, vibrating the tires, rattling my teeth.

At the north end of the overpass, I spy Bobo again. He's dead ahead. I stop the car.

The rain has slowed to a drizzle by now. I turn on the flashers. I try to open the driver's side door.

But each time a big truck rumbles past, our car shivers in its wake. Three times, I try to get out. Three times, I feel the wind of the semis and pull the door back shut.

"Don't get run over, Mommy," Ry says. "Don't die."

I slam the driver's door closed. I reach across to the passenger seat, throw my backpack and the cooler in the back seat, between the boys. I lean over and unlock the passenger door.

Slowly, carefully, I ease my way over the gear shift, climbing onto the passenger seat. I try to shove open the passenger door. But the guardrail is in the way. The door will only open partially. I squeeze out, turning my hips to clear the guardrail.

Bobo is waiting.

He's still stuck in the guardrail. A little soggy. But no visible skid marks.

I pick up that little blue elephant and squeeze him hard.

Driving back down I-75, speeding back toward Brooksville for the third time, almost an hour after we first went this way, I pull over at the now-familiar rest stop. I let the car idle. I'm still shaking.

"I just need a minute," I tell my boys. I just need to calm down.

I lean my arms on the steering wheel. Rest my head on my arms. Close my eyes.

"Mommy!" Tucker cries from the back seat. "Mommy! Mommy!"

He's thrashing around again, holding Bobo this time, trying to unbuckle his seat belt. "Mommy!" he's shouting. "Help me get out!"

"Give me a minute!" I scream. "Just give me a minute, here. Would you?" I've been on the road almost nine hours by now. I've been trying, so hard, to hold it all together. I feel myself starting to lose it.

"But Mommy!" Tucker wails. The tears start streaming again. "I have to get out!"

"Why?" I shriek, spinning around to glare at him.

Tucker clutches Bobo more tightly. He smears a satin-lined elephant ear across his wet cheeks. Then he looks up at me, his blue eyes shining.

"Me and Bobo need to give you a hug."

AFTER THE STORY

Bobo got a bath that night. I stitched up his split trunk, sewed his silk ear, which had frayed. By the time Tucker woke up, his best friend was back beside him.

For the next 14 years, Bobo slept in Tucker's bed. He was there through angst over elementary school dance recitals, tears over middle school drama, his first date, first drive, first job. When Tucker left home to attend Northwestern University, Bobo was the last thing he packed and the first thing he put in the closet of his dorm room. When COVID canceled his final semester and he had to quickly flee, he left most of his stuff at school. But Bobo came home.

As of this writing, Tucker is a dance and theater teacher at a school in Boca Raton. When he moved into his first apartment, he brought Bobo with him. His best friend lives on the bottom bookshelf beside his bed. He swears he doesn't hug that threadbare elephant anymore. But sometimes, he still hugs me.

ACKNOWLEDGMENTS

So many people helped make this book happen.

My dad, Neill Thomasson, who read the newspaper out loud every morning while I ate Cheerios before kindergarten. My mom, Clarissa Thomasson, who stayed up late helping chop words from my high school articles. My sister, Amie Thomasson, who talked to teenage me through the shower curtain, helping untangle ideas.

For more than 30 years, my husband, Dan, has heard my stories before I wrote them, sorting through them with me, poking holes, questioning and encouraging. He always improves them and often serves as my first editor.

My son Ryland challenges me with his curiosity and keeps my computer running.

My son Tucker fills my world with music and dance, sparking new story structures.

All three of my guys have put up with me and my profession, joined in my reporting adventures, and sometimes even let me share their stories.

Thank you to my favorite editors: Maria Carrillo, who saved me from a bureau, introduced me to narrative, then returned to lead me two decades later. Mike Wilson, who turned me from a reporter into a writer and helped me carve the elephant from a bar of soap. I'm indebted to you both for listening to me, believing in me, trusting me, showing me structure and helping me see the stories. Without you both, I wouldn't be me.

Tom French, you showed me what storytelling can be, how to

slow down, and you have been a marvelous mentor. Kelley Benham French, thanks for understanding me and pushing me—especially about endings—for all of the crazy conversations, awesome edits. And for getting me a puppy to sit on my feet while I type.

Neil Brown, thanks for all of the talks and beers, and for encouraging me to see stories in a different way.

Caryn Baird, Leonora LaPeter Anton and Patti Ewald, you have shared my newsroom and my life. Thank you for inspiring me with your work, listening to my angst, going on crazy road trips, and being my best friends.

I'm so grateful to the late Jim Sheeler for his words and wisdom—and, years ago, for suggesting this book.

And to my wise and infinitely patient editor at the University of Chicago Press, Mary Laur, who helped shape my vision, molded an anthology and journalism textbook into a manuscript, and shepherded it through myriad changes. Thank you for all of your support—and for making this happen.

Mollie McFee managed all of the logistics and legalities, making the complicated parts painless.

Thanks to Erin DeWitt, whose expert copyediting helped make this manuscript sing.

R. B. Brenner invited me to talk to his students at Stanford University and provided invaluable insight as a reviewer.

Thanks to Janet Keeler and her students at the University of South Florida, who sparked many of these tips with their careful questions. And to Deni Elliott, former chair of USF's journalism department, who told me I should be a teacher—and let me try.

John Pendygraft and Melissa Lyttle took many of the incredible photos and helped me see what to do with the stories. I love working with you both so much and became a better journalist—and person—by your side. Thank you for the life talks and travels.

I am lucky to have workshopped and mind-melded with Jacqui Banaszynski for decades, and so grateful that the Nieman Storyboard featured several of these stories.

And I'm honored to have known Beth Macy, prize-winning journalist and author of *Dopesick*, since we were young reporters together in Virginia. Thank you for always keeping me in awe, and for writing the foreword to this collection.

A giant hug to my friend *Tampa Bay Times* photo editor Boyzell Hosey, who helped find many of these images that had been lost and is a consummate collaborator—and source of perpetual positivity.

Thank you to the *Tampa Bay Times*, editor Mark Katches and former CEO Paul Tash for giving me permission to reprint these stories—and understanding the power of narratives.

And to my friends at the Poynter Institute, for pushing me to make the *WriteLane* podcast about nonfiction writing—and hosting the episodes on your website.

Finally, this book wouldn't be possible without the scores of strangers who let me into their lives. Thank you all for opening up, trusting me with your stories, and letting me share them.

Made in the USA
Coppell, TX
08 February 2024

28764923R00157